Dr. Louise Baker
Aiken Technical College

Sentence Power

Sentence Power

Jean Reynolds
Polk Community College

Holt, Rinehart and Winston, Inc.
Fort Worth   Chicago   San Francisco   Philadelphia
Montreal   Toronto   London   Sydney   Tokyo

Publisher   Ted Buchholz
Acquisitions Editor   Michael Rosenberg
Developmental Editor   Leslie Taggart
Production Manager   Ken Dunaway
Art and Design Supervisor   Serena Barnett
Text Designer   Impressions Publishing Services
Cover Designer   Clare & Co.

Copyright ©1991, by Holt, Rinehart and Winston, Inc.

All rights reserved. No part of this publication may be reproduced or transmitted in any form or by any means, electronic or mechanical, including photocopy, recording or any information storage and retrieval system, without permission in writing from the publisher.

Requests for permission to make copies of any part of the work should be mailed to: Permissions Department, Holt, Rinehart and Winston, Inc., 8th Floor, Orlando, Florida 32887.

Excerpt from *Make the Most of Your Best* by Dorothy Sarnoff, ©1981 by Dorothy Sarnoff. Used by permission of Doubleday, a division of Bantam, Doubleday, Dell Publishing Group, Inc.

Printed in the United States of America

Reynolds, Jean, 1945–
    Sentence power / by Jean Reynolds.
      p.   cm.
    ISBN 0-03-026333-6
      1. English language--Sentences--Problems, exercises, etc.
2. English language--Grammar--1950--Problems, exercises, etc.
3. English language--Rhetoric--Problems, exercises, etc. I. Title.
PE1441.R45   1991
428.2--dc20
                                                                                                                      90-39895
                                                                                                                        CIP

1 2 3 4 016 9 8 7 6 5 4 3 2 1

Contents

Introduction		vii
Preface		ix

Part 1 — The Importance of Writing — 1

Unit 1	Introduction to Writing	2
Unit 2	The Writing Process	16
Unit 3	The Paragraph	37
Unit 4	More About Paragraphs	51

Part 2 — Writing Effective Sentences — 63

Unit 5	The Sentence	64
Unit 6	Subjects and Verbs	71
Unit 7	More About Verbs	84
Unit 8	More About Subjects	101
Unit 9	Fragments	111
Unit 10	Sentences with *If, When, Because,* and *Although* (Subordinate Conjunctions)	127
Unit 11	Sentences with *And, But* and *Or* (Coordinate Conjunctions)	144
Unit 12	Sentences with *Who* and *Which*	155
Unit 13	Semicolons	169
Unit 14	Sentence Variety	182

Part 3 — Avoiding Common Errors — 191

Unit 15	Run-on Sentences	192
Unit 16	Present-Tense Verbs	203
Unit 17	Past-Tense Verbs	219
Unit 18	Pronouns	232
Unit 19	Adjectives and Adverbs	248
Unit 20	Apostrophes	265
Unit 21	Words Often Confused	278
Unit 22	Capital Letters	291
Index		299

Introduction

This book is divided into three parts. Part 1 describes the importance of writing for academic and professional success. You will discover some tips to make writing easier and more effective, and you'll begin to do some writing yourself.

Part 2 focuses on how to avoid common sentence errors. You will practice the four types of sentences that successful writers use.

Part 3 teaches you how to avoid the most common usage errors found in student writing. When you complete this part of the book, you'll feel confident in your ability to express yourself well in writing.

Preface

This book is designed to help students master the basic sentence patterns taught in most developmental English courses. Two assumptions shaped the overall plan for this book. First, students write more effectively when they read and talk about one another's work. Second, students benefit when new material is presented in a variety of ways.

   To help students enjoy maximum success in this course, the book contains the following features:

- A motivational unit, "Introduction to Writing," shows students how good writing can help them achieve success academically and professionally.
- Study tips demonstrate innovative approaches to new material.
- Students are encouraged to share their ideas and their written work with one another. As they try to put their knowledge into words, students improve their communication skills and increase their mastery of the material.
- The usage section focuses on the two most important areas in developmental English: avoiding sentence errors, such as fragments and run-ons, and mastering compound and complex sentence patterns.
- Students spend most of their time reading and practicing model sentences, instead of memorizing grammatical terms that are quickly forgotten.
- New concepts are taught by several approaches. For example, students are encouraged to read new sentence patterns aloud, so that the ear can guide them when they construct new sentences. A variety of exercises provides ample opportunities to practice new skills.
- Students focus on a number of writing issues not often discussed in developmental textbooks: the differences between speaking and writing, colloquial and slang words, sexism in language, and the importance of writing in business careers.

   I want to thank the many instructors who reviewed this text for their helpful and encouraging comments: Laureen Belmont, North Idaho College; Sara Blake, El Camino College; Mark Branson, Davidson County Community College; Paul Calocino, Bergen Community College; Kate Cosper, Walla Walla Community College; Barbara J. Craig, Del Mar College; Don Edge, Camden County College; Lulie E. Felder, Jones County Junior College; Ann Fields, Western Kentucky University; James Helvey, Davidson County

Community College; Robert Jenkins, Florence-Darlington Technical College; Ruth Koenig, Danville Area Community College; Paul Olubas, Southern Ohio College; Muriel Rada, Metropolitan Technical Community College; Jill Sessons, USC, Coastal Carolina College; and W. C. Truckey, Lewis and Clark Community College.

Special thanks go to Judy Sacks, who copyedited my text; Leslie Taggart, my editor; Kathleen Riley, a colleague who has taught me a great deal; Polk Community College, which granted me a sabbatical while I wrote this book; and Charles and Jade Reynolds, for their love and encouragement.

Sentence Power

Part One
The Importance of Writing

Writing at the college level may be new to you, but your past schooling introduced you to many writing skills. This course will help you review what you've already learned. In addition, it will add new skills to those you've already mastered.

Part 1 focuses on two concerns: *why* writing is important to your future, and *how* you can develop your writing skills. Part 1 provides given opportunities for sharing your future plans with other students; together you'll explore new ways to write more easily and effectively.

Unit One
Introduction to Writing

SUMMARY

1. Writing skills are important to your success in college and in your future career.

2. You don't have to be born with talent to be a good writer. This course will help you learn many of the skills you need.

3. Writing skills are different from speaking skills, and you need to apply your understanding of those differences when you write.

4. Skilled writers focus their attention on two areas: effective organization of content and correct usage.

Writing in Your Future

Right now you are probably looking forward to a challenging and well-paying career. You may even have started working in your chosen field. Chances are you can already picture yourself as a health-care professional, business manager, or electronics technician, for example. You already know that your college major will prepare you for your future career, but you may not realize that writing skills are important to your success, both now and later on.

Writing skills can help you succeed in college. You may be surprised at the amount of time you will spend writing before you graduate. Essay tests, research papers, lab reports, and book reviews require a great deal of writing skill.

After graduation, you can expect to spend a great deal of time writing on the job. Law enforcement officers need to submit reports that can be used as evidence in court. Nurses must write patient-care plans that other members of the medical team will read. Business managers often must explain in writing how they plan to increase profits. Almost every field, indeed, requires employees to write reports and answer correspondence.

Good writing skills can help you stand out in your field. Supervisors and coworkers will appreciate your ability to handle routine paperwork efficiently and effectively. Furthermore, writing can help you gain wide recognition. Many career-related journals, newsletters, and magazines need well-written articles.

As you gain experience on the job, each promotion will introduce you to new writing tasks. If you are chosen to train other employees, you may be asked to prepare job descriptions for them to follow. If you become a supervisor, you will write detailed evaluations of your employees. In the arts, grant proposals must be written to obtain funds for music festivals, dance companies, and theater productions. In any field, the people who handle money and responsibility must write well.

As you plan your future, remember that writing skills are important to your success. Remember, too, that *now* is the time to prepare. Once you enter the job market, you will probably be too busy to study paragraph organization and usage. Resolve to use this opportunity to prepare for the future.

All of your writing assignments in this course will be brief ones— sentences and paragraphs. In subsequent writing courses, your instructors will introduce you to other tasks, but you will continue to use your sentence and paragraph skills throughout college.

Exercise 1

INSTRUCTIONS: After you have completed these activities, hand your answers to your instructor.

1. Use your college catalog to identify two courses you plan to take that may require writing. List the types of assignments you may be asked to do.
2. Meet with a small group of students from your class to list as many types of writing assignments as you can think of.
3. Name a career that interests you. Then list the types of writing tasks that career may require of you.
4. Meet with a small group of students from your class to list the writing skills that might be important to all of you in the future.

How Important Is Talent?

Don't be too impressed by talent. Writing is a skill, like driving a car. With patience and concentration, you can learn to write successfully.

Perhaps some of your classmates in high school wrote elegantly with very little effort, while you had to struggle to write a single paragraph. Or you may have worked with a friend who was a gifted writer. You may have felt frustrated because your efforts produced disappointing results. The good news is that research has proven again and again that effective writing *can* be learned. By practicing the skills taught in this course, you can move confidently towards your goal of writing like a professional.

Some students worry about too many concepts at once—organization, spelling, and punctuation. Successful writers, however, concentrate on one concept at a time; they don't try to produce a good piece of writing all at once. Unit 2 introduces you to the three-step *writing process* that they use.

In this course you'll concentrate on short writing assignments, one paragraph long. Learning how to write effective paragraphs will provide the basic skills to build on in future writing courses.

Introduction to Writing

Exercise 2

INSTRUCTIONS: Write your answers to these questions and hand them to your instructor.

1. Think about a friend or relative who writes well, or a writer whose work you enjoy. What qualities do you admire in that person's writing?
2. List *three* habits you plan to develop to improve your own writing.
3. Imagine that a friend has told you that he's worried about college because he finds writing difficult. Write him a short letter of encouragement.
4. Meet with a small group of students from your class to discuss this question: Which is more important to good writing, talent or effort? Appoint one group member to be secretary and write down the group's ideas. Be ready to share your group's thoughts with the rest of the class.

Comparing Speaking and Writing

Writing skills are very different from speaking skills, so you must develop language skills that are different from your speaking skills. First, some of the words used in conversation are not acceptable in college and professional writing. Slang words, such as *ain't* or *bad* (meaning *good*), are examples of words that are acceptable in conversation with your friends, but they should never appear in college writing. You also need to avoid colloquial expressions in your writing assignments. *Colloquial* refers to colorful, everyday words and expressions like *dork*, *wimp*, and *spaced-out*. These words are amusing in conversation, but they won't enhance your professional image. Instead of saying that you frequently "hang around with the gang," in a college paper you might write "I enjoy spending time with a few close friends."

Second, usage rules—the rules that govern grammar—are stricter in writing than in conversation. You don't have to think about punctuation when you talk, but when you write, you must use commas, periods, and other punctuation marks correctly. Furthermore, writers must follow detailed rules about such matters as verb endings and pronouns, but in conversation your friends may not mind if you make verb or pronoun errors.

A third difference is that college writing requires *planning*, but conversation doesn't. When you talk with friends, you can say almost anything that comes into your head. Most conversations aren't organized into paragraphs, so you're free to change the subject any time you want to; furthermore, conversations don't require you to develop all your ideas. For example, it's okay to say that you like horseback riding and then switch to another idea. But when you write a paragraph, you must plan and organize your ideas carefully. First, you must follow through on one subject. Resist the impulse to stray onto another subject as you write. Second, you must develop your ideas with several sentences. It's not enough to say that you like horseback riding, for example; you must provide more information. What do you particularly like about it? You might mention the fresh air, your feeling of independence, and the scenery in the countryside.

You spend more time speaking than writing, so your speaking habits may show up in your writing and create problems. The following exercises will help increase your awareness of the differences between writing and speaking. When you understand these differences, you can develop your writing skills.

Exercise 3

INSTRUCTIONS: Write your answers to the following questions, and be prepared to discuss your ideas in class.

1. *Control* is an important factor in speaking and writing. Which activity allows you more control over your words—speaking or writing? Why?

2. Look up the words *colloquial* and *slang* in the dictionary. Then, in your own words, write a definition of each.

3. Explain why colloquial and slang words are not normally acceptable in college writing.

4. Make a list of colloquial and slang words that you might use in conversation but not in college writing.

5. Do you pay more attention to usage when you write or when you speak? Why?

6. Write out a brief conversation that contains colloquial words. Then rewrite the conversation in words suitable for college writing.

7. Write out a brief conversation in which the topic changes several times. Then list the ideas that were not fully developed in conversation.

The Importance of Organization and Usage

Here is a well-written paragraph done by a student named Karen for her first writing course in college. Her instructor had asked the students to write about their favorite pastime. Notice that Karen's paragraph is carefully organized and that all of her usage is correct:

My Favorite Pastime

I listen to the radio as often as I can. First, it is good company. When I'm sitting home alone or driving to class, the radio keeps me from feeling lonely. The announcers and disc jockeys seem like old friends. Second, the radio lifts my spirits. If things go wrong, I go off by myself and turn on my radio. Soon I'm singing and feeling better. Whether the songs are old or new, they usually cheer me up. Most of all, the radio gives me something to talk about. I can discuss new songs with my friends because all of them have radios too. When I started college, I made friends quickly by starting conversations about my favorite radio station. Throughout the day, listening to the radio is an important part of my life.

Learning More About Organization

Reread Karen's paragraph, noticing how carefully she organized it. First, the paragraph has *unity*, because Karen stuck to her subject. Everything in her paragraph explains why she enjoys listening to the radio. Second, Karen's paragraph has *coherence*, because she was careful to put related ideas together. After she wrote that the radio lifts her spirits, she explained how: it makes her feel like singing. Finally, Karen used the "organizing words" *first, second,* and *most of all* to sort her ideas. In this course you will learn more about both organizing words and paragraph writing. Naturally, you will not use the same organizing words in everything you write. As you become more skilled, you will develop other ways to organize your ideas. For now, you will find these organizing words useful tools.

Learning More About Usage

Karen's paragraph shows that she cared about correct usage. Throughout the paragraph, she paid attention to small but important sentence details such as spelling and punctuation. Karen spelled every word correctly, and she was careful to complete every sentence. She used commas and periods properly throughout her paragraph.

Correct usage is important for two reasons. First, it shows that you are serious about your work. Successful college students edit their assignments in order to make a good impression. Second, correct usage makes your writing easier to read.

The following sentence demonstrates the confusion that arises from faulty punctuation. What does the restaurant serve? Even if you read the sentence carefully, you're not sure:

> **Coffee ice cream chocolate cake and apple pie are served at the restaurant.** *Commas needed*

Does the writer mean *coffee ice cream*, or does he mean *coffee* and *ice cream*? Commas clarify the meaning: Coffee ice cream, chocolate cake, and apple pie are served at the restaurant.

Here's another example. Without a comma, this sentence is confusing:

> **When we finished eating the squirrel hopped away from our picnic table.** *Comma needed*

The sentence is easier to understand when you add a comma after *eating*:

> **When we finished eating, the squirrel hopped away from our picnic table.**

Exercise 4

INSTRUCTIONS: Write your answers to the following questions, and hand them to your instructor.

1. Clip out a well-written paragraph from a magazine article or newspaper. Make a list of its good qualities.

2. Write three sentences explaining why you enjoy weekends. Use the organizing words *first*, *second*, and *most of all* in your sentences.

3. In a sentence or two, explain how correct usage can enhance the professionalism of your writing.

Getting the Most Out of This Writing Course

This course focuses on the two qualities of good writing discussed earlier: organization and usage. Unit 2 introduces the three steps of the writing process: planning, writing a rough draft, and editing. Units 3 and 4 address how to organize a short paragraph. Unit 5 covers four basic types of sentences. The rest of this book gives more information about writing effective sentences. In addition, the course provides many opportunities for practicing writing short paragraphs.

Your success in this course depends on you. The following suggestions will help you master the organization and usage skills taught in this course:

1. Ask questions.

Most instructors welcome questions from their students. If something puzzles you while you're studying this text or listening in class, ask about it. If you need more information from your instructor, make an appointment to see him or her during office hours.

2. Take notes.

Your instructor knows a great deal about good writing. Benefit from that knowledge by taking careful notes in class. Pay particularly close attention to anything written on the chalkboard during a lecture.

3. Read each assignment at least twice.

Each reading has a different purpose. When you read an assignment for the first time, you're becoming familiar with new information. On the second reading, you should underline important material that needs special attention.

4. Make your own study aids.

If a page in your notes seems particularly important, photocopy it to carry with you and study in your spare moments. When a usage rule seems particularly important, copy it onto a piece of posterboard and hang it in your room. Make flash cards with questions on one side and answers on the back. Some students make small flash cards and punch a hold in one end. Then they carry the cards on a key ring for frequent review. You will especially appreciate these study aids when you are studying for a major test.

5. Improve your spelling skills by making a spelling notebook.

To make a spelling notebook, buy a pocket-sized notebook and write one letter from the alphabet on top of each page. On the "A" page, write down the "A" words you find hard to spell—for example, you might write *accommodate, all right,* and *ancient.* Keep adding new words to your notebook. Every time you look up a word in the dictionary, record the correct spelling in your notebook. Keep it with you whenever you work on a writing assignment, and carry it with you to study in your spare moments. It's easier to look up a word in a spelling notebook than in a big dictionary. The spelling notebook will also remind you of the spelling words you need to study.

6. If you have a cassette recorder, use it as a study aid.

You can make a tape of important information and play it back several times a day. Some students play a study tape while getting ready for class in the morning and before going to sleep at night. Listening to a tape several times a day is an excellent way to memorize new material.

If your car has a tape deck, you can play your recording while you're driving. If you don't have a tape deck, consider buying an inexpensive adapter so that you can plug your cassette player into the cigarette lighter. Students with busy schedules say that they can memorize a great deal of information while they are commuting.

7. Make studying a daily habit.

Don't wait until the day before a test to begin studying. Even if your instructor doesn't give you an assignment, spend some time studying every day. Plan to use this time reviewing your flash cards, learning a few words from your spelling notebook, and studying a chapter from this book. If you have a cassette player, spend some additional time every day listening to a study tape.

Introduction to Writing

8. Use a team approach to learning.

Of course, you will need to study by yourself every day, but try to organize a small group of friends to meet with regularly for studying. Working together, you can help one another understand new material. Team members can also build your confidence and help you enjoy learning.

9. Plan ahead.

Develop a realistic study plan and follow it during your spare time. Establishing a consistent routine will help you get into the mood to study. Make your plan flexible enough to allow for interruptions and regular breaks. A workable plan is one of the best tools you can have during your college years.

Exercise 5

INSTRUCTIONS: Write out your answers to all of the following questions. Be prepared to share them with other class members.

1. Reread all nine study suggestions. Which two would be most helpful for you to adopt immediately? Explain why.

2. What are ten words that you feel doubtful about when you are spelling them? Explain how you plan to avoid doubts about them in the future.

3. Which study suggestions would be most difficult for you to adopt immediately? Explain why, and then describe your plan for overcoming the difficulty.

4. What is a study technique you've used in the past and found helpful? Explain how you plan to use the technique in the future.

Glimpsing into Your Future

The following story, about former President Jimmy Carter, illustrates the importance of preparing *now* for future success. Dorothy Sarnoff, a speech consultant, wrote this account after working with president Carter on one of his speeches. Jimmy Carter's speech-making difficulties emphasize the importance of developing communication skills now, while you are still in college. Although you are studying writing rather than speaking in this course, Dorothy Sarnoff's advice should still prove useful to you:

Rehearsing a President
by Dorothy Sarnoff

It was early in the summer of 1979.

"This is Gerry Rafshoon," the pleasant voice on the phone said. "I'd like to ask you if you would work with the President."

"What do you think he needs?" I asked.

"Everything," said Mr. Rafshoon. "How much time will you need?"

"Well," I said, "I would not like to do a Band-Aid operation to get him through one speech. I'd like to do the basics with him."

"That's very sensible. Sounds good."

I told Mr. Rafshoon I'd need at least four hours, preferably two hours on two days, and that I also would want to meet with the President's writers and anybody else who was involved in his speeches.

I flew down to Washington on a Friday, the weekend before the President was to deliver a major speech on television—only I didn't know that then. In the Map Room of the White House, I checked out the videotaping equipment I'd requested. Everything looked perfect for the next day.

On Saturday morning I met Mr. Carter in the Map Room. He entered with Gerry Rafshoon and one of his aides. He was beaming.

"Okay," I said. "We're ready. Good-bye, everybody."

"Yes," said the President. "Everybody out."

"What would you like to accomplish during my time here?" I asked when we were alone.

He leaned back in his chair and smiled. "Well," he drawled, "everybody tells me I'm pretty good."

"Then," I said kiddingly, "I can turn around and go home, right?"

"I never took a course in this, you know," Mr. Carter said.

I handed him an unmarked copy of an earlier speech of his. Mr. Carter delivered it in a choppy fashion, no flowing phrasing and the famous smile was there.

"I think I have something you'll like," I said and showed him the same speech separated into phrases. "Here's the first rule," I said. "Don't stop the breath until you get to margin right. Finish the phrase, finish the phrase, finish the phrase."

We worked on the speech for nearly an hour.

"This is marvelous," he said.

"One thing to try to get rid of," I said, "is shifting on your feet every time you shift phrases." I suggested he keep his body firm, weight evenly distributed on the balls of both feet, ribcage erect.

"Nobody ever told me that," he said.

"And try to go down in pitch at the ends of phrases and when you want to emphasize."

"They told me to go up to emphasize," said President Carter.

"I don't know who 'they' is," I said, turning on the videotape machine for his next run-through, "but down in pitch will work much better for you."

We watched the playback of his speech. I pointed out to him that the camera exaggerated his warm smile into a grin, and that—grin or smile—it often seemed inappropriate.

"Some day I'd like to deliver a speech that gives me something to smile about," he said ruefully.

The following day, I was struck by the inhumanely hectic pace of the President's schedule, the rushing from one appointment to another. When could he, or any President, have time to think, to mull things over?

We worked for about two hours. Much of that time was devoted to looking over a new speech. It concerned the crisis in Cuba, and Mr. Carter planned to deliver the talk on Monday night. I showed the President how to shorten the overlong sentences, and why they were not spoken sentences. "Could you please come to Camp David tomorrow so that we can work on it some more?" he asked me.

"Of course," I said.

The next day I met with President Carter in his Camp David Office. He handed me the new draft of his Cuba speech. He had worked on it all night; it was considerably improved, but it also was considerably changed. We went over it together.

"We need a closing on this," I said. "It just fades away. By the way, you really should have a collection of quotes and anecdotes you can draw on."

"We really should," said the President appreciatively.

"And the word *important*," I said, "it's used at least six times in this talk. Do you have a thesaurus here at Camp David?"

"Susan," he called to his secretary, "call Rosalynn and get the thesaurus." When the book arrived, he read to me from it. *"Crucial? Critical?"* He was an eager student; he had a huge appetite for improvement.

On Monday afternoon I was back at the White House. I worked with the people who were preparing the Teleprompter roll. The trick is to synchronize the Teleprompter with the notes the speaker has in front of him. That was nicely under control when the President walked in with what amounted to a whole new speech. There was hardly time for two run-throughs. The TV staff had to race to put together a new Teleprompter script while the President and I started rehearsing. When the script finally arrived, it did not match the President's.

That night in the Oval Office, the President delivered his speech to the world, putting into practice many of the principles on which we had worked. President Carter never did develop into a Franklin Delano Roosevelt or a Winston Churchill, but the speaker who delivered the Presidential State of the Union message in 1980 had come a long way from the speaker of 1976.

Speaking and communicating skills should be sharpened before you sit in the big leather chair, behind the big executive desk, in the big executive office. Once you get there, the demands of public and corporate life are so consuming that there's little time to develop those needed skills.

Exercise 6

INSTRUCTIONS: The following questions relate to the selection you just read. Answer each question. Then, when you are finished, be prepared to discuss your answers with a group of other students.

1. In her last paragraph, Dorothy Sarnoff stresses the importance of sharpening your communication skills early in life. What are the communication skills that will be most important in your career?

2. Participating in class and studying your textbook are two ways to sharpen your communication skills now. What other ways can you think of? Be as creative as you can.

3. Imagine that the time is ten years from now. You have been extremely successful in your career. Write a brief imaginary newspaper account about yourself as you hope to be in the future.

Introduction to Writing

Reviewing What You Have Learned

Exercise 7

INSTRUCTIONS: Answer these questions.

1. In a sentence or two, explain why writing is important to your future plans.
2. Fill in the blank:
   Successful writers recognize the importance of both
   _____ and _____ .
3. True or false:
   Most successful writers follow a three-step writing process.
4. Give two reasons why correct usage is important in college writing.
5. List three ways in which spoken English is different from the written English used in college assignments.
6. Describe a procedure you can follow to improve your spelling skills.
7. Explain how team studying can increase your chances of success in college.
8. Give one reason for sharpening your writing skills before you enter the professional world.
9. Explain how your writing skills can help you succeed in college.
10. Describe one change you plan to make in your study habits as you take this writing course.

Unit Two
The Writing Process

SUMMARY

1. You can improve your writing by following the three-step process that successful college students use: planning, writing, and revising.

2. Because each of the steps has a different purpose, you should concentrate on one writing task at a time.

3. Be flexible as you go through the steps. Make changes as you write, even if they're messy, and repeat the steps as many times as you need to.

In Unit 1 you learned that successful students use *the writing process* when they prepare their assignments. In this process, you tackle a writing assignment in three steps. Each step has a different purpose, so you can concentrate on one task at a time. Now you're going to learn in more detail how to use the writing process to write a good paragraph.

Many students fear writing assignments because they try to write a perfect paper all in one step—an almost impossible task. A good paragraph takes shape gradually. You'll develop confidence and skill as you practice breaking down the writing process into three steps.

To get an overview of this process, think of three pieces of paper. (Of course you won't always use *exactly* three sheets of paper every time you work on a writing assignment, but this example may help you understand the process.) You'll begin by *planning* your assignment on one sheet of paper. At this stage it's perfectly all right to be messy. You don't even have to write complete sentences yet; you're warming up and experimenting with ideas.

After you've finished planning, you'll get another sheet of paper and start *writing*—the second step. Now you're putting your thoughts into complete sentences. It's still all right to be messy; a rough draft doesn't have to be perfect.

Finally you'll begin the third step, *revising*. Working from your rough draft, you may change some of your ideas to make them more effective. You'll probably rewrite some of your sentences to improve them, and you'll correct spelling errors by using your dictionary. When you've finished making these changes, you'll neatly write out your assignment on the third piece of paper and hand it in.

Making the Writing Process Work for You

Be flexible as you go through the writing process. Most successful writers—both college students and professionals—jump back and forth between the steps, improving their writing each time. After you've written your rough draft, feel free to return to the planning step to discover more ideas. Later, as you revise your paragraph, you can write another draft or change some ideas.

In the past you may have tried to make your paragraphs perfect the first time, without any false starts, cross-outs, and sentence errors.

Perfectionism doesn't work well in college writing, however. Your assignments will probably demand more planning, more rough drafts, and more revising changes than you may be accustomed to. Resolve now to take all the time you need, and all the steps that are necessary, to produce an effective piece of writing.

Getting Involved in the Writing Process

Good writing draws upon your own personality and life experience. Often you will write about events that have happened to you and people you know, and you will draw upon thoughts born from your intellect and your imagination. Even when you write about an issue outside of your own experience, your lifestyle and belief system will shape your words and ideas. Think of the diverse responses a group discussion could elicit about topics such as these: white-collar crime, nuclear disarmament, the divorce rate, and alcoholism. If you listened to a discussion about one of these topics, you could develop opinions about the participants, their personalities, and their backgrounds.

To avoid snap judgments and oversimplifications in your writing, draw upon your personality and experience. You know from your own educational experiences that generalizing about students is almost impossible because there are so many differences in age, goals, habits, tastes, and lifestyles. Remember that every group has diversity, whether it is ethnic, national, religious, or political.

Remember, too, that successful writers choose subjects that they know well or have researched carefully. You can achieve success by following their example.

Express your individuality by choosing topics that interest you, and search for ideas and examples that reflect your personality. A topic such as alcoholism can be handled in a multitude of ways. For example, you could take a compassionate look at some victims of alcohol, or you could write persuasively about the need for legislation and new programs—or you could choose a totally different viewpoint. Your personal experiences and outlook on life will guide your choice of the approach that works best for you.

Before you begin to write, spend some time thinking about your topic. Suppose that you want to write a paragraph about your favorite type of popular music. You may describe how music fits into your lifestyle at home, with your friends, and at work. Perhaps a special song reminds you of an inspiring moment, a romantic evening, or a hilarious weekend with friends. You may be able to remember a time when music lifted you out of a depression. You may also have earned money as a performer, or amused your friends by imitating a popular singer, or worked in a music store. Whatever your experience has been, it's unique to you—and you can describe it better than anyone else can.

Be creative as you search for material to write about. If the topic is largely outside your personal experience, do some research. The library is a great resource; so is the telephone book, which can put you in touch with people who know firsthand about your subject.

Many of the topics in this course center around your personal experience. Here, too, preparation can be extremely helpful. If you're writing about a vacation, for example, reread any letters you have about it. Look at your postcards and photographs, and talk with someone who was there with you. Most important, try to recall and relive the experience. As memories start to flow, jot them down on a piece of paper so you'll be able to remember them later. Train yourself to search for the most vivid, powerful details you can think of—the best examples to illustrate the point you want to make. More than any other writing technique, preparation will bring your writing to life.

The following activities will guide you through the experience of bringing something from the past to life so that you can write about it.

Exercise 1

1. Search your memory to recall a story about yourself that you want to share with others. You may choose a story from childhood, adolescence, or adulthood. The story might relate to your sense of humor, compassion, love of fun, ambition, loyalty, intelligence, versatility, or some other trait.

2. Relive as much of the story as you can, either by thinking about it or telling it to someone else. Take notes at this step so that you don't forget anything important.

3. Write the story. Don't worry about usage or organization; just try to put as much as you can on paper so that you can share your story with others.

4. Make copies of your story to share with two or three other students; then meet in a group and take turns reading your stories aloud while group members read along silently. Following each story, give each listener a chance to comment about a particularly effective part of the story. Then suggest

how the story could be improved. Finally, ask group members to explain how and why they chose their particular stories.

5. Write down the names of group members. After each name, jot down a few words describing a special quality the person has that showed up in the story he or she told.

Step 1: Planning

The preparation you do before you write is called the *planning step*. Preparation makes your writing more effective by encouraging you to dig into your own experience for material. As you research your subject and explore your memories, you are getting ready to write. As you saw in Exercise 1, prewriting activities help you get in touch with ideas you didn't even know you had.

Stimulating the flow of new ideas is one of the most important purposes of the planning step. You've probably had several experiences like this one: You disagree with a friend about an idea, and suddenly you raise points you'd never thought of before. The disagreement stimulated you to produce new ideas: you could describe it as a discovery process. Writing is also a discovery process—a way of generating new thoughts. Throughout college and your professional life, you will often learn something new as you write.

As you plan, give yourself permission to discover new thoughts by writing down *everything* that comes into your head. If an idea is unworkable, you can always cross it out later. When you allow yourself to think freely, your imagination and creativity spring into action.

Learning How to Plan

The planning step can include a variety of activities to quicken new ideas and organize your thoughts. You may choose one planning activity, or you can combine several. As you follow the tips given here, you will jot down many ideas on scratch paper. These pieces of paper are called your "planning sheets." Save them to use later as a guide.

One helpful planning technique is called *freewriting*. Begin by writing down your topic in a few words. Then write as many ideas as you can about your topic. Don't aim for elegance with this technique (or any planning technique), and don't stop to cross out material or correct errors. Just keep writing until you have run out of ideas.

Another helpful technique is *listing*. Just write your subject at the top of a sheet of paper and then list everything you can think of about it. Don't try to write complete sentences: your only purpose is to produce ideas. If you're writing about a car you want to buy, for example, list everything you like about the car. If your subject is the dangers of drinking and driving, list every danger you can imagine.

Still another strategy is to list these words on a planning sheet: *Who, What, Where, When, Why, How.* Put a question mark after each one, and then answer each question with ideas about your subject. Suppose, for example, you are writing a paragraph about teenage marriage. Under *Who?* you could jot down the name of some married teenagers you know. Under *What?* you could list some observations you've made about teenage marriages. The questions *When? Why?* and *How?* can be answered the same way. By the time you've finished, you should have a solid list of possible ideas for a paragraph.

Remember that *details create interest*, and search for specific details as you plan. Do you remember Karen's paragraph about listening to the radio? To make her ideas more interesting, she included several specific details. Her paragraph tells us that she listens to the radio often, that she sings along, and that her friends have radios, too. Be as specific as possible while you're generating ideas.

Making Your Own Planning Sheet

You are going to write a paragraph about your favorite pastime. Begin by thinking about activities you enjoy; then choose a favorite for your freewriting. The pastime you choose is called the topic or subject of your paragraph.

In Unit 1, you read Karen's paragraph about listening to the radio. Here is the list she prepared as she planned her paragraph:

My Favorite Pastime

singing with the radio
I listen in the car
I listen at home
I don't feel lonely
I have a cassette player, too
my father complains about the noise
talking about songs in the
  Student Center
the disc jockeys are like old friends

sometimes the news comes on
I sing advertising jingles
the radio cheers me up
hearing the latest songs
I take my radio to the beach

Karen didn't use all of these ideas in her paragraph; some of them didn't explain why she enjoyed the radio. Since enjoyment was her main idea, she crossed out the comments about the cassette player and her father's complaints. She dropped other items on the list because they would have made her paragraph too long—advertising jingles, news reports, the beach.

You should choose just as selectively when you plan your own paragraph. Every paragraph needs *unity*—it must stick to one idea. Cross out any irrelevant and weak material before you begin the writing step. If you can't find enough strong ideas to write about, pick another topic. Remember that the best ideas and examples are those that come from your life experience, your personality, and your belief system.

Learning More About Unity

Here's a student paragraph that lacks unity. Cross out any ideas that don't develop the main idea:

Mornings

I need to be better organized in the morning. My whole day goes badly when I get off to a bad start. But sometimes I wake up early and feel terrific all day. First, I need to eat a good breakfast. Even though I'm dieting, I can find something nutritious to eat in the morning. My grandmother used to make fantastic homemade biscuits. They were probably loaded with calories. Second, I should lay my clothes out the night before. I waste valuable time looking for my favorite shirts and shoes. I have found some wonderful bargains at consignment stores. My pleated wool skirt cost only three dollars. Most of all, I need an appointment calendar. Sometimes I forget the classes and meetings I've scheduled for the day. Then I leave the house without the papers I need. Maybe I should cut back on some of my outside activities, too. These simple changes will make my whole life less hectic and more enjoyable.

You should have crossed out these sentences:

But sometimes I wake up early and feel terrific all day.

My grandmother used to make fantastic homemade biscuits.

They were probably loaded with calories.

I have found some wonderful bargains in consignment stores.

My pleated wool skirt cost only three dollars.

Maybe I should cut back on some of my outside activities.

Learning About Coherence

Paragraphs also need *coherence*: Ideas must be grouped together logically. Good writers avoid jumping from one idea to another.

The following paragraph has unity but lacks coherence. Regroup the ideas so that they are organized coherently:

Visiting Walt Disney World

My family enjoyed our trip to Walt Disney World last summer. We enjoyed meeting all the Disney characters. At MGM Studios, my parents got excited about the film sets and movie-star displays. Our visit triggered many memories for them, and I enjoyed hearing them reminisce. We swam, danced, and ate exotic meals. Minnie Mouse visited us at breakfast one morning. We saw Pluto in a French beret and Donald Duck in a space suit. The characters were always friendly and fun to watch. I enjoyed seeing my parents so relaxed and full of fun. The fun never stopped. There was always a show or parade to entertain us. We never went to sleep before 2 A.M. Although we just got back two weeks ago, I can't wait for our next visit.

Here's an improved version of the same paragraph. This time, ideas have been grouped coherently with the help of the words *first*, *second*, and *most of all*:

Visiting Walt Disney World

My family enjoyed our trip to Walt Disney World last summer. First, we enjoyed meeting all the Disney characters. Minnie Mouse visited us at breakfast one morning. We saw Pluto in a French beret and Donald Duck in a space suit. The characters were always friendly and fun to watch. Second, I enjoyed seeing my parents so relaxed and full of fun. At MGM Studios, they got excited about the film sets and movie-star displays. Our visit triggered many memories for them, and I enjoyed hearing them reminisce. Most of all, the fun never stopped. We swam, danced, and ate exotic meals. There was always a show or parade to entertain us. We never went to sleep before 2 A.M. Although we just got back two weeks ago, I can't wait for our next visit.

Good organization doesn't happen automatically—it takes planning. You probably have felt frustrated when listening to a speaker who randomly jumped from one idea to another—a problem with coherence. Or you may have tried to follow your friend's recounting of a cave-diving adventure, but her ideas weren't unified: she wandered off the subject to talk about the ridiculous price she paid for her equipment. The following exercise will help you increase your understanding of unity and coherence.

Exercise 2

INSTRUCTIONS: Four paragraphs appear here. Two are correctly organized, but two have problems with unity and coherence. Label each paragraph *correct* or *incorrect* and be prepared to meet with other students to explain your choices.

Paragraph 1

I'm trying to save enough money to take a trip to France next summer. First, I quit smoking. The money I save on cigarettes will pay for my airplane tickets. Second, I'm not sure I want to go next summer. If I wait until I graduate, I'll have more money to spend in France. Most of all, I want to buy clothing in Paris. I'll be able to impress all my friends with my French wardrobe.

Paragraph 2

I'm trying to save enough money to go to France next summer. First, I quit smoking. The money I save on cigarettes will pay for my airplane tickets. Second, I started working as a waitress. My salary and tips will pay some of my expenses in Paris. Finally, I moved back home with my parents. Because it's inexpensive to live with them, I hope to build up my vacation fund rapidly.

Paragraph 3

My parents are sorry they had a swimming pool built in our back yard. First, it cost more than they had expected. The contractor's original estimate wasn't very accurate. Second, pool maintenance is very difficult. We spend hours every week trying to keep the water clear. Most of all, we don't have enough time to use the pool much. It takes us over an hour to change our clothes, swim, and then blow-dry our hair afterwards.

Paragraph 4

My parents are sorry they had a swimming pool built in our back yard. First, it cost more than they had expected. Second, pool maintenance is difficult. My parents put the pool in so that our family could swim together. When my brothers and I were small, we begged our parents to get a pool. My brother Mark swims before breakfast every morning during the summer. My other brother and I swim a few times a week. It takes over an hour to change our clothes, swim, and blow-dry our hair afterwards.

Gathering Ideas

Since you're writing about a favorite pastime, it's important for you to get close to this experience. If at all possible, do it! Go to the bowling alley, shoot a roll of film, play a piano piece—engage in the activity you've chosen. Take a notebook with you and take notes. If you can't do the activity at this time, you have two choices. Use your imagination and other aids (photos, perhaps, or a telephone call to a friend) to remember how the activity feels. Or choose another pastime as your subject—one that you can experience right now.

Exercise 3

INSTRUCTIONS: Prepare a planning sheet about your favorite pastime. *Participate* in the pastime if at all possible. Take notes and use your imagination. When you've finished writing down your ideas, exchange papers with another student. As you read each other's papers, check to see that you both have included some vivid details.

Writing a Topic Sentence

After reading over your planning sheet, write a general sentence about your favorite pastime. (If you've already filled up one piece of paper, use another one.) This sentence is called your *topic sentence* because it explains the topic of your paragraph. It's not just a title; it is a sentence that demonstrates your attitude towards the pastime. Later it will be the first sentence (and the most general) in your paragraph. Here is Karen's topic sentence:

I listen to the radio as often as I can.

Exercise 4

INSTRUCTIONS: Write a topic sentence that shows how you feel about your favorite pastime. After you have written your topic sentence on your planning sheet, meet with three or four other students from your class to look over your topic sentences. Then have your instructor check these sentences.

Supporting Your Ideas

Take a moment right now to review the planning you have done. Surprise—you have already finished most of the preparation needed to write your paragraph. The topic sentence you wrote in Exercise 3 will be the first sentence in your paragraph. The other ideas you jotted down will become *supporting ideas;* they will explain why you enjoy the activity. You should have crossed out any ideas that did not fit your topic sentence. For example, don't include anything negative about your favorite pastime (it tires you out, costs too much money, or interferes with your college work). Make sure your outline has *unity*— that all your ideas are consistent.

Reread the planning you have already done, grouping similar ideas together. Look for the three biggest reasons why you enjoy your favorite pastime. Cross out ideas that don't fit with those three major reasons. This grouping of ideas gives your paragraph coherence. Instead of jumping from one idea to another, you develop each idea separately.

Write the three reasons you have chosen underneath your topic sentence. If you have trouble thinking of these reasons, you may find it helpful to write the word *Why* three times on your planning sheet. Then explain *Why* three times, and your three supporting ideas will be ready.

Here are Karen's topic sentence and supporting ideas:

I listen to the radio as often as I can.   *Topic Sentence*

(Why?) It is good company.   *Supporting Idea*

(Why?) It gives me something to talk about.   *Supporting Idea*

(Why?) It lifts my spirits.   *Supporting Idea*

Exercise 5

INSTRUCTIONS: On a planning sheet, write the word *Why* three times after your topic sentence. After each *Why*, write one reason why you enjoy your favorite activity. Check your outline for unity and coherence.

Organizing Your Ideas

You've already been introduced to the organizing words *first*, *second*, and *most of all*. These words help you group your ideas and examples logically so that your writing has coherence. To use them, think about your three supporting ideas again, and decide which is the most important. (Karen decided that talking about new songs with her friends was most important to her.) Put a star (☆) in front of that reason, like this:

☆ **It gives me something to talk about.**

Now write your three reasons again, putting the starred reason *last*, as Karen did:

I listen to the radio as often as I can.   *Topic Sentence*

It lifts my spirits.   *Supporting Idea*

It is good company.   *Supporting Idea*

☆ **It gives me something to talk about.**   *Supporting Idea*

Now put organizing words before your reasons. To do this, label your reasons *first*, *second*, and *most of all*, as Karen did:

I listen to the radio as often as I can.   *Topic Sentence*

First, it lifts my spirits.   *Supporting Idea*

Second, it is good company   *Supporting Idea*

Most of all, it gives me something to talk about.   *Supporting Idea*

These four sentences—Karen's topic sentence and supporting ideas—are her *outline*. Now she has completed planning her paragraph, and she is ready to move on to the second step in the writing process. You should be ready, too.

Exercise 6

INSTRUCTIONS: Write your outline here.

_____ Topic Sentence
_____ First Supporting Idea
_____ Second Supporting Idea
_____ Most Important Supporting Idea

Now that you have finished the planning step, you are ready for the next step—writing a rough draft of your paragraph. Be sure to save your planning sheets, since you will be referring to them again when you go on to the next step.

Exercise 7

INSTRUCTIONS: Meet with three or four students from your class to check your outlines. Make sure you have used the organizing words correctly.

Step 2: Writing Your Rough Draft

In this step you will write a "rough draft"—a messy first version of your paragraph. Don't use a dictionary in this step, and don't be concerned about usage rules yet. Concentrate on writing complete sentences about the ideas you listed in your outline.

You need enough working space for two pieces of paper. Your outline will serve as a guide, and you'll use a clean sheet of paper to write your rough draft on. Follow the pattern you set up in your outline, but your rough draft will look quite different when you are finished: each part of your outline will become a complete sentence. In addition, you will develop your ideas by adding examples. Sometimes a paragraph will also have a final sentence called a *conclusion*, as Karen's does.

When Karen wrote her first draft, she copied her topic sentence from her outline. She also copied her reasons and organizing words, but she made them into complete sentences—and she developed each one.

Here is Karen's rough draft:

My Favorite Pastime

I listen to the radio as often as I can. First, the radio is good company. Sometimes the radio seems like a friend. Second, it lifts my spirits. Things go wrong, and I turn on my radio. Soon I'm singing and feeling better. Most of all, the radio gives me something to talk about. I can discuss new songs with my friends. Listening to the radio is an important part of my life.

Exercise 8

INSTRUCTIONS: Read Karen's rough draft again and label each part:

A. Title, topic sentence

B. First reason, first development

C. Second reason, second development

D. Third reason, third development

E. Conclusion

Developing Your Ideas

Before you start your rough draft, think about each reason in your outline. What details can you think of to support each reason? Write these details as complete sentences, and include them in your rough draft. If you have diffficulty thinking of suitable details, try asking *When?* and *How?* after each of your reasons. Make sure your reasons and details have coherence—that you have grouped them together logically with the organizing words *first, second,* and *most of all.*

Bob, a college freshman, decided to write a paragraph about his favorite pastime, coaching his brother Joey's softball team. He used this outline to write his rough draft:

Topic Sentence   *I enjoy coaching my brother's softball team.*

First Reason   *First, I enjoy the sunshine and fresh air.*

Second Reason   *Second, it feels good to have Joey and his friends look up to me.*

Most Important Reason   *Most of all, the games are always exciting.*

Bob needed some examples to make his paragraph interesting. The planning sheet he had prepared earlier listed several good ideas. This is what he had written:

Planning Sheet

sunshine, fresh air
Joey and his friends look up to me
I remember when I was
  ten years old
the whole team gets excited
  when we win
yelling when there's a home run

teaching the boys new skills
I make sure everyone gets to play
  each game
they're learning sportsmanship
we encourage everyone on
  the team
I get a suntan

Now he felt that he was ready for the writing step. Here is his rough draft:

My Favorite Pastime

I enjoy coaching my brother's softball team. First, I enjoy the sunshine and fresh air. I haven't been to the beach yet, and I have a suntan already. Second, it feels good to have Joey and his friends look up to me. I'm teaching them about sportsmanship. Most of all, the games are exciting. We all yell when someone hits a home run. When I started coaching Joey's team, I expected the boys to have fun. The surprise was how much I enjoyed it, too. Because coaching has been such a good experience, I'm already looking forward to the softball season next spring.

Exercise 9

INSTRUCTIONS: Read Bob's rough draft again and label each part:

A. Title, topic sentence

B. First reason, first development

C. Second reason, second development

D. Third reason, third development

E. Conclusion

Exercise 10

INSTRUCTIONS: Using the planning sheets you have already prepared, write a rough draft about your favorite pastime. Keep your sentences short and simple. When you are finished, label each part of your paragraph:

A. Title, topic sentence

B. First reason, first development

C. Second reason, second development

D. Third reason, third development

E. Conclusion

Then meet with two or three other students to read your rough drafts. Make sure that each part of the paragraph is labeled correctly. Make sure the paragraph has coherence: Ideas should be grouped together logically. Also, check the paragraph for unity: cross out any ideas that stray from your main idea.

Step 3: Revising

After you complete the writing step (your rough draft), you are ready to revise your paper and hand it in. During the revising step, you will make changes in your paragraph to be sure that it is effectively written. You will also *edit* your paper to ensure that it is free of spelling and usage errors. (You will learn more about usage in later units of this book.)

Revising can be a time-consuming process. You will have to reread your paper several times, and perhaps rewrite it several times, before you can hand it in. You will find it helpful to ask friends to help you revise your papers. Most professional writers depend on colleagues to help them polish their writing. You would be wise to follow their example, unless, of course, an instructor asks you to work entirely on your own. For example, if you're taking an essay test, you won't be permitted to ask other students for help!

Be aware that you may need to go back to the planning and writing steps. As you revise, try to write the best possible paper. Feel free to change ideas, cross out material, and add new sentences if necessary.

Learning How to Revise

You will need your rough draft, a pen or pencil, your notes, and at least one clean sheet of paper. Your working area should be spacious enough so that you can spread your materials out in front of you.

You will probably make most of your corrections on your rough draft. Later, when you are satisfied with your paragraph, you will copy it onto a clean sheet of paper to hand in.

First, evaluate the content of your paper. It's best to read your paragraph aloud to one or two other students, paying close attention to their suggestions. First, ask your friends to help you evaluate the quality of your ideas. Two helpful questions to ask are, "Is it intelligent?" and "Is it interesting?" If your paper lacks either quality, go back to the planning step to search for better ideas and examples.

Next, check the organization of your paper. You can begin by looking for unity. If you went off the subject at some point in your paragraph, eliminate the detour. Every sentence in your paragraph should relate to your topic sentence. As you have seen, coherence is another essential quality. Your paragraph should make sense. As you revise, cross out any ideas that weaken your topic sentence. Check your supporting ideas to make sure that each is developed thoroughly.

Finally, edit your paper for sentence errors. Evaluate the effectiveness of your sentences. If your friends tell you that an idea is unclear, or if they misunderstood something, clarify it. Rewrite any awkward sentences, and correct sentence mistakes.

With the help of a dictionary, check and correct the spelling of any word you're not sure about. Write the words you've checked in your spelling notebook so that you can study them later.

If you're unsure about a punctuation mark or another usage question, check your notes or textbook. (During this writing course, you will thoroughly review punctuation and usage.)

Read your paper aloud one last time—either to yourself or to a friend—but do it differently this time: start with the last sentence, and read backwards until you finish with the first sentence. This useful trick helps many students spot sentence errors they otherwise might have missed.

When you're finished with your corrections, write or type the final draft on fresh paper. Then check it one last time before you hand it to your instructor.

Neatness

Aim to hand in a paper that looks professional. If you're writing by hand, skip lines as you write. If you make an error, cross it out neatly with a single line and make a correction above the line or after it. If you make more than two errors, throw the paper away and begin again. Do not scribble, erase, trace over, or use correction fluid.

If you're typing, double space. If you make an error, correct it neatly with correction tape or correction fluid. If you find an error after you take the paper out of the typewriter, correct it neatly with a pen. If you find more than two errors, retype the page.

Exercise 11

INSTRUCTIONS: Reread Karen's rough draft, comparing it to her revised paragraph. Write your answers to these two questions:
1. What changes did Karen make in her revision?
2. Why do you think she made these changes?

Then discuss your answers with two or three other students.

Karen's rough draft:

My Favorite Pastime

I listen to the radio as often as I can. First, the radio is good company. Sometimes the radio seems like a friend. Second, it lifts my spirits. Things go wrong, and I turn on my radio. Soon I'm singing and feeling better. Most of all, the radio gives me something to talk about. I can discuss new songs with my friends. Listening to the radio is an important part of my life.

Karen's revised paragraph:

My Favorite Pastime

I listen to the radio as often as I can. First, it is good company. When I'm sitting home alone or driving to class, the radio keeps me from feeling lonely. The announcers and disc jockeys seem like old friends. Second, the radio lifts my spirits. If things go wrong, I go off by myself and turn on my radio. Soon I'm singing and feeling better. Whether the songs are old or new, they usually cheer me up. Most of all, the radio gives me something to talk about. I can discuss new songs with my friends because all of them have radios too. When I started college, I made friends quickly by starting conversations about my favorite radio station. Throughout the day, listening to the radio is an important part of my life.

Exercise 12

INSTRUCTIONS: Compare Bob's rough draft, which you have already read, and his revised paragraph. Answer these questions; then meet with two or three other students to discuss your answers.

1. What changes did Bob make when he revised his paragraph?
2. Why did he make these changes?

Bob's rough draft:

My Favorite Pastime

I enjoy coaching my brother's softball team. First, I enjoy the sunshine and fresh air. I haven't been to the beach yet, and I have a suntan already. Second, it feels good to have Joey and his friends look up to me. I'm teaching them about sportsmanship. Most of all, the games are exciting. We all yell when someone hits a home run. When I started coaching Joey's team, I expected the boys to have fun. The surprise was how much I enjoyed it, too. Because coaching has been such a good experience, I'm already looking forward to the softball season next spring.

Bob's revised paragraph:

My Favorite Pastime

I enjoy coaching my brother Joey's softball team. First, the sunshine and fresh air are wonderful. I haven't been to the beach yet, but I have a suntan already. Second, I feel important when Joey and his friends look up to me. I'm teaching them about sportsmanship because I believe in team spirit. Most of all, the games are exciting. We jump up and yell when someone hits a home run. When I started coaching Joey's team, I expected the boys to have fun. The surprise was how much I enjoyed it, too. Because coaching has been such a good experience, I'm already looking forward to the softball season next spring.

Exercise 13

INSTRUCTIONS: With the help of another student, revise your rough draft and make a neat final copy. Then meet with two or three other students and discuss the changes you made.

Reviewing What You Have Learned

Exercise 14

INSTRUCTIONS: Column A lists the three steps in the writing process. Column B lists writing tasks. Match the writing tasks in Column B with the steps in Column A. Notice that you will list two tasks under each step.

Column A	Column B
Planning Step	Evaluate content
Writing Step	"Warming up"
Revising Step	Write a rough draft
	Check spelling in a dictionary
	Put ideas into complete sentences
	Explore ideas

Exercise 15

INSTRUCTIONS: Imagine that a classmate is having trouble with writing because he can't get started. He has never heard of the writing process. Write him a brief note, explaining how planning his paragraph ahead of time can help him get off to a good start.

Exercise 16

INSTRUCTIONS: Write a letter to a newspaper describing your views on an issue that concerns you. Use the writing process to plan your letter, make a rough draft, and revise your work. When you are finished, meet with a small group of students to discuss the steps you followed. Did you find the writing process helpful? Explain your answer.

Unit Three
The Paragraph

SUMMARY

1. A paragraph is a short unit of writing about a single idea.

2. The paragraphs you will write for this course will be from seven to ten sentences long.

3. A paragraph has three parts: the *topic sentence, supporting ideas,* and *examples.*

4. The topic sentence states the main idea in a paragraph.

5. The topic sentence is usually the most general sentence in a paragraph.

6. Supporting ideas and examples develop the topic sentence.

Every time you open a book, magazine, or newspaper, you are likely to find paragraphs. A paragraph is a short unit of writing about a central idea. In both college and professional writing, paragraphs must be carefully planned and organized.

The paragraphs that you write for this course will contain from seven to ten sentences. This unit shows you how to recognize the main parts of a paragraph. You will also learn how to arrange them so that they are organized effectively.

The most general sentence in a paragraph is called the *topic sentence*. It states the main idea of the paragraph. Other sentences, called *supporting ideas* and *examples*, develop the topic sentence. Later in this unit you will learn how to identify these parts of a paragraph.

When you're reading, it is easy to spot the beginning of a paragraph, because it starts with an *indentation*—a short space on the first line. If you look back to the first line of this paragraph, you will find an indentation before the word *When*. As you write, you will indent your paragraphs in the same way.

You will find it worthwhile to spend a great deal of time and effort mastering paragraphs because you will write so many of them in college. Sometimes you will write a single paragraph for an assignment; on other occasions you will write papers that contain five or six paragraphs (or even more).

Throughout this course, you will concentrate on single paragraphs such as the one below, which was written by a student named Tim. His instructor had asked the class to write about the worst job they'd ever had. Tim's paragraph will serve as a model for the paragraphs you will be writing. Once you understand how Tim put his ideas together, you can organize your paragraphs in the same way:

Paragraph 1

The worst job I ever had was typing for an insurance firm. First, the work exhausted me. I sat in an uncomfortable chair all day and typed envelopes. Second, my supervisor disliked me. Although I was the best typist in the office, she often complained about my work. Most of all, the pay was low. My hourly wage was only ten cents more than the minimum wage.

Identifying the Parts of a Paragraph

Every paragraph you write in this course consists of three parts. First, it needs a *topic sentence* that tells what the paragraph is about. Here is Tim's topic sentence:

> **The worst job I ever had was typing envelopes for an insurance firm.** *Topic Sentence*

In this writing course, you will put your topic sentence at the beginning of the paragraph, as Tim did. (In future courses, the topic sentence may be placed in other positions.)

Your paragraph also needs another type of sentence called a *supporting idea*. A supporting idea develops your topic sentence. Here is Tim's paragraph again, with his supporting ideas underlined:

> The worst job I ever had was typing for an insurance firm. <u>First, the work exhausted me.</u> I sat in an uncomfortable chair all day and typed envelopes. <u>Second, my supervisor disliked me.</u> Although I was the best typist in the office, she often complained about my work. <u>Most of all, the pay was low.</u> My hourly wage was only ten cents more than the minimum wage.

Notice that Tim had a sentence after each of his supporting ideas. These sentences, which give details that explain your three supporting ideas, are called *examples*. Here's Tim's paragraph again, with his examples underlined:

> The worst job I ever had was typing for an insurance firm. First, the work exhausted me. <u>I sat in an uncomfortable chair all day and typed envelopes.</u> Second, my supervisor disliked me. <u>Although I was the best typist in the office, she often complained about my work.</u> Most of all, the pay was low. <u>My hourly wage was only ten cents more than minimum wage.</u>

In subsequent writing courses you may learn other ways to organize paragraphs. The basic parts of a paragraph always are the same, however: topic sentence, supporting ideas, and examples.

Learning More About Topic Sentences

The topic sentence usually is the most general statement in your paragraph. It tells your reader what you plan to write about and what idea you have about it. If your topic is computers, your topic might look like this:

Every college student should take an introductory computer course.

Everything else in your paragraph will develop the topic sentence with specific information. In the paragraph about computers, you would explain *why* students should learn about computers. You could develop your topic sentence with *examples* from college life and careers.

Here are some topic sentences that one group of students used when they wrote about the worst jobs they'd ever had:

I never want to baby-sit again.   *Topic Sentence*

I spent the most miserable summer of my life selling magazines.   *Topic Sentence*

Cleaning the attic for my mother was the worst job I've ever had.   *Topic Sentence*

Each of these sentences would make a good topic sentence for a paragraph because each can be developed with specific information. The student writing about baby sitting could describe some of the difficult children she worked with. The magazine salesperson could discuss the frustrations involved in selling door-to-door. The young man who cleaned the attic could recall the exhausting hours he spent moving trunks and cartons for his mother.

Exercise 1

INSTRUCTIONS: On a piece of scratch paper, jot down some ideas about an unpleasant job you remember. (The job could be one you did for money or one you did without pay for a relative or friend.) Then write a topic sentence about it. Make sure your topic sentence is general enough to be backed up with specific information. Finally, meet with two or three other students to evaluate your topic sentences, making sure that you can support and develop them.

Learning More About Supportive Ideas

Your paragraph needs three supporting ideas to develop your topic sentence. It's a good practice to begin these sentences with the organizing words *first, second, most of all*. Take another look at Tim's topic sentence. Notice that his supporting ideas explain why his topic sentence is true:

The worst job I ever had was typing for an insurance firm.
Topic Sentence

(Why?) The work exhausted me.   *Supporting Idea*

(Why?) My supervisor disliked me.   *Supporting Idea*

(Why?) The pay was low.   *Supporting Idea*

The topic sentences presented earlier about baby-sitting, selling magazines, and cleaning the attic also can be supported in the same way—by answering the question *Why?* three times, as shown here:

I never want to baby-sit again.   *Topic Sentence*

(Why?) The children were rude to me.   *Supporting Idea*

(Why?) The pay was low.   *Supporting Idea*

(Why?) The time dragged.   *Supporting Idea*

Here is a complete paragraph about baby-sitting. The topic sentence and supporting ideas have been underlined. Notice that they are the same ones you just read:

Paragraph 2

<u>I never want to baby-sit again. First, the children were rude to me.</u> They argued with me when I told them it was bedtime. Although they finally went to bed, I was in such a bad mood that I couldn't study or watch TV. <u>Second, the pay was low.</u> I didn't even make minimum wage, and there were never any tips. <u>Worst of all, the time dragged.</u> I felt bored sitting all alone late at night. I much prefer having my friends or family with me. I finally decided to stop baby-sitting and to find a job I enjoyed.

Exercise 2

INSTRUCTIONS: Label the topic sentences and supporting ideas in paragraphs 3 and 4. Then meet with a small group of other students to explain your answers.

Paragraph 3

I spent the most miserable summer of my life selling magazines. First, I felt embarrassed all the time. I was so shy that it was difficult to talk to my customers. Second, I made very little money. The people I talked to couldn't afford the magazines I was selling. Worst of all, I was too exhausted to enjoy my time off. Walking up and down the street in the heat of summer wore me out. Next summer I'm going to look for a well-paying job in an office.

Paragraph 4

Cleaning the attic for my mother was the worst job I've ever had. First, the job was backbreaking. I hauled huge piles of magazines and old clothes out to the trash. In one weekend I cleaned out seven years of accumulated junk. Second, I felt sick the whole time. The dust and mildew in the attic irritated my nose and eyes. Worst of all, the job was dangerous. I fell down the stairs twice while I was carrying boxes outside. I dropped an old typewriter on my foot, and I limped for three days. The next time my mother wants to empty the attic, I'm going to suggest that she hire a cleaning service.

Exercise 3

INSTRUCTIONS: Several topic sentences appear here. Each one is followed by a supporting idea. Write two additional supporting ideas for each topic sentence.

I'm hoping to make some good friends while I'm in college.
Topic Sentence

First, I'm going to get involved in campus activities.
Supporting Idea

_____*Supporting Idea*

_____*Supporting Idea*

Last Saturday's car wash was a success.   *Topic Sentence*

First, we had a good location.   *Supporting Idea*

_____*Supporting Idea*

_____*Supporting Idea*

College students need a place of their own to live.   *Topic Sentence*

Students need a private place to entertain their friends.   *Supporting Idea*

_____*Supporting Idea*

_____*Supporting Idea*

I'd like to visit Europe after I graduate.   *Topic Sentence*

First, I'd like to see some of the countries I've been hearing about.   *Supporting Idea*

_____*Supporting Idea*

_____*Supporting Idea*

Exercise 4

INSTRUCTIONS: Write three supporting ideas for your topic sentence from Exercise 1. Remember that your supporting ideas should explain why you disliked that particular job. When you are finished, meet with a small group of other students to discuss your supporting ideas.

Learning More About Examples

Examples are the most specific sentences in a paragraph. They clarify your supporting ideas by providing specific details. They also add interest because they describe particular places, people, and events.

To see how examples add interest, compare these two paragraphs. Paragraph 5 lacks examples, but examples are included in Paragraph 6. Because we know more about the mother's enthusiasm for the Beatles, we find her more interesting. As a result, we enjoy reading Paragraph 6 more than Paragraph 5:

Paragraph 5

Although my mother is over forty, she is still a devoted Beatles fan. First, she admires their musical talent. Second, she loves their classic films. Most of all, she likes to remember the fun she used to have watching their concerts and television appearances.

Paragraph 6

Although my mother is over forty, she is a devoted Beatles fan. First, she admires their musical talent. *Rubber Soul* and *Sergeant Pepper's Lonely Hearts Club Band* are still her favorite albums. I've often heard her talk about the creativity the Beatles brought to popular music. Second, she loves their classic films. She's seen *A Hard Day's Night* more than a dozen times. John Lennon's puns always make her laugh. Most of all, she likes to remember the fun she used to have watching their concerts and television appearances. She still talks about the night she watched the Beatles perform in New York's Shea Stadium. I think it's pretty neat having a mother who's such a devoted Beatles fan.

Exercise 5

INSTRUCTIONS: Read Paragraph 6 again, and label the topic sentence, the supporting ideas, and the examples.

Exercise 6

INSTRUCTIONS: Go back to the topic sentence and supporting ideas you wrote in Exercise 4. Now write an example for each supporting idea. When you are finished, meet with a small group of students to discuss what you've written.

Exercise 7

INSTRUCTIONS: The topic sentences used in Exercise 3 appear again here. You have already written supporting ideas for each of these topic sentences. Copy the supporting ideas you have already used; then add an example for each.

The Paragraph 45

I'm hoping to make some good friends while I'm in college.
Topic Sentence

First, I'm going to get involved in campus activities.
Supporting Idea

_____ *Example*

_____ *Supporting Idea*

_____ *Example*

_____ *Supporting Idea*

_____ *Example*

Last Saturday's car wash was a success.   *Topic Sentence*

First, we had a good location.   *Supporting Idea*

_____ *Example*

_____ *Supporting Idea*

_____ *Example*

_____ *Supporting Idea*

_____ *Example*

College students need a place of their own to live.   *Topic Sentence*

First, students need a private place to entertain their friends.
Supporting Idea

_____ *Example*

_____ *Supporting Idea*

_____ *Example*

_____ *Supporting Idea*

_____ *Example*

I'd like to visit Europe after I graduate.　　*Topic Sentence*

First, I'd like to see some of the countries I've been learning about.　　*Supporting Idea*

_____ *Example*

_____ *Supporting Idea*

_____ *Example*

_____ *Supporting Idea*

_____ *Example*

Exercise 8

INSTRUCTIONS: Label the topic sentence, the supporting ideas, and the examples in both of the following paragraphs:

Paragraph 7

I'm glad I decided to take a word-processing course. First, I'm saving time on my college writing assignments. I don't have to retype a whole page when I want to change a sentence. Second, my grades are better. Because editing on a computer is so easy, I'm handing in better papers. Most of all, I'm practicing a skill that will benefit me later on. Many companies are interested in hiring people with word-processing skills.

Paragraph 8

Learning how to apply makeup is not as easy as it looks. First, you must choose the appropriate colors. You have to consider your skin, your eyes, and the clothing you will be wearing. Second, you have to experiment with makeup so that it looks natural. If you apply a little too much foundation or blusher, your makeup may look garish. Most of all, you must practice using a variety of brushes and other makeup tools. You will probably discover that it is difficult to put eye shadow and eyeliner on without smearing them.

The Paragraph 47

Reviewing What You Have Learned

Exercise 9

INSTRUCTIONS: Fill in the blank space in each sentence with information you have learned about paragraphs.

1. The most general sentence in a paragraph is called the _____.

2. Examples of organizing words are _____, _____, and _____.

3. Organizing words are generally used with the sentences called _____.

4. Each *supporting idea* should be followed by one _____.

5. Usually the most specific sentences in a paragraph are the _____.

Exercise 10

INSTRUCTIONS: Go back to Exercise 6. Write out your topic sentence, supporting ideas, and examples in paragraph form. Label each sentence.

Exercise 11

INSTRUCTIONS: The topic sentences in the following paragraphs are missing. Read each paragraph carefully, and then write a suitable topic for it. (Remember that a topic sentence is the most general sentence in the paragraph.)

Paragraph 9

First, housework bores me. There's nothing interesting about vacuuming a floor or scrubbing a bathtub. Second, housework exhausts me. After I've cleaned the whole house, I don't have the energy to enjoy myself that evening. Most of all, I'm embarrassed to have my friends see me doing housework. I wish I could tell them that my parents are rich enough to afford a cleaning service.

Paragraph 10

First, I don't have a quiet place to study. My younger brother, who shares my bedroom, insists on having the radio on all the time. Second, I don't have any privacy. Because our house is small, I don't have a place to be alone with my friends. Most of all, there are too many interruptions at home. Every time I sit down to study or call a friend, someone in my family wants to talk to me.

Exercise 12

INSTRUCTIONS: The next three paragraphs need additional supporting ideas and examples. First, read the paragraph carefully. Next, decide what is missing--a supporting idea or an example. Finally, write a suitable sentence in the space provided.

Paragraph 11

Keeping a pet is more expensive than many people realize. First, cats and dogs need routine veterinary care. A pet should be neutered and should have vaccinations every year. Second, pets sometimes need special medical attention. _____.
Most of all, the daily upkeep of a cat or dog can be expensive. _____.

The Paragraph

Paragraph 12

I've decided to start taking better care of my car. _____. The hoses and belts are four years old. Second, I'm going to wash and wax it regularly. _____.

_____. Most of all, I'm going to look under the hood more often. I think I have an oil leak, and that could cause serious problems.

Paragraph 13

I'm finding it hard to work and go to college at the same time. First, I had trouble arranging my work hours with my boss. _____. Second, I'm more tired than I expected to be. Last night I started to get sleepy while I was studying.

_____. Although I used to eat lunch with my friends several times a week, I rarely see them anymore.

Exercise 13

INSTRUCTIONS: Three scrambled paragraphs appear here: the sentences have been placed in the wrong order. Follow these steps to rewrite the paragraphs in the correct order:

1. Read each scrambled paragraph carefully.
2. Look for the topic sentence and label it. (Remember that it is the most general sentence in the paragraph.)
3. Label the three supporting ideas. (They are more specific than the topic sentence and explain why the topic sentence is true.) Usually they begin with organizing words: *first, second, most of all.*
4. Label the three examples. (Remember that they are specific incidents that back up supporting ideas and are always the most specific sentences in a paragraph.) An example should follow each supporting idea.

5. Rewrite the scrambled sentences as a paragraph. (Remember to indent the first sentence.) Be sure to write the sentences in the correct order. You may find it helpful to use the paragraphs in Exercise 5 as a model.

Scrambled Paragraph 1

Most of all, I feel proud of my mechanical knowledge. Because I've done the work myself, I don't have to worry that a mechanic made an error. My friends are impressed when I tell them that I replaced a water pump myself. First, I save money. I'm glad I've learned how to do my own car repairs. Most garages are charging at least twenty dollars an hour for labor. Second, I know that the repairs have been done properly.

Scrambled Paragraph 2

If I'm constantly late for work, I may not be considered for promotions. Twice last month she got mad at me because we were late for a movie. Second, lateness annoys my girlfriend. Last week I missed some important information in my chemistry class because I was late. First, lateness is affecting my schoolwork. I need to work on my lateness problem. Most of all, lateness could damage my future.

Scrambled Paragraph 3

She thinks the adult language is unsuitable for family viewing. She just had our living room redocorated, and she doesn't want it spoiled by a black cable. Second, she disapproves of some of the movies shown on cable. First, she says we don't need to watch more television. My mother refuses to have cable television installed in our house. Most of all, she says the black television cable is unsightly. My younger brother is having trouble in school because television cuts into his study time.

Unit Four
More About Paragraphs

SUMMARY

1. In the planning step of the writing process, you need to choose the type of paragraph that best suits your purpose.

2. A *descriptive* paragraph develops an idea by creating a word-picture for your readers.

3. In a *narrative* paragraph, you make your point by telling readers an appropriate story.

4. In a *persuasive* paragraph, you use strong evidence to support a position that you are advocating.

In the last unit, you learned how to develop a topic sentence through supporting ideas and examples. This unit introduces you to three more types of paragraphs. *Descriptive* paragraphs provide a vivid word-picture for your readers. *Narratives* tell a story, and *persuasive* paragraphs present strong evidence to support a particular point of view.

These three types of paragraphs share a common characteristic: they are organized around a central idea. Suppose you choose to write a paragraph about beauty pageants. If you are in favor of them, you could write a descriptive paragraph showing how much fun they are for participants and audiences. You could also write a narrative telling an upbeat story about one of the winners. Or you could write a persuasive paragraph arguing that beauty pageants are a worthwhile tradition: contestants learn poise in front of an audience, win scholarship money, and develop self-confidence.

You could also write a descriptive, narrative, or persuasive paragraph that takes a stand against beauty pageants. A descriptive paragraph might focus on the relentless competition and false glamour backstage. In a narrative, you could tell a depressing story about a disappointed contestant who didn't win. A persuasive paragraph might argue that beauty pageants exploit women, trivialize their talent, and destroy their self-esteem. The choice is yours, and so is the responsibility for developing your viewpoint clearly and effectively.

Introducing Descriptive Paragraphs

A descriptive paragraph makes a point by helping readers imagine the person, place, or thing you are describing. In both college and your career, you can expect to write many descriptive paragraphs. A humanities professor may ask you to describe an art show you visited; a manager may need a description about new office equipment; a police sergeant will want to know what a particular crime scene looked like.

Here is a sample of a descriptive paragraph:

The Dance Studio

Last January my husband and I started loking for ways to be more active and make new friends. We decided to go to a dance studio to learn ballroom dancing. The dance studio has become one of my favorite places. First, it's elegant. Potted plants line a wall of shining mirrors. We dance on a beautiful, old-fashioned parquet floor. Second, the studio is friendly. Most of the students know one another. They drop in to say hello when they're in the neighborhood. Once a month we get together for a party. Most of all, it's a magical place. When tango music is playing, I feel mysterious and exotic. When we're gliding to a waltz, I feel like a princess. I've discovered a whole new world at the dance studio.

Good descriptive writing is an extremely useful skill. In your personal life, letters and diaries with powerful descriptions are worth rereading and saving for future generations. Descriptive writing is helpful at work, too. In applying for a grant, evaluating an employee, or promoting a product, you must create a convincing word-picture for your reader. Résumés also require descriptive writing. How can you convince a prospective employer that you are responsible, intelligent, and creative? The answer is to write vivid sentences describing the tasks you have performed: perhaps you *led a project, designed a program, supervised a budget,* or *trained a team.*

Good descriptions are frequently visual, asking readers to use their imagination to *see* what you are describing. Visual descriptions can also help you describe feelings, character traits, and abstract qualities, such as excellence and integrity. How does a person act when she is angry, curious, skeptical, or spiritual? Search for vivid examples that your readers can visualize, and encourage them to use their other four senses as well: hearing, tasting, smelling, touching.

The following writing activities will help you develop your ability to write descriptions by asking you to describe someone you know well—yourself.

Exercise 1

1. Imagine that you are applying for a job that you would especially enjoy doing. Be creative as you imagine the job—it can be either paid or voluntary, full time or part time. It can involve any area that interests you: athletics, crafts, the academic world, social problems, business, or any other field. Write a letter introducing yourself and your qualifications. In your letter, describe a few accomplishments that qualify you for the job. Focus on specific activities to make your letter convincing.

2. Choose a photograph of yourself and write five sentences that describe what you were like when the picture was taken. Before you start writing, spend some time recalling that period in your life. What were your goals, interests, personality traits, achievements, and problems? You don't have to mention all of these, but they should provide some vivid details to use in your description.

Writing Descriptive Paragraphs

After you've done a few planning activities to explore your subject, you can start organizing your ideas. The topic sentence should state your subject and controlling idea. You may need to give some background information in a sentence or two. If you're writing about a person, mention her age and occupation. A descriptive paragraph about a car, for example, should give its make, model, and color.

Details and examples bring descriptions to life. Convey what your favorite beach looks like, or how exhausted you feel after frying hamburgers for an eight-hour shift, or what makes you enjoy tinkering with your car so much. The organizing words you have already learned—*first, second,* and *most of all*—probably will be useful.

As you read the following descriptive paragraph, notice how the writer's main point, supporting ideas, and details add interest and clarity:

A Troubled Person

My cousin Oliver, a nineteen-year-old auto mechanic, is a troubled young man. Three months ago he entered a drug rehabilitation program. When my parents and I visited him at the treatment center last week, we saw that he has a long struggle ahead of him. First, Oliver is too angry to cooperate with the center's program. I saw him clench his fists when the Director was talking to him. Twice during the visit he started an argument with my father. Second, Oliver lacks self-control. He isn't used to looking ahead at the consequences of his actions. During Sunday's visit, he told us that he'd lost his privileges several times for breaking the center's rules. He didn't want to get into trouble, but he couldn't stop himself. Worst of all, Oliver has low self-esteem. When I reminded him that he was my favorite cousin, he shrugged and changed the subject. Oliver is an expert mechanic and a talented musician, but he denies having any special talent. Oliver is going to need a great deal of help to turn his life around.

Exercise 2

1. Describe an annoying or pleasing trait you've observed in another person. Use specific facts and details to enliven your description.
2. Think of a quality your family has that makes it special. Then write a paragraph describing that quality. Make your paragraph convincing by using specific examples.
3. Write a paragraph describing one of the following: a room in your house, a place you remember from childhood, your place of worship, a place you've visited, your vehicle, or the place where you work.
4. Write a paragraph describing one of the following: a sports team, a school or community group you've joined, or your carpool.
5. Write a paragraph describing one of the following: a perfect college, job, house, vacation, friend, or spouse.

Introducing Narrative Paragraphs

Once you are familiar with descriptive paragraphs, you can begin another type, the narrative. Although you may not have tried writing a narrative before, developing an idea in this way is not really new to you. Every story is a narrative—even the fairy tales of childhood. Here's a narrative paragraph:

My Prison Visit

Two months ago my sociology professor arranged a class trip to a state prison. As a result of that visit, I've become interested in learning more about criminal justice. When we arrived at the visitor's building, a stern officer read a long list of rules to us. No pocket knives, cameras, or valuables were allowed in the visitor's room. Two officers were assigned to search us. Then we nervously took seats in the visitors' room, where a group of inmates talked to us about prison life. At first we were afraid to ask questions. But after a half hour, we felt more comfortable. I learned a lot about everyday prison life. By the time we left, several of us had made friends with inmates. I'm still writing to Bob, who is serving a sentence for armed robbery. Lately I've been reading more about the penal system. Our prison visit aroused my curiosity about the men and women who live behind bars.

When you think about narratives, you may associate them with entertainment. You probably enjoyed stories as a child, and now you appreciate more sophisticated narratives in novels, television shows, plays, and movies. You may know—or be—a gifted storyteller who turns everyday happenings into delightful stories.

However, narratives do more than entertain—they shape and define the events of our lives. As you look back on your life, you may have changed the way you tell some of your own stories. A frightening or embarrassing story from the past may now seem humorous or poignant. An event that seemed insignificant or bewildering five years ago may now have a central place in your life's story.

Every narrative requires interpreting and shaping; in a sense, it is impossible to tell a story objectively. Selecting and discarding always are necessary, for a story crammed with irrelevant details lacks focus. In addition, the storyteller must always choose a beginning and an end point, and these decisions likewise shape the story.

When you plan a narrative, your first task is to reflect on your story to decide what it means. Then you can select the details that emphasize your story's meaning. Think of a police officer preparing a report about a marital argument, for example. Before she begins to write, the officer must decide what the story means. Was it really an argument? Or was it an assault or an attempted homicide? The officer must choose the category that best fits the story she is writing. To give her story unity and coherence, she must decide what to include and what to omit. She noticed a heavy skillet on the kitchen counter. Should it be mentioned in the report? When the angry husband opened the door, he was buckling on a heavy belt. That might be an insignificant detail, or it could transform the story into a tale of violence.

Of course, this marital argument could be told differently by a psychologist, minister, newspaper reporter, or novelist. The arguing husband and wife would have different versions, and so might an eavesdropping neighbor. Writing is power—the power to define and interpret events according to your unique experience and outlook.

Professionals often use narratives to convey a message to their readers. After a tour of a distant factory, a manager might write a narrative about the organizational problems she noticed there. Supervisors frequently include narratives in personnel evaluations; the story of a good or bad job performance can serve as useful documentation later on.

When you write a narrative paragraph, be aware of your power to shape and interpret the events you are describing. Use your imagination to relive your story and get in touch with its meaning; then select details that will convey the story's significance to your readers.

Writing Narrative Paragraphs

In planning your narrative, you will decide what the story means. Incorporate that meaning into your topic sentence, telling your reader two things: what your story is about, and what it means. Here are some sample topic sentences:

When I was fired from my first job, I learned an important lesson about cooperation.   *Topic Sentence*

I'm glad I was able to overcome my nervousness about the speech contest last year.   *Topic Sentence*

The most fun I ever had was tubing down the Peace River with my friends.   *Topic Sentence*

After you've written the topic sentence, decide how your story began, and start your narrative there. Remember to use "time words" to organize your story: for example, *first, next, after,* and *when*. You won't use *first, second,* and *most of all* in a narrative.

During the revising step, make sure you told your story clearly, and look closely at the details you included. Do they bring your story to life? If not, search for better ones. When you're finished, read your story to a classmate or family member and ask for suggestions.

Now read the following narrative, and label the topic sentence and organizing words:

Money Problems

Cutting up my credit cards was one of the smartest things I ever did. I started having money problems two yeras ago when I got my first credit card. A department store downtown was trying to attract student business, and they opened an account for me. I didn't use the card for three months. But right before Christmas, I ran out of money for gifts. Then I remembered the card and started spending. Two months later I received a gasoline credit card in the mail. Before long, I was charging all my gas and car repairs. Then my bank offered me one of their cards. Somehow I forgot that I'd have to pay for everything eventually, and I went on a spending spree. Finally the truth hit me. The interest charges kept piling up, and sometimes I couldn't even pay the minimum monthly charges. One night, with a friend cheering me on, I cut all my credit cards in half. Since that day, I've paid off two of the credit cards. I plan never to make the same mistake again

Exercise 3

1. Write a narrative about an experience that taught you something important.

2. Choose an emotion, either positive or negative (anger, joy, sadness, frustration, love, hate, fear—or any other). Write a story about a time that you or someone else experienced that emotion.

3. Ask a friend or family member to tell you about an experience that shaped his or her life. Tell the story in a narrative paragraph.

4. Tell the plot of a television show in a narrative paragraph. Avoid the trap of merely recording a sequence of events: make sure you give the story meaning.

5. Write a narrative about a memorable event you participated in or witnessed. (Think about these categories to help you select an event: travel, school, work, recreation.)

6. Recall a piece of advice you might give another person. Then write a narrative illustrating your advice.

Introducing Persuasive Paragraphs

Now you're ready to begin writing persuasive paragraphs. You write persuasively every time you argue your point of view with someone else. Here's a typical persuasive paragraph.

Corporal Punishment is Obsolete

It's time for parents to stop using corporal punishment. Hitting kids does not help them become responsible citizens. First, corporal punishment is unnecessary. Many fine parents rear their children without striking them. Books and parenting classes can suggest many other discipline methods. Second, corporal punishment has limited usefulness. When a child is too big to hit anymore, her parents lose control over her. It's best to use alternative methods from the beginning. Most of all, corporal punishment can lead to child abuse. Too many kids are seriously hurt and even killed by their parents every year. Our society needs to make a strong commitment to other types of discipline.

You've probably noticed that the different paragraph types overlap. Many paragraphs describe, persuade, and tell a story all at once. The difference lies in the writer's purpose.

Like most types of writing, the persuasive paragraph is designed to make a point. What distinguishes persuasive writing is the directness with which the writer makes the main point. A persuasive paragraph clearly states its central idea and supporting arguments. The writer states the purpose in the topic sentence and develops the argument in the rest of the paragraph. Newspaper editorials are good examples of persuasive writing.

Persuasive writing is an important way of exercising the power that words can instill in you. People in responsible positions use persuasive writing to advocate change, win supporters for their beliefs, and increase their budgets and staff size. As a professional, you will often want to influence others. Persuasive skills are essential to success.

Writing Persuasive Paragraphs

The planning step is extremely important, because you'll need convincing evidence to advance your argument. Choose a subject you know well; if possible, read and listen to opposing arguments as well. Knowing what the opposition is saying often can give you ideas for your own paragraph. For example, you can argue against a proposed law by reading and answering the people who want it to pass.

Three supporting points seem to work well, so aim to include three in your paragraph. (The organizing words *first, second,* and *most of all* will probably be useful.) Each point then should be backed up with evidence.

Developing good supporting points and examples is an important goal of the planning step.

Studying your audience is equally important. You may choose to adjust your arguments to your readers' age, occupation, sex, and background. A paragraph about cleaning up the water supply, for example, might be pitched one way for young married couples, another way for business leaders, and yet a third way for the scientists.

After you've read the following persuasive paragraph, label the topic sentence, supporting ideas, and evidence.

Irresponsible Advertising

Advertising agencies need to take more responsibility for the attitudes they transmit to the public. First, automobile advertisers should stop glorifying reckless driving. The drivers on television ads often ignore road hazards, perform stunts, and take sharp turns at high speeds. They imply that driving is a sport rather than a responsibility. Second, the alcohol industry needs to tone down its fun-filled image. Ads make wine coolers sound as harmless as soft drinks. Wine is associated with wealth and glamour; beer is advertised as convivial and masculine. Most importantly, advertisers need to stop implying that their products provide instant solutions to life's problems. Extravagant claims for toys, appliances, pain relievers and beauty products can subtly alter consumers' attitudes to life. Americans may avoid searching for long-term solutions to problems because advertising keeps promising instant cures. How can a child develop his imagination if he believes that only an elaborate toy can relieve his boredom? Many adults are just as deceived by the gadgets in advertisements. Advertisers need to examine these issues and promote their products more responsibly.

Exercise 4

1. Write a paragraph persuading someone you know to change an opinion you disagree with. The issue could relate to lifestyle, politics, family life, religious beliefs, college, sports, or any other area.

2. Write a paragraph persuading someone you know to change a practice or behavior you disagree with. The issue could relate to parenting, work, recreation, the community, or any other area.

3. Take a position about one of the topics listed here. Then write a paragraph arguing your position. At the beginning of your paragraph, be sure to explain exactly what your position is.

   the drinking age   legalization of drugs
   early marriage   cheating in school
   the prison system   poverty
   abortion   the death penalty
   homosexuality   college rules

4. Write a paragraph arguing for or against one of the following positions:

   Telephone soliciting should be outlawed.

   Support Americans' right to bear arms.

   College students should be free to choose their own lifestyle.

   Religion should play a greater part in American life.

   All college courses should be pass/fail.

   The speed limit should be raised to 65.

Part Two
Writing Effective Sentences

Now that you've spent some time thinking about the importance of good writing, you're ready to sharpen your sentence skills. In Part 2 you'll learn to spot and correct common sentence problems, such as fragments and comma errors. Even more important, you'll master the four sentence patterns that successful writers use. Your sentences will begin to sound more mature, and you'll build on your ability to use commas and semicolons confidently.

Unit Five
The Sentence

> SUMMARY
>
> *1.* To succeed in college, you must be able to write effective sentences.
>
> *2.* Skilled writers use a variety of sophisticated sentence patterns.
>
> *3.* As you learn the four most important patterns, you will discover that each pattern has its own punctuation and usage rules.

Writing Effective Sentences

In Unit 1, you learned that good writing always has two important qualities: effective organization and good usage. Units 2, 3, and 4 showed you how to produce an effective paragraph in three steps. Now you're ready to learn about English usage. This unit shows you how sentence variety adds maturity and polish to your paragraphs. You will practice writing and punctuating four sentence patterns, along with a few variations. As you master these four sentence patterns, your writing will improve in two ways: you will follow the principles of correct usage, and you will develop skill in using a variety of sentence patterns, just as professional writers do.

Learning About Sentence Patterns

Successful writers value *sentence variety*. Instead of using short, choppy sentences, they connect their ideas in a variety of interesting ways. To see how mastering different sentence patterns can improve your writing, read the following two short, choppy sentences. Then read on to see how they can be combined into more sophisticated sentences:

Harriet wants to buy a new car. She can't afford the monthly payments.   *Short, choppy sentences*

Now see how a skilled writer might use more sophisticated sentences to present the same information:

Harriet wants to buy a new car although she can't afford the monthly payments.   *Example*

Although she wants to buy a new car, Harriet can't afford the monthly payments.   *Example*

Harriet wants to buy a new car; she can't afford the monthly payments.   *Example*

Harriet wants to buy a new car; however, she can't afford the monthly payments.   *Example*

Harriet wants to buy a new car, but she can't afford the monthly payments.   *Example*

Harriet, who wants to buy a new car, can't afford the monthly payments.   *Example*

You may be surprised that an idea can be written in so many ways. Good writers use a variety of sentence patterns because they want to keep their ideas interesting. Just as a dinner consisting of nothing but white foods would be dull (white chicken, white sauce, mashed potatoes, and cauliflower), a piece of writing with too many similar sentences can be boring.

Good writers, therefore, avoid using just one or two sentence patterns over and over. For example, skilled writers usually avoid writing three *because* sentences in a row. Knowing a variety of sentence patterns, they can change a string of *because* sentences to something different.

Here are three sentences that use the same pattern—ideas connected with *and*. Notice that the sentences sound monotonous:

Sentences Lacking Variety

Frank is studying photography, and he hopes to open his own studio eventually. He's still in college, and he's already earning money with his photography skills. A dancing school hired him to photograph its students, and he made enough money to pay his school fees this semester.

Now read the same ideas, expressed with a variety of sentence patterns. Notice that the monotony is gone—the variety of sentence patterns enlivens the ideas:

Sentences with Variety

Frank is studying photography because he hopes to open his own studio eventually. He is still in college, but he's already earning money with his photography skills. A dancing school hired him to photograph its students; he made enough money to pay his school fees this semester.

This textbook covers four sentence patterns, along with their variations, that are useful in both college and professional writing. While you study each sentence pattern, you will become familiar with its punctuation rules and its special words. For example, one sentence pattern uses the words *who* and *which* and often requires a comma. You will practice writing *who* and *which* sentences, and you will learn when the comma is required. Each sentence pattern is presented in a separate unit so that you can master it thoroughly.

To appreciate the advantages of knowing all four sentence patterns, think of a student of auto mechanics who is gradually becoming familiar with various makes of cars and their special features. Once he understands the characteristics of the Mercedes line, he knows what to expect when a car of that make comes into his shop. Similarly, after you have been introduced to a particular sentence pattern, you will know what to look for every time you work with that type of sentence. Your confidence will grow as you gradually master all four of the sentence patterns taught in this course.

Here are the four sentence patterns and variations, along with their examples:

1. Sentences with *although, if, when, because* (subordinate conjunctions)

    Harriet wants to buy a new car although she can't afford the monthly payments.

    Variation **Although she can't afford the monthly payments, Harriet wants to buy a new car.**

2. Sentences with semicolons

    Harriet wants to buy a new car; she can't afford the monthly payments.

    Variation **Harriet wants to buy a new car; however, she can't afford the monthly payments.**

3. Sentences with *and, but, or* (coordinate conjunctions)

    Harriet wants to buy a new car, but she can't afford the monthly payments.

4. Sentences with *who* and *which*

    Harriet, who wants to buy a new car, can't afford the monthly payments.

Chances are you've been using some (or all) of these patterns most of your life. Now you will learn them more thoroughly so that they can form the foundation for your college writing assignments.

Learning About Sentence Correctness

In addition to learning the four sentence patterns and their variations, you need to master the principles of usage (sentence correctness). When you hand in your college assignments, your professors will look for sentences that follow all the rules of English usage. In this course, you will learn procedures to ensure that your punctuation, capitalization, verb endings, pronouns, and other details are correct.

College students often make errors of usage in their writing, but even professional writers frequently have to correct their work. Effective writers focus on finding and correcting every error in their writing. To succeed in college, you need to decide now that you will work on each writing assignment until it is error free. You can eliminate almost all sentence errors by resolving to check your written work—just as you would check math assignments—before you hand it to your professor. As you learned in the last unit, you will make corrections in the final step in the writing process: the revising step.

As you study the procedures for correcting errors, you will probably appreciate their consistency. It is frustrating to work with a vague rule, such as "Use a comma every time you pause." You and the student sitting next to you may choose different places for a pause—how can you tell who is right? In this writing course, you will learn consistent usage rules that will always produce the correct answer.

Reviewing What You Have Learned

Exercise 1

INSTRUCTIONS: Read the four paragraphs. Two of them have sentence variety; two do not. Put a check before each paragraph that has sentence variety. Be prepared to explain your choices in class.

Writing Effective Sentences

President Theodore Roosevelt had a fun-loving teenaged daughter named Alice. She jumped off the deck of a ship with all her clothes on. She went to parties constantly. She shocked people with her sharp tongue. President Roosevelt jokingly tried to explain why he didn't interfere with her. He said, "I can run the country or control Alice. I cannot do both."

My mother's thrifty habits always embarrass me. She always has at least twenty coupons for the cashier when she pays for her groceries. My parents earn good salaries, but my mother shops at Goodwill every weekend. She goes to every garage sale in town; once a year she even holds her own garage sale to finance our family vacation. Although I enjoy the benefits of her thrift, I wish she would change her shopping habits.

Because our doctors wanted us to be slimmer, my friends and I started a dieting club last year. The club helped me lose twenty-five pounds, but it also caused me to become obsessed with food. When our club met each week, food was the main topic we discussed. Now I count calories every day, but I don't go to the dieting club any more.

My parents disagree about my sister's high school education. My mother wants her to go to a private school, but my father disagrees. Mom says the private school is worth the expense, but he wants to spend the money on educational trips instead. My sister wants to go to public school, but my parents don't want her to make that decision herself.

Exercise 2

INSTRUCTIONS: Fill in each blank by choosing an answer from the list.

1. To write effective sentences you must be skilled in the areas of _____ and _____.

2. In this course you will study four _____ and some of their _____.

3. To master each sentence pattern, you must learn its _____ and _____.

Answers
sentence patterns
sentence variety
sentence correctness
special words
variations
punctuation rules

Exercise 3

INSTRUCTIONS: Write two short sentences of your own. Then combine them in as many variations as you can, using the sentence patterns in this unit as a guide.

Unit Six
Subjects and Verbs

SUMMARY

1. Every sentence needs a subject and a verb.

2. If the subject or verb is missing, the sentence is incomplete.

3. The subject and verb must make sense together.

4. The subject tells *who* or *what* the sentence is about.

5. Most verbs are *action* or *existence* words.

6. An understanding of subjects and verbs will help you in the revising step of the writing process.

Subjects and verbs are important because they are the basic parts of any sentence. When you understand subjects and verbs, you can build on that knowledge to learn the basic sentence patterns that were introduced in Unit 5.

An understanding of subjects and verbs can also help you correct incomplete sentences (usually called *fragments*) when you revise a paragraph. The following exercise will help you understand what a fragment is. Two versions of a student's paragraph appear here. The first paragraph has some sentence errors because several subjects and verbs are missing. In the second version, every sentence is correct. Read both paragraphs *aloud* two or three times. As you read, try to hear the difference between the complete and incomplete sentences:

First Version

My friend Erika needs a part-time job. Only a small allowance from her parents. First, wants a nicer wardrobe for weekends. She doesn't have the right clothes for parties. Second, Erika doesn't always like the dorm food. Wants extra money for McDonald's and Taco Bell. Worst of all, gasoline very expensive. One morning last week she ran out of gas.

Correct Version

My friend Erika needs a part-time job. She gets only a small allowance from her parents. First, Erika wants a nicer wardrobe for weekends. She doesn't have the right clothes for parties. Second, she doesn't always like the dorm food. Erika wants extra money for McDonald's and Taco Bell. Worst of all, gasoline is very expensive. One morning last week she ran out of gas.

Here is the paragraph again, with the fragments underlined:

My friend Erika needs a part-time job. <u>Only a small allowance from her parents. First, wants a nicer wardrobe for weekends.</u> She doesn't have the right clothes for parties. Second, Erika doesn't always like the dorm food. <u>Wants extra money for McDonald's and Taco Bell. Worst of all, gasoline very expensive.</u> One morning last week she ran out of gas.

The following sentence pairs will give you another opportunity to hear the difference between complete and incomplete sentences. Read the pairs of sentences aloud. The first sentence in every pair is incomplete. The second sentence is correct. As you read, try to hear the difference between the incomplete and complete sentences:

Only a small allowance from her parents   *Incomplete*
She gets only a small allowance from her parents.   *Complete*
First, wants a nicer wardrobe for weekends.   *Incomplete*
First, she wants a nicer wardrobe for weekends.   *Complete*
Wants extra money for McDonald's and Taco Bell.
   Incomplete
Erika wants extra money for McDonald's and Taco Bell.
   Complete
Worst of all, gasoline very expensive.   *Incomplete*
Worst of all, gasoline is very expensive.   *Complete*

Exercise 1

INSTRUCTIONS: Write a paragraph explaining why you would like to have more money. Use only the first two steps of the writing process (planning and writing a first draft) that you have already learned. Save your planning sheet and rough draft. You will revise your paragraph later in this unit, when you have learned how to check each sentence to make sure it has a subject and a verb.

Defining Subjects and Verbs

To learn more about complete sentences, you need to understand the two most important parts of a sentence—the *subject* and the *verb*. Although you don't think about subjects and verbs as you speak, you use them both constantly. Every conversation, and everything you write, contains sentences with subjects and verbs.

The subject tells *who* or *what* the sentence is about. In the following sentences, *Janet* is the subject:

Janet goes to an exercise class twice a week.   *Example*
Janet is an excellent dancer.   *Example*

A verb is an *action* or *existence* word that completes the main idea of the sentence:

Janet <u>goes</u> to an exercise class twice a week.   *Example*

Janet <u>is</u> an excellent dancer.   *Example*

The first sentence has an action verb—*goes*. The second sentence has an existence verb—*is*. Notice that the subject and verb together form a "miniature sentence" that makes sense by itself:

Janet goes.   *Subject and Verb*

Janet is.   *Subject and Verb*

Learning More About Verbs

Most verbs are action or existence words that go with the subject. Common action words are *go, drive, study, eat,* and *work*. Common existence words are *am, is, are, was,* and *were*.

STUDY TIP: The five existence verbs appear very often in sentences. Learn them now so that you can recognize them easily. Write all five (*am, is, are, was, were*) on an index card. Then practice turning the card over and writing on scratch paper as many existence verbs as you can remember. Practice until you've memorized all five.

In the following exercise, use your knowledge of action and existence words to find the verb in each sentence:

Exercise 2

INSTRUCTIONS: Draw two lines under each verb in the following sentences. Remember to look for action and existence verbs.

1. My friends are creative people.
2. Chris paints wildlife pictures.
3. Birds are his favorite subjects.
4. Maria designs her own dresses.
5. Sometimes she makes a gown for a friend too.
6. Francesca decorates hats for her friends.
7. Last year I wore one of her hats to a wedding.
8. Donald is a cartoonist.
9. He draws cartoons for the campus paper.

Subjects and Verbs 75

10. Carl invents exotic recipes.
11. A restaurant manager offered him a chef's job.
12. Gerry writes poetry.
13. She finds ideas in everyday experiences.
14. Stanley does woodcarving.
15. I love his woodland animals.
16. Pam sells flower arrangements.
17. Usually she buys her flowers from a wholesaler.
18. I enjoy needlework.
19. Embroidered pillows are excellent gifts.
20. Last month I gave three of them to friends.

Exercise 3

INSTRUCTIONS: Put a check in front of all the action and existence verbs in the following list.

1. _____ cook
2. _____ plan
3. _____ was
4. _____ green
5. _____ is
6. _____ erase
7. _____ month
8. _____ change
9. _____ grow
10. _____ when
11. _____ pretty
12. _____ are
13. _____ travel
14. _____ near
15. _____ over
16. _____ were
17. _____ go
18. _____ bathtub
19. _____ steal
20. _____ am

Learning About Contractions

Sometimes a verb is joined with another word in a shortened combination called a *contraction*. The words *haven't, didn't,* and *I'm* are examples of contractions. When two words are combined in a contraction, letters are omitted and replaced by apostrophes:

I am = **I'm** (an apostrophe replaces the *a*)

have not = **haven't** (an apostrophe replaces the *o*)

did not = **didn't** (an apostrophe replaces the *o*)

When you look for verbs in a sentence, pay careful attention to contractions. Study the following examples:

> Jerry<u>'s</u> on his way to fame and fortune as a movie star. (The '<u>s</u> stands for *is*)
>
> You<u>'re</u> one of the winners. (The '<u>re</u> stands for *are*)
>
> We could<u>n't</u> see anything because we bought cheap tickets to the show. (The <u>n't</u> stands for *not*)

Exercise 4

INSTRUCTIONS: Draw two lines under the verbs in each of the following sentences.

1. He'll help you with your suitcase in a minute.
2. You've learned a great deal about chemistry this semester.
3. She'd enjoy an evening at the bluegrass festival with you.
4. Kathy's planning on a wedding at the beach.
5. We'd tried every plumber in town, with no luck.
6. I couldn't learn those medical abbreviations for the test.
7. They're the first watercolors I ever painted.
8. We'll try to get Professor Winston off the subject again today.
9. It's a perfect day for the space shot.
10. Somehow Gilbert hasn't bothered me once today.

Learning More About Subjects

You already know that the subject tells who or what a sentence is about. A subject can be a person, a place, or a thing. To find the subject of a sentence, look for the verb first. Then ask *Who?* or *What?* before the verb, like this:

> **Jennifer drove her aunt to the airport.** *Example*
>
> (The verb is *drove*. Who drove? Jennifer.)

Remember that the subject and verb form a miniature sentence that makes sense by itself. In the example you just read, the miniature sentence is *Jennifer drove*. Now study the following examples. What is the miniature sentence for each one?

Alan jogs at five o'clock in the morning.   *Example*

(The verb is *jogs*. Who jogs? Alan.)   *Miniature sentence: Alan jogs.*

Notice that the miniature sentence is the same even if you change the sentence around:

At five o'clock in the morning, Alan jogs.

The telephone wakes up my baby brother.   *Example*

(The verb is *wakes*. What wakes my baby brother? The telephone.)   *Miniature sentence: The telephone wakes.*

Flea markets are interesting places.   *Example*

(The verb is *are*. What are interesting places? Flea markets.) *Miniature sentence: Flea markets are.*

Be careful: the subject isn't always the first word in the sentence. Compare the following pairs of sentences. Although they begin differently, the subject in each pair is the same. No matter where it appears in a sentence, the subject always tells who or what the sentence is about:

<u>Jennifer</u> **drove her aunt to the airport.**   First, <u>Jennifer</u> drove her aunt to the airport.

<u>Alan</u> **jogs at five o'clock in the morning.**   As a rule, <u>Alan</u> jogs at five o'clock in the morning.

The <u>telephone</u> wakes up my baby brother.   Worst of all, <u>the telephone</u> wakes up my baby brother.

<u>Flea markets</u> are interesting places.   Sometimes <u>flea markets</u> are interesting places.

Exercise 5

INSTRUCTIONS: Draw one line under the subject in the following sentences. You'll find it helpful to draw two lines under the verb first. Then ask *Who?* or

What?, as discussed above. When you have found the subject and verb, put them together to see if you have a miniature sentence that makes sense.

1. My friends are creative people.
2. First, Chris paints wildlife pictures.
3. Birds are his favorite subjects.
4. Second, Maria designs her own dresses.
5. Sometimes she makes a gown for a friend too.
6. Most interesting of all, Francesca decorates hats for her friends.
7. Last year I wore one of her hats to a wedding.

Exercise 6

INSTRUCTIONS: In Exercise 2, you found the verbs in these sentences. Now draw one line under the *subject* in each one. Finally, write a miniature sentence for each one.

1. Donald is a cartoonist.
2. He draws cartoons for the campus paper.
3. Carl invents exotic recipes.
4. A restaurant manager offered him a chef's job.
5. Gerry writes poetry.
6. She finds ideas in everyday experiences.
7. Stanley does wood carving.
8. I love his woodland animals.
9. Pam sells flower arrangements.
10. Usually she buys her flowers from a wholesaler.
11. I enjoy needlework.
12. Embroidered pillows are excellent gifts.
13. Last month I gave three of them to friends.

Exercise 7

INSTRUCTIONS: Find the verb in each sentence and underline it twice. Then put one line under the subject. You'll find it helpful to ask *Who?* or *What?* about each verb. Check your work by writing a miniature sentence for each example.

Subjects and Verbs

1. Last year I read *The Scarlet Letter*.
2. Nathaniel Hawthorne wrote it.
3. Later I learned about his youngest daughter, Rose.
4. In 1871 she married George Lathrop.
5. But their marriage was not a happy one.
6. In 1895 they agreed on a separation.
7. Rose wondered about her future.
8. She decided on a nursing career.
9. First she nursed poor cancer patients in their homes.
10. Then she opened a private hospital for them.
11. In 1899 she started a religious order.
12. Many friends became nuns.
13. Slowly the order grew larger.
14. The nuns spent all their time with cancer patients.
15. Today her religious order cares for many cancer patients.

Exercise 8

INSTRUCTIONS: Write five sentences about people you know. On a sheet of paper, list the names of five people—friends, relatives, and family members. (These names will be the subjects of your sentences.) Then write a sentence telling what each person does on weekends. Finally, put one line under the subject and two lines under the verb, like this:

<u>Aunt Teresa</u> <u>loses</u> her car keys.   *Example*

<u>Gina</u> <u>argues</u> with her in-laws.   *Example*

<u>Grandpa</u> <u>ignores</u> his doctor's orders.   *Example*

Using Subjects and Verbs to Edit Sentences

Subjects and verbs are the basic parts of a sentence and can be called a miniature sentence. Stripped down to those basic parts, a sentence may not be particularly interesting. However, it is still a sentence, just as a hamburger without catsup, onions, and relish is still a hamburger.

Usually you will build up your sentences to make them as interesting as possible, just as you might add toppings to a hamburger to make it taste better. But when you look for sentence errors during the revising step, you will simplify your sentences. When the sentences are "stripped down," you can discover if they are complete by looking for the subjects and verbs and ignoring everything else. If you come to a sentence that doesn't have a verb or lacks a subject, you know you must fix it. As an additional aid, read your sentences aloud so that you can hear the difference between complete and incomplete sentences. Complete sentences have both a subject and a verb, but incomplete sentences lack a subject, or a verb, or both.

Here is a paragraph written by a student named Don. When it was time to revise the paragraph, Don underlined all the subjects and verbs. He found several incomplete sentences in this paragraph. After you have read Don's paragraph, underline the subjects once and the verbs twice. Then label the incomplete sentences:

Cable Television (rough draft)

Last month I installed cable television in my apartment. First, cable television offers excellent sports coverage. Watch an exciting game almost every evening. I've learned a great deal about hockey and soccer since I started watching them on cable. Second, my girlfriend likes old situation comedies. Enjoys *Mr. Ed* and *Leave it to Beaver*. I like sitting beside her and laughing at those shows. Most of all, movies cheaper on cable than in a theater. On my student's budget, I appreciate the savings. The selection is better, too.

Here is Don's paragraph again, along with the lines he drew under the subjects and verbs. Compare your underlining to his:

Cable Television (rough draft)

Last month I installed cable television in my apartment. First, cable television offers excellent sports coverage. Watch an exciting game almost every evening. I've learned a great deal about hockey and soccer since I started watching them on cable. Second, my girlfriend likes old situation comedies. Enjoys *Mr. Ed* and *Leave it to Beaver*. I like sitting beside her and laughing at those shows. Most of all, movies cheaper on cable than in a theater. On my student's budget, I appreciate the savings. The selection is better, too.

Notice that three of Don's sentences are incomplete:

Watch an exciting game almost every evening.   *No Subject*

Enjoys *Mr. Ed* and *Leave it to Beaver*.   *No Subject*

Most of all, **movies** cheaper on cable than in a theater.
No Verb

Finally, here is Don's corrected paragraph:

Cable Television (edited version)

Last month I installed cable television in my apartment. First, cable television offers excellent sports coverage. I watch an exciting game almost every evening. I've learned a great deal about hockey and soccer since I started watching them on cable. Second, my girlfriend likes old situation comedies. She enjoys *Mr. Ed* and *Leave it to Beaver*. I like sitting beside her and laughing at those shows. Most of all, movies are cheaper on cable than in a theater. On my student's budget, I appreciate the savings. The selection is better, too.

Exercise 9

INSTRUCTIONS: Check the sentences to make sure each one contains a subject and a verb. First, underline all the verbs twice. Second, underline the subjects. Finally, label the incomplete sentences. (Remember that reading aloud is helpful when you're looking for incomplete sentences.)

Paragraph 1

I need a new wardrobe. First, my old clothes not suitable for college. Styles different in my old high school. I want to look like a college student. Second, I know more about fashion now. Want coordinated outfits in bright colors. I need to start developing my own unique style. Most of all, I wear a smaller size. Lost fifteen pounds during the summer. My old clothes look limp and saggy on me now.

Paragraph 2

Franco worries too much. First, he frets about school. Has no confidence in his scholastic abilities. He trembles before every test. Second, he is uneasy about his personal life. Worries about the quality of his friendships. He keeps expecting to lose his friends. Most of all, he dreads the future. Doesn't look forward to starting his business career. He is paralyzed by the fear of failure.

Paragraph 3

My weekends are too busy. First, do all my housework. I struggle for hours with laundry, meals, and other chores. The house needs a lot of attention. Second, visit with my friends. I drive all over town from one house to another. Try to see most of them every weekend. Most of all, my schoolwork keeps me busy. Study for hours on Saturday and Sunday nights.

Using Subjects and Verbs to Edit Paragraphs

In Exercise 1, you wrote a paragraph explaining why you'd like to have more money. Now you are ready for revising.

1. Read your paper aloud (to another student if possible). Be sure to read what is actually on the page, not just what you think is there! Pay close attention to any suggestions you are given. If no one is available to listen, read your paper aloud by yourself. You may hear awkward spots and devise some ideas for improvements.

2. Check and correct the spelling of any word you're not sure about. Write the words you've checked in your spelling notebook so that you can study them later.

3. Underline all your subjects once and verbs twice. If a sentence lacks a subject or verb, or both, it is incomplete. Add a subject or verb to correct it.

4. Read your paragraph aloud one more time, but start with the last sentence and end with the first. Many students find that this simple technique helps them spot and correct sentence problems easily.

5. When you're finished with your corrections, write or type your final draft on fresh paper. Then check it one last time before you hand it to your instructor.

Subjects and Verbs

Reviewing What You Have Learned

Exercise 10

INSTRUCTIONS: Answer each of the questions listed here. When you are finished, read your answers aloud to another student. If your answers are different, find out why.
1. What are two ways in which your knowledge of subjects and verbs can help you improve your writing?
2. What is the *subject* of a sentence?
3. What is an *incomplete sentence*?
4. What are two types of verbs? Give five examples of each.
5. What is a "miniature sentence"?

Exercise 11

INSTRUCTIONS: Draw one line under the subject and two lines under each verb in the following sentences. (Remember to look for action and existence words.)
1. Last week I bought a kitchen timer.
2. It helps me with my evening schedule.
3. After dinner I set it for each subject.
4. I study in thirty-minute blocks.
5. My friend Ramona gave me the idea.
6. She has a wristwatch with an alarm.
7. Her watch reminds her about the time.
8. She is never late anymore.
9. We are determined clock-watchers.
10. Punctuality is important to us.

Unit Seven
More About Verbs

> SUMMARY
>
> *1.* College writing involves two additional types of verbs: *actions of the mind* and *helping* verbs.
>
> *2.* Although *infinitives* and *-ing* words often look like verbs, they aren't verbs at all.
>
> *3.* A sentence may have more than one verb.
>
> *4.* A verb may be more than one word long.

More About Verbs

You have learned several important facts about verbs. First, every complete sentence contains at least one verb. Second, an understanding of verbs can help you write varied sentences. Finally, underlining verbs twice can help you in the revising step of the writing process.

You are already familiar with action verbs. Most of these are easy to identify—for example, *sew, read, jog,* and *help.* Each is an actual physical activity. Another type of verbs is *existence* verbs: *am, is, are, was,* and *were.* This unit presents two additional types of verbs: *actions of the mind* and *helping verbs.* After you have learned these verbs, you should be able to identify the verbs in almost any sentence you read or write.

Learning About Actions of the Mind

Actions of the mind includes such verbs as *expect, hope, remember, wait, memorize, forget,* and *think.* All of these are mental rather than physical activities. When you are revising a paragraph and underlining verbs, remember to look for these verbs as well as the ones you've already learned.

Exercise 1

INSTRUCTIONS: Draw two lines under each verb in the following sentences.
1. We want a three-bedroom house with a large yard.
2. I believe all the information in that book.
3. This year many students need financial assistance.
4. The children learned the multiplication tables very quickly.
5. Joan's parents plan their vacations a year ahead.
6. Derek decided on an accounting career.
7. Sometimes I daydream during class.
8. In December, little children think constantly about the holidays.
9. The college expects a large freshman class next year.
10. My grandparents remember many happy events from the early years of their marriage.

Exercise 2

INSTRUCTIONS: Write a sentence of your own containing each of these verbs: *expect, hope, wait, remember, think*. When you are finished, draw two lines under each verb.

Learning About Helping Verbs

In previous English classes, you probably encountered a group of verbs called *helping* verbs. These verbs received their name because they "help" other words that appear in a sentence.

To learn more about helping verbs, compare these sentence pairs:

I seen the movie twice.   *Incorrect*

I have seen the movie twice.   *Correct*

My mother done gone to the store.   *Incorrect*

My mother has gone to the store.   *Correct*

In the second sentence, the verb *have* "helps" *seen*, which is incorrect by itself. In the fourth sentence, the verb *has* "helps" *gone* in the same way. Of course these verbs can be used by themselves, too; they don't always act as "helpers." You'll find it useful to memorize these verbs so that you can spot them quickly in the sentences you write:

Helping Verbs

am	could
is	must
are	will
was	would
were	do
may	does
might	did
ought	has
should	have
can	had

More About Verbs 87

> STUDY TIP: You can learn these words quickly by grouping them together on flash cards and then studying them during spare moments throughout the day. When you examine the list of helping verbs, notice that many of them have related meanings. For example, *do, does,* and *did* can go together on one card. You can list *has, have,* and *had* together on another card. Develop your own groupings (rhyming verbs are one possibility) as you memorize these verbs.

Exercise 3

INSTRUCTIONS: Draw two lines under each verb in these sentences.
1. I have a new electronic typewriter.
2. It is helpful to me in many ways.
3. First, it has a memory function.
4. Corrections and changes are easy.
5. Second, my typewriter has a built-in dictionary.
6. It does spelling checks automatically.
7. Finally, it does underlining and centering.
8. I am a more efficient typist now.
9. I was never a good student before.
10. Typewriters were never this good before either.

Exercise 4

INSTRUCTIONS: Choose ten helping verbs from the list, and write a sentence for each one. When you're finished, underline the subject and verb in each sentence. Meet with another student to check your work.

Finding Verbs in Sentences

When you look for verbs in sentences that you've written, you will want to be as efficient as possible. The following suggestions will help you.

First, make sure you can instantly recognize the helping verbs. They are probably the most common verbs in the English language. Second, familiarize yourself with common words and phrases that are different from verbs, and remember *not* to underline them. You have already learned several of these: *first, second,* and *most of all.* Other words and phrases to watch for are *not, never, always, sometimes, usually,* and *often.* Time words are different from verbs, too: *yesterday, tomorrow, next week, last year, Tuesday,* and so on. *Never* underline these words as verbs.

Exercise 5

INSTRUCTIONS: Draw two lines under each verb in the following sentences. Watch out for common words and phrases that are different from verbs.

1. Every week I take my preschool children to a nursing home for an hour.
2. The residents enjoy our visits.
3. They always think of us as their family.
4. My children usually learn something from the residents.
5. Sometimes an elderly person fascinates them with a true story from the past.
6. I am refreshed by my visits to the nursing home.
7. Last Thursday I was worried about some money problems.
8. A woman there listened to all my concerns.
9. She understood my worries from her own experience.
10. I appreciated her friendship and support.

Exercise 6

INSTRUCTIONS: Put a checkmark in the blank space in front of each verb in this list.

More About Verbs

_____ was	_____ could	_____ fix
_____ always	_____ sleep	_____ type
_____ first	_____ take	_____ solve
_____ feel	_____ add	_____ not
_____ have	_____ finally	_____ hang
_____ see	_____ might	_____ door
_____ often	_____ care	_____ make
_____ touch	_____ never	_____ beside
_____ arrange	_____ choose	_____ lake
_____ play	_____ ought	_____ win
_____ encourage	_____ pass	_____ change
_____ now	_____ pick	_____ stir

Verb Look-Alikes

By now you should feel confident about your ability to spot verbs in sentences. Before you complete your study of verbs, you will find it helpful to learn to recognize *verb look-alikes*. These look-alikes should not be called verbs even though they may resemble them. Although they are useful words, they are not verbs.

Infinitives

One group of verb look-alikes is called *infinitives*. An infinitive is an action word with *to* in front. For example, *to go*, *to study*, and *to swim* are infinitives. In the example presented next, find both the verb look alike (the infinitive) and the verb:

I want to sell my bicycle.   *Example*

You should have noticed that *to sell* is an infinitive, not a verb. The true verb in this sentence is *want*.

Here is another example:

Sonya plans to work all summer.   *Example*

The infinitive is *to work*; the verb is *plans*.

By learning about infinitives you can find verbs more efficiently when you are revising your sentences. Just skip over the infinitive and make sure a verb is present somewhere else in the sentence.

Exercise 7

INSTRUCTIONS: Draw two lines under each verb in these sentences. Remember that infinitives are *not* verbs: do not underline them.

1. My family always loves to eat in restaurants.
2. We like to try different places in our town.
3. On weekends someone usually asks to go out for dinner.
4. My father is likely to choose a seafood restaurant.
5. My mother prefers to dine in Italian places.
6. My little brothers always beg to go out for fast food.
7. I am happy to be in almost any restaurant.
8. To please everyone, we have to take turns choosing.
9. It is fun to visit a variety of eating places.
10. I hope to eat in every restaurant in town this year.

Learning About Verb Look-Alikes Ending in *-ing*

Words with *-ing* attached to the end may look like verbs, but they are not. (They are classified as present participles, verbal adjectives, or gerunds.) Notice that this example is not a complete sentence because it lacks a verb:

Jeanine studying for an algebra test.   *Incomplete*

When a verb is added, the sentence is correct:

Jeanine is studying for an algebra test.   *Complete*

Here is another example. In the next sentence, notice that the word ending in *-ing* is not the verb:

Weightlifting helps me stay in shape.   *Example*

In this sentence, *helps* is the verb. *Weightlifting* is not a verb because *-ing* has been added to the end.

Now find the verb in this sentence:

I spend a few quiet minutes every day writing in my journal.
Example

The verb here is *spend*. *Writing* is not a verb because of its *-ing* ending.

Like infinitives, words with *-ing* endings can create confusion when you are looking for verbs. As you revise your papers, you will check each sentence to make sure it has a verb. Avoid underlining any verb look-alikes in the revising step. (However, some instructors ask their students to underline *-ing* words when they appear with helping verbs. Follow your instructor's guidelines as you work through this unit.)

Janet looking for her glasses. *Incomplete*

Janet <u>was</u> looking for her glasses. *Complete*

Joel going to the beach for the weekend. *Incomplete*

Joel <u>is</u> going to the beach for the weekend. *Complete*

Exercise 8

INSTRUCTIONS: Draw two lines under each verb. Do not underline verb look-alikes.

1. Reading biographies helps me learn about history.
2. Ed plans to buy a new car next year.
3. Last week I spent two evenings working on a term paper.
4. To err is human.
5. I never learned how to sew a zipper into a dress.
6. Health-care professionals need to keep informed about new medical discoveries.
7. Years ago my grandparents dreamed of finding new opportunities in America.
8. Fixing a leaky faucet is not always an easy undertaking.
9. College students benefit from having good notetaking and listening skills.
10. Every weekend I like to sail on the bay near my house.

Learning About Verb Look-Alikes with *A, An, The*

Read the following example carefully. What is the verb?

The dance ended at three in the morning. *Example*

You probably discovered that the verb is *ended*. *Dance* is not the verb because *the* appears in front of it. When you place *a, an,* or *the* in front of a verb, it becomes a verb look-alike. Be careful not to underline one of these look-alikes when you're revising your sentences.

Exercise 9

INSTRUCTIONS: Draw two lines under each verb. Do not underline verb look-alikes.
1. Some of my friends party every weekend.
2. For others, studying is more important than fun.
3. I try to mix parties and schoolwork on weekends.
4. But I often sigh over the work waiting for me on my desk.
5. At the end of a term, the rush is always too much for me.
6. Chores also tend to weigh me down.
7. On Saturday mornings, the wash keeps me busy for hours.
8. The research for my history class fills up Saturday afternoon.
9. Last week I researched one question for two hours.
10. I'm looking forward to the end of the semester.

Finding Fragments (Incomplete Sentences)

Your knowledge of verbs and verb look-alikes can help you fix incomplete sentences. Notice that this incomplete sentence has no verb. (*Dreaming* is a verb look-alike, not a verb):

Dreaming of a career in motion pictures.   *Incomplete*

In the corrected version, two words have been added, including the verb *is*:

Eric is dreaming of a career in motion pictures.   *Complete*

More About Verbs

Here is another incomplete sentence that needs a verb. The word *hoping* is a verb look-alike, not a verb:

College graduates hoping to find challenging jobs.
Incomplete

In the corrected version, the sentence now contains the verb *are*:

College graduates <u>are</u> hoping to find challenging jobs.
Complete

The next two exercises require you to identify and correct incomplete sentences that contain verb look-alikes.

Exercise 10

INSTRUCTIONS: Draw two lines under each verb in the following sentences. Then label each complete sentence **C**, and label each incomplete sentence **I**. When you are finished, compare your answers with another student's. Be prepared to explain how you decided which sentences were incomplete.

_____ 1. To understand the reasons for his decision.
_____ 2. Singing always makes me happy.
_____ 3. Changing a tire in a raging thunderstorm.
_____ 4. I never tried to barefoot water-ski before.
_____ 5. My grandmother enjoys dozing in front of the fireplace.
_____ 6. Children pretending to be wild animals in a jungle.
_____ 7. To own a successful business is my greatest dream.
_____ 8. To surprise me on my eighteenth birthday with a car.
_____ 9. Playing with dolls keeps my niece busy for hours.
_____ 10. A rag doll wearing an old-fashioned dress and apron.

Exercise 11

INSTRUCTIONS: Go back to Exercise 7 and rewrite all the incomplete sentences, adding a verb and any other words you need to make them complete.

Exercise 12

INSTRUCTIONS: The following paragraphs contain some incomplete sentences that need verbs. Read each paragraph and underline all the verbs twice. Then look for the incomplete sentences and correct them, making sure that each sentence has a verb. Finally, compare your answers with another student's. Be prepared to explain how you decided which sentences were incomplete.

Paragraph 1

Jeffrey planning to open his own business after college. First, he has made friends with many successful owners of small businesses. To get a great deal of practical knowledge beforehand. Second, he works hard in all his business courses. To take advantage of his years in college. Most of all, spending his spare time on small business projects. To gain experience before his graduation from college.

Paragraph 2

I made many mistakes learning how to do my own laundry. First, measuring out too much detergent. I had to call a repair service to fix the clogged machine. Second, forgetting to sort my clothes ahead of time. My white shirts came out with blue and red streaks on them. Worst of all, selecting hot water for my wool sweaters. They shrank to the size of doll's clothes.

Paragraph 3

My mother has trouble coping with modern technology. First, our cable television channels baffling to her. Trouble remembering the channels for her favorite programs. Every night my father and I have to help her. Second, unable to operate our VCR. She complains endlessly about all its buttons and functions. Worst of all, helpless with our home computer. My father has to do all the family's bookkeeping and paperwork. To keep up with our bills and tax records.

Learning About Verbs More Than One Word Long

So far, you have worked with one-word verbs, such as *hopes, is,* and *work*. However, sometimes verbs are more than one word long. Usually the first verb will be one of the helping verbs. Study the verbs in the following sentences:

> I <u>can do</u> all the math problems on this page.   *Example*
>
> We <u>may go</u> to Fort Lauderdale in April.   *Example*
>
> Drivers <u>must renew</u> their licenses every three years.   *Example*

In some sentences, another word will appear between the two verbs, as shown here:

> Marcia <u>can</u> never <u>pay</u> her rent on time.   *Example*

Often a helping verb will appear with a verb look-alike, as in these sentences:

> The football team <u>is</u> hoping to win tomorrow.   *Example*
>
> Computers <u>are</u> helping students in many academic fields.   *Example*

Exercise 13

INSTRUCTIONS: Draw two lines under each verb in the following sentences.

1. All students must take at least four English courses.
2. Many students will benefit from an introductory computer course.
3. You can always choose a foreign language as an elective.
4. Some colleges are allowing students to design their own courses.
5. Susan would like to study French in Paris.
6. But I would not enjoy going to school in another country.
7. I would miss my family and friends too much.

8. Next year Hal and Greg are transferring to a university.
9. I may decide to continue my education in a university too.
10. I am planning to get as much education as possible.

Learning About Sentences with More Than One Verb

You can avoid choppiness by expanding sentences with additional verbs. Compare these sentence pairs, noticing that the second sentence contains an extra verb:

Joe <u>entered</u> the contest.

Joe <u>entered</u> the contest and <u>won</u> a ten-speed bicycle.

Gail <u>wrote</u> a poem.

Gail <u>wrote</u> a poem and <u>sent</u> it to the campus magazine.

Amy <u>forgot</u> her books.

Amy <u>forgot</u> her books and <u>went</u> home for them.

Exercise 14

INSTRUCTIONS: Draw two lines under each verb. Several (but not all) sentences have more than one verb. Do not underline any verb look-alikes.

1. Every weekend I buy the Sunday paper and read it.
2. First I find the comics and read them all.
3. I smile at most and laugh at a few of them.
4. I always enjoy reading *Peanuts* and *Doonesbury*.
5. Next I look at the headlines and the news stories in the first section of the newspaper.
6. I read some stories carefully but skip others.
7. Gradually I pick up and read each section of the newspaper.
8. Finally the time comes to read the sports section.
9. I spend twenty or thirty minutes reading stories and looking at scores.
10. Then I stack up the newspaper sections and put them outside.

More About Verbs

Adding Power to Your Sentences

So far you've been using your knowledge of verbs to make sure your sentences are complete. There's another advantage to spotting verbs quickly: verbs are the power words in sentences, and you can often improve your writing with verbs.

Read these sentence pairs, noticing that the second sentence conveys more vitality than the first:

Marcus loves pro football.

Marcus puts two television sets side-by-side so he can watch two football games at once.

Leonard is an orderly person.

Leonard uses a Phillips screwdriver to line up all the screws in his refrigerator.

Lynette wants to make money by investing in stocks.

Lynette read the *Wall Street Journal* so that she can make money by investing in stocks.

Verbs can be the key to vivid writing. Add interest to your paragraph by writing about people (including yourself!) who behave in intersting ways.

Exercise 15

INSTRUCTIONS: List five qualities or facts about yourself. Then illustrate each item with a sentence about yourself. Be sure to write about things you've actually done. For example, if you listed the quality of friendliness, you could write:

I made three new friends my first day at college.   *Example*

When you're finished, share your sentences with another student.

Reviewing What You Have Learned

1. Write ten verbs that are *actions of the mind*.
2. Without looking at your book or notes, write as many *helping verbs* as you can remember.
3. Explain why it is important to be able to identify verb look-alikes.
4. Define *infinitive*, and give two examples.
5. Write four verb look-alikes.
6. Write two sentences containing verbs more than one word long.
7. Write two sentences containing more than one verb.

Exercise 16

INSTRUCTIONS: Draw two lines under each verb in these sentences.
1. Bethune-Cookman College is located in Florida.
2. Mary McLeod Bethune was one of its founders.
3. Years ago she labored for equal education for all.
4. She was an African-American teacher with a vision for the future.
5. Two centuries ago Anna Zenger was another woman with a vision.
6. In New York City she struggled to win freedom of the press for Americans.
7. Famous for her spying disguises was Emma E. Edmonds.
8. Looking like a waterboy, she walked across a Confederate battlefield and listened to military talk.
9. Then she sent war information to the Union side.
10. Surprisingly, she also nursed Confederate soldiers.

Exercise 17

INSTRUCTIONS: The following paragraph contains incomplete sentences that need verbs. Read the paragraph and underline all the verbs. Then look for the incomplete sentences and correct them, making sure that each sentence has a verb. Finally, be ready to explain your answers to another student.

More About Verbs

Last month my brother had some problems building a doghouse for his poodle. First, making the house too large. The dog's body heat would not keep him warm in the winter. Second, nailing the boards for the roof too far apart. Wind, rain, and snow could come in. Worst of all, the doghouse would not fit through his workshop door. My brother not careful enough designing the doghouse.

Exercise 18

INSTRUCTIONS: Plan and write a paragraph describing a person who's been important in your life. During the revising step, make sure your examples show this person in action. (Take another look at Exercise 15 if you need help with this.) When you do the final editing of your paragraph, underline all of your verbs. (Do not underline any verb look-alikes.) Then work with another student to make sure that each sentence has at least one verb.

Unit Eight
More About Subjects

SUMMARY

1. Subjects are more interesting when they are expanded by an *in* or *of* phrase (a prepositional phrase).

2. Some sentences have more than one subject.

3. The words *here* and *there* are never the subjects of sentences.

4. In commands, *you* is the "invisible" subject.

You know that the subject of a sentence tells who or what a sentence is about. This unit further explores the subjects of sentences.

First, spend a few moments reviewing what you have learned. One quick way to find the subject of a sentence is to look for the verb first. Then ask yourself which word in the sentence goes with the verb. (The questions *Who?* and *What?* are helpful.) Having studied verbs in some detail, you probably can find most subjects and verbs this way. The helping verbs you memorized in the last unit are especially useful.

Check your answers after you think you've found the subject and verb. Put the subject and verb together into a "miniature sentence." If your miniature sentence doesn't make sense, something is wrong. You need to find a different subject, or verb, or both.

The following examples will help refresh your memory about subjects. The verb is underlined for you. Remember, after you find the verb, you can easily spot the subject:

Next summer my family will travel to Europe for a month.
Example

(Who will travel? My family—the subject.)

Tina's love overcame all of Smitty's bad habits. *Example*

(What overcame? Tina's love—the subject.)

The subject often appears at the beginning of the sentence, but it can be placed in other parts of the sentence, too. What is the subject in this sentence? The verb is underlined for you.)

Sleeping in the back row were three weary students.
Example

The verb here is *were*. (Did you remember that *sleeping* is a verb look-alike?) Ask yourself the question "Who were?" The answer tells you the subject of the sentence—three weary students.

Exercise 1

INSTRUCTIONS: In each sentence, find the verb first and draw two lines under it. Then find the subject that goes with it, and underline it once. Finally, write a miniature sentence and check your work.

More About Subjects

1. Talent scouts spotted Babe Ruth during a baseball game at a reform school.
2. Before long Babe Ruth was pitching for the Baltimore Orioles.
3. At first Babe Ruth had trouble with his curve ball.
4. Somehow the opposing players always expected it.
5. For hours every day, the coaches worked with Ruth.
6. They never could uncover the problem.
7. Then one afternoon an outfielder solved the mystery.
8. Babe Ruth always made a face just before a curve ball.
9. Quickly the coaches convinced Ruth to be careful about his facial expressions.
10. Throughout his long career, Babe Ruth was a superstar.

Introducing Sentences With More Than One Subject

Sentences with more than one subject are very common. Here is one that you probably remember from childhood:

Jack and Jill went up the hill to fetch a pail of water.
Example

This sentence has two subjects—*Jack* and *Jill*. In sentences like these, be sure to underline both subjects that go with the verb. The following examples will give you more practice with sentences that have more than one subject:

Fleas and mosquitoes cause many health problems in dogs.
Example

Stability and spotting are basic skills for skydivers.
Example

Amsterdam and Venice delight tourists with their canals.
Example

Exercise 2

INSTRUCTIONS: Write ten sentences with more than one subject. Underline the verbs twice and subjects once in each sentence.

Introducing Sentences with Prepositional Phrases

You probably use the words *of* and *in* frequently when you write and talk. These words are called *prepositions*. A preposition is a word—often a short one—that indicates direction or purpose. Prepositions include these words: *in, of, on, by, with, for, to, over, under.*

In the next examples, both the subject and verb are underlined. Notice that *of* appears right after the subject and that it is followed by other words:

> **<u>Some</u> of your paintings <u>are</u> good enough to hang in an art gallery.** *Example*
>
> **<u>One</u> of my brothers <u>has</u> a beautiful Arabian horse.** *Example*

The words that appear directly after *of* are called a prepositional phrase. Prepositional phrases add interesting information to sentences. Examine the following pairs of sentences. The first sentence does not have a prepositional phrase, but the second one does. Notice the improvement from adding the prepositional phrase:

> **Some belong here.** *Example*
>
> **Some of your paintings belong here.** *Example*
>
> **One owns an Arabian horse.** *Example*
>
> **One of my brothers owns an Arabian horse.** *Example*
>
> **The books are hers.** *Example*
>
> **The books in my car are hers.** *Example*
>
> **A vacation excites me.** *Example*
>
> **A vacation in the Virgin Islands excites me.** *Example*

Because you want to write varied sentences, you won't use prepositional phrases all the time. When you do use them, however, be sure to follow the rules of correct usage. These guidelines will help you:

1. Remember that the subject and verb always are *outside* of a prepositional phrase.

More About Subjects

2. When looking for the subject and verb in a sentence, lightly cross out any prepositional phrases. You will find the subject and verb among the remaining words in the sentence.

The next examples demonstrate this cross-out technique. Notice that the prepositional phrase in each example is crossed out. Can you find the subject and verb? (Look for the verb before you find the subject.)

Skydivers ~~of all ages~~ always must wear an emergency parachute.   *Example*

People ~~in skydiving organizations~~ learn many freefall maneuvers.   *Example*

Every year thousands ~~of skydivers~~ earn licenses and awards.   *Example*

Here are the sentences once again, with subjects and verbs underlined:

Every year <u>thousands</u> ~~of skydivers~~ <u>earn</u> licenses and awards.   *Example*

<u>Skydivers</u> ~~of all ages~~ always <u>must wear</u> an emergency parachute.   *Example*

<u>People</u> ~~in skydiving organizations~~ <u>learn</u> many freefall maneuvers.   *Example*

Exercise 3

INSTRUCTIONS: Lightly cross out the *in* and *of* phrases in these sentences. Then draw two lines under the verb and one line under the subject. Write a miniature sentence for each to check your work.

1. Every Sunday morning one of my neighbors wakes me up running his power tools.
2. A walk in the rain doesn't seem very romantic to me.
3. Last week one of my classmates visited my girlfriend.
4. Usually half of my free time is spent studying.
5. Sad moments in movies always move me.
6. A year in Germany certainly would improve my German.

7. Two years in military school didn't help Buddy one bit.
8. A steady supply of pizza and Pepsi is all I need to survive college.
9. Six months in jail seems like a short sentence.
10. An hour of shopping is usually enough to exhaust my father.

Read both of the following short sentences, and then rewrite them with an *of* or *in* phrase after each subject. (Both the subjects and verbs are underlined already.)

A photograph won first prize. *Example*

A photograph _____ won first prize.

The trophy is mine. *Example*

The trophy _____ is mine.

Your sentences should look something like these:

A photograph of an antique car won first prize. *Example*
The trophy in the glass case is mine. *Example*

Exercise 4

INSTRUCTIONS: Draw one line under each subject and two lines under each verb. Then expand each sentence by adding an *of* or *in* phrase after the subject. The sentences shown before may be helpful to use as models.

1. A student always helps me study.
2. Later today the rest will audition as ballerinas.
3. Last year one joined an NFL team.
4. Two women designed a mural.
5. Recently children received free Sea World tickets.
6. Bottles crashed to the floor, startling the burglar.
7. Suddenly the pastor spoke out.
8. The ingredients are always fresh.
9. Next year the members had better change their "men only" policy.
10. The loud laughter angered the librarian.

Exercise 5

INSTRUCTIONS: Write five sentences with *of* phrases after the subject. Then write five sentences with *in* phrases after the subject. Underline the subjects and verbs.

Introducing Sentences Beginning with There and Here

You need to know that *there* and *here* can never be the subject of a sentence. To find the subject, look elsewhere in the sentence. As you've already learned, it's usually helpful to find your verb before you look for the subject. What is the verb in the following sentences—and what is the subject?

There is a package for you on the kitchen table. *Example*
The verb is *is*, and the subject is *package*.

Here are three reasons why you need this course. *Example*
The verb is *are*, and the subject is *three reasons*.

There go my two best friends. *Example*
The verb is *go*, and the subject is *two best friends*.

Exercise 6

INSTRUCTIONS: Underline the verb twice and subject once in each sentence. Remember *there* and *here* are never the subjects of sentences.

1. There was a strange phone call for you last night.
2. Here are several books about horticulture.
3. There is no reason for admitting that I broke the lamp.
4. Here comes the bride.
5. In the attic there is a box of old photographs.
6. There were two hundred angry people at the meeting.
7. Last April there were confusing new tax rules.

8. Here is your bill.
9. There were at that time several problems with your account.
10. There stands the man responsible for this problem.

Introducing Sentences with "Invisible" Subjects

What is the subject of the following sentences? (The verbs are underlined for you.)

<u>Have</u> some pie.   *Example*

<u>Memorize</u> this list.   *Example*

<u>Stop</u>.   *Example*

Who is going to have some pie, memorize the list, and stop? The subject is never stated, but it is obvious: *you*. Sentences like these (they're actually commands) have an "invisible" or "understood" subject: *you*. The next time you see a "Stop" sign, or a flashing "Don't walk" sign, think about the invisible subject—you.

Exercise 7

INSTRUCTIONS: Look around for signs that have invisible subjects. Write down the messages on ten of them, if you can. If you can't find ten, write your own sentences with invisible subjects.

Reviewing What You Have Learned

Exercise 8

INSTRUCTIONS: Draw one line under each subject and two lines under each verb. Check your work by writing a miniature sentence for each. When you're finished, compare your answers to another student's, and be prepared to explain them.

More About Subjects

1. Playing in a mud puddle behind our house was my little nephew.
2. There go my ex-boyfriend and his wife.
3. Have some peanuts.
4. First the newlyweds will need to find a place to live.
5. Every afternoon the 3:45 train arrives from Memphis.
6. Last week some of my friends talked about picketing the dean's office.
7. Wait a minute.
8. Chuckling to himself, the young father hid the Easter eggs.
9. Stan and Joy were arrested for ticket-scalping.
10. Here at last are the compact discs I lent to Barney.

Exercise 9

INSTRUCTIONS: Label each statement *true* or *false*.

_____ 1. In a command, the subject is always *you*.
_____ 2. The first word of a sentence is always the subject.
_____ 3. Sometimes you must look inside a prepositional phrase to find the subject of a sentence.
_____ 4. The words *there* and *here* can never be the subject of a sentence.
_____ 5. It's best to find the subject of a sentence before you look for the verb.

Exercise 10

INSTRUCTIONS: Underline the verb twice and the subject once in these sentences. To check your work, write a miniature sentence for each.

1. Here are the wedding invitations from Lynn and Barry.
2. Next week four of us will go rafting together.
3. There were several reasons for our decision to change to another computer system.
4. The boxes in the back room need new labels.
5. A vacation in the Virgin Islands appeals to me.
6. The first of many changes in our procedures is beginning this week.
7. The best of the art contest entries will hang in the president's office.

8. The books in my car belong to my friend Anna.
9. There are twelve Apple computers in the Learning Center.
10. Here is the money from the bake sale.

Exercise 11

INSTRUCTIONS: Write a paragraph describing a gift you enjoyed receiving. As you plan your paragraph, try to think of three reasons why the gift was special. Then use the words *first, second,* and *most of all* to organize your ideas. In the editing step, draw one line under each subject and two under each verb. (Remember that it's helpful to look for your verbs first.) If you have written any fragments, correct them by adding a subject or verb.

Unit Nine
Fragments

> SUMMARY
>
> 1. A *fragment* is a group of words that looks like a sentence but is actually incomplete.
>
> 2. Skillful writers know how to identify and correct four types of fragments: fragments lacking a subject; fragments lacking a verb; fragments beginning with *if, when, because,* or *although* (subordinate conjunctions); and fragments beginning with *who* or *which*.

A fragment is an incomplete sentence. In college work, you must check your sentences carefully to make sure that they are complete. Even a short sentence can be complete, as shown here:

Jack did. *Complete sentence*

This sentence has a subject—*Jack*—and a verb—*did*. It is complete even though the reader may not know who Jack is and what he did. In contrast, this group of words is *not* complete:

If Jack did his own car repairs. *Fragment*

This group of words needs another subject and verb because it begins with *if*. Read the complete version:

If Jack did his own car repairs, he would save hundreds of dollars every year. *Complete sentence*

This unit shows you specific ways to identify and correct four types of fragments:

1. Fragments lacking a subject
2. Fragments lacking a verb
3. Fragments beginning with *if, when, because,* or *although* (subordinate conjunctions)
4. Fragments beginning with *who* or *which*

You can often spot fragments if you read your sentences aloud before handing them in to the professor. It's especially helpful to read your papers in reverse order, starting with the last sentence and ending with the first—a trick you encountered earlier in this course. Often you can correct a fragment by attaching it to the sentence in front or in back of it, as shown here:

I always enjoy the beach. Although I don't swim well.
Fragment

I always enjoy the beach although I don't swim well.
Complete sentence

As you study this unit, read both sentences and fragments aloud to develop proficiency with this "read aloud" technique.

Introducing Fragments Lacking A Subject

As you know, every sentence must contain a subject. In the short sentence *David reads*, the subject is *David*. You could make the sentence longer, like this:

David reads a new book at least once a month. *Example*

The subject is still *David*. A group of words that lacks a subject is called a fragment. As you write, check each clause (word group) carefully to make sure that it has a subject. If the subject is missing, then you must add it to the fragment.

Compare the following sentences and fragments:

Bought a used heap last week. *Fragment (no subject)*

Mary bought a used heap last week. *Complete sentence.*

Next year will go to a four-year college. *Fragment (no subject)*

Next year I will go to a four-year college. *Complete sentence*

Exercise 1

INSTRUCTIONS: The same paragraph has been written twice. In version A, all the sentences are correct, but in version B, some subjects are missing. Read both versions aloud to hear the difference between sentences and fragments that lack a subject. Underline the fragments in version B.

A. Correct version

Everyone in our house likes to watch television. Almost every room in our house has a TV. We can't imagine life without our favorite programs. My nine-year-old brother likes adventure shows. He also enjoys reruns of old sitcoms. My parents like sports, movies, and news shows. They have a small TV in their bathroom for Dad to watch while he's shaving. I like just about everything. Sometimes I have trouble getting assignments done because of my TV habits.

B. Incorrect version

Everyone in our house likes to watch television. Almost every room in our house has a TV. Can't imagine life without our favorite programs. My nine-year-old brother likes adventure shows. Also enjoys reruns of old sitcoms. My parents like sports, movies, and news shows. Have a small TV in their bathroom for Dad to watch while he's shaving. I like just about everything. Sometimes have trouble getting assignments done because of my TV habits.

Exercise 2

INSTRUCTIONS: Mark each sentence **S**. Mark each fragment **F**. Then add a subject to each fragment.

_____ 1. Donna is moving into her own apartment this weekend.
_____ 2. Her father is helping her move her things.
_____ 3. But isn't looking forward to seeing her move away.
_____ 4. She is the last of his children still living at home.
_____ 5. Will miss her and find the house empty without her.
_____ 6. Donna's mother won't be able to help her move this weekend.
_____ 7. Flew to Atlanta for a business conference.
_____ 8. She thinks Donna needs to be on her own now.
_____ 9. Has encouraged all three of her children to be independent.
_____ 10. Set a good example by pursuing a career in marketing.

Exercise 3

INSTRUCTIONS: Mark each sentence **S**, and mark each fragment **F**. Then add a subject to each fragment.

_____ 1. I am trying to get into a good exercise routine.
_____ 2. So far have been frustrated.
_____ 3. Tried jogging but got exhausted and sore right away.
_____ 4. Then a friend urged me to try swimming.
_____ 5. Convinced me that it was a perfect exercise.
_____ 6. But the hours at the swimming pool aren't convenient.

Fragments   115

_____ 7. Interfere with my part-time job at the Student Center.
_____ 8. Also I don't like to get my hair wet and tangled.
_____ 9. Calisthenics have never appealed to me.
_____ 10. Always make me feel awkward and silly.

Exercise 4

INSTRUCTIONS: Mark each sentence **S** and each fragment **F**. Then add a subject to each fragment.

_____ 1. Finally, after many failures, set up an exercise routine that works for me.
_____ 2. My friends decided that we should exercise together.
_____ 3. Take a brisk two-mile walk three times a week.
_____ 4. A friend on the boxing team had another good idea.
_____ 5. Suggested that I work out with a jump rope.
_____ 6. Early every morning I do a hundred jumps.
_____ 7. In the beginning felt clumsy and embarrassed.
_____ 8. But quickly improved both my skill and my figure.
_____ 9. Now my friends envy my skills.
_____ 10. One even bought a jump rope and works out with me.

Introducing Fragments Lacking a Verb

Every sentence, long or short, requires a verb. In the sentence *David reads*, the verb is *reads*. If you make the sentence longer, the verb is still *reads*:

David reads a new book at least once a month.

A group of words that lacks a verb is called a fragment. As you write, check each clause carefully to see that it has a verb. Watch especially for constructions that look like verbs but aren't. As you saw earlier, *infinitives* (*to* plus a verb) are never verbs. Notice that the following group of words is not a sentence:

The desire <u>to obtain</u> a good job quickly.   *Fragment*

The phrase *to obtain* is not a verb—it is an infinitive. Corrected, the sentence might read:

He has the desire to obtain a good job quickly.   *Complete sentence*

The subject is *he*, and the verb is *has*.

Also, watch out for verb look-alikes (such as *jogging* and *to jog*), because they do not function as verbs in a sentence. The following group of words is actually a fragment because it lacks a verb:

The girls <u>jogging</u> around the lake.   *Fragment*

Jogging is not a verb, because it ends in *ing*. The correct version would be:

The girls enjoy jogging around the lake.   *Complete sentence*

Enjoy is a verb; now the sentence is complete.

Exercise 5

INSTRUCTIONS: The same paragraph has been written twice. In version A, each sentence is complete, but in version B, some of the verbs are missing. Read both versions aloud so that you can hear the difference between a complete sentence and a fragment that is missing a verb. Underline each fragment in version B.

A

John hopes to go to pharmacy school next year. The desire to become a successful pharmacist has inspired him throughout college. Right now he is finishing the courses for a bachelor's degree. Completing pharmacy school is his most important goal.

B

John hopes to go to pharmacy school next year. The desire to become a successful pharmacist throughout college. Right now he is finishing the courses for a bachelor's degree. Completing pharmacy school his most important goal.

Correcting Fragments with Missing Verbs

You are free to add any words you choose when you correct a fragment. Just make sure that your sentence has both a subject and a verb and is complete when you finish. Read the following fragment, and then note the two ways to correct it:

The need to have some spending money for college.
Fragment

This clause is a fragment, because it lacks a verb: *to have* is an infinitive, not a verb. To correct it, you may add a verb (*causes*) and some other words:

The need to have some spending money for college causes problems for many students. *Complete sentence*

The subject is *the need;* the verb is *causes*. A second choice is to add both a subject (*Most students*) and a verb (*feel*):

Most students feel the need to have some spending money for college. *Complete sentence*

Of course, you might try many other solutions. Just make sure that the sentence has both a subject and a verb when you are finished.

Exercise 6

INSTRUCTIONS: Mark each sentence **S** and each fragment **F**. Then make each fragment into a complete sentence by adding any words you choose. Be ready to compare your answers and explain them to another student.

_____ 1. The necessity of knowing how to type reasonably well.

_____ 2. I finally decided to enroll in a typing course.

_____ 3. Hoping to avoid paying a typist every semester.

_____ 4. The determination to do anything necessary to succeed at typing.

_____ 5. My mother had pointed out the advantages of doing my own typing.

_____ 6. Not to be dependent on someone else to prepare my assignments.
_____ 7. Having the option of doing last-minute typing jobs myself.
_____ 8. But in the typing classroom, doubts and fears.
_____ 9. Fingers quaking, I struggled at the keyboard.
_____ 10. Finally, though, I achieved a speed of forty words per minute.

Exercise 7

INSTRUCTIONS: Mark each sentence **S** and each fragment **F**. Then make each fragment a complete sentence by adding any words you choose.

_____ 1. Laurie's friend Bob taught her how to drive this summer.
_____ 2. She was tired of depending on public transportation.
_____ 3. Worrying that a bus drivers' strike would cause her to miss classes.
_____ 4. Passing her road test was a great source of worry.
_____ 5. To calm herself down before the test.
_____ 6. She tried everything she could think of, including a nap.
_____ 7. Unfortunately she was nervous anyway.
_____ 8. Going through a stop sign without stopping.
_____ 9. She confessed to the examiner that she hadn't even seen it.
_____ 10. A firm resolution to concentrate more on her driving next time.

Introducing Fragments Beginning With If, When, Because, and Although (Subordinate Conjunctions)

A *conjunction* is a connecting word. A *subordinate* conjunction is a word that connects a subordinate (less important) idea to a main sentence. The words *if, when, because,* and *although* are subordinate conjunctions. Ideas beginnning with these words cannot stand alone; they are not as important as the main idea of the sentence. When left alone, they are fragments.

You will study sentences with *if, when, because,* and *although* in detail. For now, you need to learn only two basic principles. First, memorize the four subordinate conjunctions *if, when, because,* and *although*. Second, note that a clause beginning with one of these words *never* contains the main subject or verb of a sentence. It is subordinate to the main idea, so the main subject and verb appear elsewhere in the sentence. Look at this example:

When my clock was broken.   *Fragment*

To complete this sentence, you must add a subject and verb outside of the *if* clause:

When my clock was broken, I missed chemistry class.
Complete sentence

The main subject is *I*, and the main verb is *missed*.

It's helpful to think of these words as *hanging* words: Any idea that begins with a subordinate conjunction seems to be hanging in the air, waiting to be attached to a complete sentence. Read the following example:

Because Gail helped me.   *Fragment beginning with because*

This word group is a hanging fragment that needs to attach to a complete sentence. Now read the corrected version:

Because Gail helped me, I survived biology.   *Complete sentence*

(Notice that it is perfectly all right to start a sentence with a subordinate conjunction such as *because*.) In this sentence, you might think that *Gail* is the subject and that *helped* is the verb. But actually the subject is *I*, and the verb is *survived*. You must skip over the words that immediately follow *because*.

Often you can spot these hanging fragments simply by reading your written work aloud. Check your work by following this procedure. First, make a light pencil line through *because* and the words that immediately follow it, like this:

~~Because Gail helped me~~, I survived biology.

Then look *outside* the pencil line to find another subject and a verb. What if you make your pencil line and then find no subject or verb? In that case, you have written a fragment. Study this example:

~~If my car payments are too high~~.   *Fragment*

This group of words is not a complete sentence because it does not tell what will happen as a result of the high car payments. Here is the correct version:

~~If my car payments are too high~~, I will find a part-time job.   *Complete sentence*

The subject is *I,* and the verb is *will find.*
Check carefully any clause beginning with a subordinate conjunction to be sure that it has a subject and verb. Study the following examples:

~~When I get angry at my roommate~~.   *Fragment*

~~When I get angry at my roommate~~, I write him an angry note.   *Complete sentence*

The subject is *I,* and the verb is *write.*

~~Although Beth wants to move out~~.   *Fragment*

~~Although Beth wants to move out~~, she doesn't have enough money.   *Complete sentence*

The subject is *she,* and the verb is *doesn't have.*

Exercise 8

INSTRUCTIONS: Two versions of the same paragraph appear here. The first version is correct, but the second version contains fragments. Read both versions aloud to hear the difference between the correct and incorrect use of subordinate conjunctions. Find the fragments in version B.

A

Because car maintenance is so expensive, I ride a bicycle to college and to work. When my friends talk about the high prices they pay for oil changes and tune-ups, I just smile. If my bicycle needs an adjustment, I can usually take care of it myself. Although the bicycle is inconvenient in bad weather, the savings are well worth it.

Fragments

B

Because car maintenance is so expensive. I ride a bicycle to college and to work. When my friends talk about the high prices they pay for oil changes and tune-ups. I just smile. If my bicycle needs an adjustment. I can usually take care of it myself. Although the bicycle is inconvenient in bad weather. The savings are well worth it.

Exercise 9

INSTRUCTIONS: Each clause that follows begins with a subordinate conjunction. Some clauses are fragments; others are complete sentences. Mark each sentence **S** and each fragment **F**. Be prepared to explain your answers to a classmate.

_____ 1. Although I started early on my sociology assignment, as usual.

_____ 2. Because I had problems with the library, I didn't finish it.

_____ 3. When the professor talked about microfilm, I panicked.

_____ 4. If I have to use a piece of library equipment, I freeze.

_____ 5. Although I'd used microfilm before, in another course.

_____ 6. Because I was nervous, I forgot the procedure.

_____ 7. If I could have talked to the librarian, Mrs. Henry.

_____ 8. When she's there, microfilm is no problem.

_____ 9. Because the assistant, who wasn't familiar with the machine.

_____ 10. When the assignment was due, I still hadn't read it on the machine.

Exercise 10

INSTRUCTIONS: Mark each sentence below **S** and each fragment **F**. Then correct each fragment by adding a subject and verb or combining it with a complete sentence. (Hint: Because this exercise is actually a paragraph, it may be helpful to work in reverse order, starting with the last sentence and ending with the first.) Be prepared to explain your answers to another student.

_____ 1. Jill is an animal activist.

_____ 2. Although she doesn't have much money.

_____ 3. If she has a few extra dollars.

_____ 4. She sends a donation to an animal organization.
_____ 5. Because she was at the vet's office all the time.
_____ 6. He hired her as his assistant.
_____ 7. When she sees a lost dog or cat, she tries to find the owner.
_____ 8. If her efforts fail.
_____ 9. She advertises for a new home.
_____ 10. Because she cares, she tries to help.

Introducing Fragments Beginning With Who and Which

Any group of words beginning with *who* or *which* is a fragment *unless* it ends with a question mark. Study these examples:

Who spilled milk all over the floor.   *Fragment*
Who spilled milk all over the floor?   *Sentence*

Fragments beginning with *who* or *which* can be corrected in either of two ways. If you want to change the fragment to a question, just change the period to a question mark, as shown. If you don't want the fragment to become a question, add it to another sentence, like this:

Susan is a friend. Who is always there when I need her.
Incorrect

Susan is a friend who is always there when I need her.
Correct

Exercise 11

INSTRUCTIONS: Two versions of the same paragraph appear here. In version A, all of the sentences are correct. In version B, several fragments appear that begin with *who* and *which*. Read both versions carefully to identify the fragments.

A. Correct Version

The telephone is an invention which has improved my life. First, it enables me to talk to friends who have moved away from my neighborhood. Second, it is handy for ordering catalog merchandise which isn't sold in local stores. Most importantly, it can help me handle emergencies which might arise at any time. For example, I can use the telephone to call for a doctor, a police officer, or a firefighter.

B. Incorrect Version

The telephone is an invention. Which has improved my life. First, it enables me to talk to friends. Who have moved away from my neighborhood. Second, it is handy for ordering catalog merchandise. Which isn't sold in local stores. Most importantly, it can help me handle emergencies. Which might arise at any time. For example, I can use the telephone to call for a doctor, a police officer, or a firefighter.

Exercise 12

INSTRUCTIONS: Mark each sentence **S**. Mark each fragment **F**. Be prepared to explain your answers to a classmate.

1. Which sport is your favorite?
2. I've always been crazy about baseball.
3. Which offers suspense, colorful personalities, and humor.
4. I like to look at the homemade banners.
5. Which fans bring to the baseball park.
6. Which team is your favorite?
7. My favorite baseball team is the Boston Red Sox.
8. Who never give up hoping and trying.
9. Carl Yastremski is a baseball hero.
10. Who has inspired countless young baseball players.

Exercise 13

INSTRUCTIONS: Underline each fragment that begins with *who* or *which*. Be prepared to explain your answers to a classmate.

My Career Decision

Next year I'm going to New York to study the culinary arts. Who inspired me? I got the idea from a friend of my mother's. Who's a business manager for a cruise line. She said that cruise ships are always looking for chefs. Who can prepare excellent food for the ship's passengers. Cruises build their reputation on the meals they serve. Which have to be superbly cooked and served. Which cruise line do I plan to work for? I haven't decided yet. But I'm sure I'll be paid well, and I know I'll have a chance to see the world.

Reviewing What You Have Learned

Exercise 14

INSTRUCTIONS: Mark each statement either *true* or *false*.

_____ 1. If you're not sure what a sentence means, it is a fragment.

_____ 2. If a clause has both a subject and a verb, it is a complete sentence.

_____ 3. If a clause lacks a subject, it is a fragment.

_____ 4. You should never start a sentence with a subordinate conjunction.

_____ 5. If a fragment begins with the words *who* or *which*, one possibility is to correct it with a question mark.

_____ 6. Checking the first word in every sentence you've written can help you find fragments.

_____ 7. Reading paragraphs in reverse order, starting with the last sentence, can help you spot fragments.

Exercise 15

INSTRUCTIONS: Mark each of the following clauses with the appropriate letter:

a. No subject
b. No verb
c. Fragment with *if, when, because* or *although*
d. Fragment beginning with *who* or *which*
e. Correct sentence

_____ 1. I became interested in photography a year ago.
_____ 2. Bought a used 35-millimeter camera.
_____ 3. On a friend's advice, I bought fifty rolls of black-and-white film.
_____ 4. Which took up so much space in our refrigerator that my mother complained.
_____ 5. My friend assured me that I'd learn a lot about photography as I used up all that film.
_____ 6. He was right.
_____ 7. While I was learning the basic principles of photography.
_____ 8. Many dull, overexposed, out-of-focus pictures.
_____ 9. Gradually my skills improved.
_____ 10. Which technique helped me the most?
_____ 11. Looking at famous photographs in books from the library.
_____ 12. To attempt the same effects myself.
_____ 13. Although I often felt discouraged, even hopeless.
_____ 14. Began to feel proud of my photographs.
_____ 15. When one of my pictures won a prize, I celebrated.
_____ 16. It was a photograph of a small child.
_____ 17. Who was crouched over his family's cat.
_____ 18. If you've ever struggled to perfect a new skill.
_____ 19. You can understand my excitement about the prize.
_____ 20. Hoping to continue to improve my photography skills.

Exercise 16

INSTRUCTIONS: Plan and write a paragraph about a project that didn't turn out as you had expected. In the revising step, go through these procedures with a classmate:

1. Slowly read each sentence aloud, making sure that it is complete. Often your ear will warn you when a sentence needs to be changed.

2. Read your sentences a second time, underlining all the verbs twice. Be careful to avoid infinitives (*to* plus a verb) and verbs with *ing* endings—remember, these two constructions are not really verbs. If one of your clauses lacks a verb, correct it by adding a verb.

3. Underline all the subjects. If one of your clauses lacks a subject, correct it by adding a subject.

4. Ask yourself whether any of your clauses begin with a subordinate conjunction such as *because, if, when,* or *although*. If so, make a light pencil line through the words following your subordinate conjunction. Then make sure you have a subject and verb outside of your pencil line.

5. Ask yourself whether any of your clauses begin with *who* or *which*. If so, correct them in one of two possible ways. If you have written a question, put a question mark at the end. Or you may add the *who* or *which* clause to another sentence.

6. Read your paragraph aloud again, this time in reverse order—start with the last sentence and end with the first. Your ear may help you spot sentence errors that you had missed earlier.

7. Before you hand in your sentences, use a dictionary to look for misspelled words.

Unit Ten
Sentences with If, When, Because, *and* Although (Subordinate Conjunctions)

SUMMARY

1. The words *if, when, because,* and *although* are subordinate conjunctions.

2. Subordinate conjunctions add maturity to your writing.

3. A sentence may begin with one of these four words.

4. A group of words beginning with *if, when, because,* or *although* is called a *subordinate clause*.

5. Punctuating subordinate clauses involves applying a rule about commas.

6. The main subject and verb in a sentence *never* appear in a subordinate clause.

Introducing If, When, Because, and *Although*

Subordinate conjunctions, such as *if, when, because,* and *although,* combine short, choppy sentences into longer and more interesting ones. In addition, they enable readers to connect related ideas. To understand how these subordinate conjunctions work, read the following sentence pairs aloud. Notice how much better the second sentence in each pair sounds:

You study hard. You will make good progress.   *Choppy*

If you study hard, you will make good progress.   *Better*

My dog trembles. He hears a loud clap of thunder.   *Choppy*

My dog trembles when he hears a loud clap of thunder.   *Better*

I'm careful with money. I work hard for it.   *Choppy*

I'm careful with money because I work hard for it.   *Better*

Alice loves candy. She doesn't eat it often.   *Choppy*

Although Alice loves candy, she doesn't eat it often.   *Better*

The second sentences in each pair is better, for two reasons. First, it is smoother. Short, choppy sentences (the first kind) often sound childish. Second, the second sentence includes a connecting word—*if, when, because,* or *although*—that links the two ideas that form the sentence. Some of the second sentences have commas, but others do not. These commas will be discussed later.

To understand more clearly the meaningful connection in these sentences, compare the following examples:

I studied drama for six years. I won an acting scholarship.
   Example

Because I studied drama for six years, I won an acting scholarship.   *Example*

The first example just states two facts. The second example is better, because it shows that the two facts have a cause-and-effect relationship: I won the scholarship as a result of my drama studies. Mature writers use words like *because* to show how facts relate to one another.

Notice that the last example sentence begins with *because*, as do many sentences in this unit and this textbook. As we mentioned in Unit 8, it is perfectly correct to begin sentences with words such as *if*, *when*, *because*, and *although*. In fact, because you want to vary your sentence patterns, you may often put a subordinate conjunction at the beginning of a sentence. Another good reason for starting a sentence with *if*, *when*, *because*, or *although* is that this type of word signals readers, telling them what to expect. Readers can follow your ideas more easily.

Here are two more sentences that can be joined effectively with *because*:

> **Antonio won the game with a foul shot. The team cheered him.** *Example*

> **Because Antonio won the game with a foul shot, the team cheered him.** *Example*

Again, the first example just states the facts. The second example is better, because it shows that the successful foul shot led to the cheering.

Learning More About *If* and *When*

If and *when* are words that join ideas in a meaningful way. *If* indicates that something might happen, as in this sentence:

> **I will spend a week at the beach if I can earn enough money.** *Example*

When has two meanings. First, it can show two things happening at the same time, as in this sentence:

> **The dog barked when I rang the doorbell.** *Example*

When can also indicate that something is definitely going to happen, as in this sentence:

> **I will spend a week at the beach when the semester is over.** *Example*

Exercise 1

INSTRUCTIONS: Complete the following sentences by adding either *if* or *when* and any other words you think are appropriate. When you are finished, be prepared to explain your choices to another student.

1. Sarah will win a gold medal for figure skating _____.

2. I always get a headache _____.

3. My makeup runs _____.

4. My car stalled _____.

5. Get in touch with the doctor _____.

6. We will eat dinner _____.

7. Jacques helped me with my French _____.

8. The police officer won't give me a ticket _____.

9. I understood the lesson _____.

10. I'm always in a good mood _____.

Learning More About *Because* and *Although*

The words *because* and *although* signal readers to look for certain kinds of information. *Because* tells readers to look for a logical connection between two ideas. In contrast, *although* tells readers that an unexpected piece of information will appear in the sentence. To learn more about *although* and *because*, try completing both of these sentences:

Although Georgette studies hard, _____.	*Example*
Because Georgette studies hard, _____.	*Example*

Sentences with *If, When, Because,* and *Although*   131

Your sentences are probably similar to these:

Although Georgette studies hard, she makes low grades.
   Example

Because Georgette studies hard, she makes high grades.
   Example

The first example begins with *although*. Therefore, it contains unexpected information: A student who studies hard earns low grades. The second example, however, begins with *because*. Therefore, it tells us what we expect to learn: Georgette, who studies hard, earns high grades.

Here are two more sentences to try:

Because the weathercaster predicted rain, _____

   _____ .   *Example*

Although the weathercaster predicted rain, _____

   _____ .   *Example*

Your sentences are probably similar to these:

Because the weathercaster predicted rain, we cancelled our camping trip.   *Example*

Although the weathercaster predicted rain, we went ahead with our camping trip.   *Example*

We expect people to cancel a camping trip when rain is predicted. Therefore, the first example (with *because*) continues with an expected result. We don't expect people to go camping when rain is coming. Therefore, the second example (with *although*) shows an unexpected result.

In the next four examples, place either *because* or *although* in the blank spaces:

I enjoyed the movie _____**Meryl Streep is my favorite actress.**   *Example*

The baby slept peacefully _____**the party next door was a noisy one.**   *Example*

_____Chicago is an interesting place, I don't want to live there.   *Example*

_____I want to buy a new wardrobe, I decided to get a part-time job.

Your sentences should look like these:

I enjoyed the movie <u>because</u> Meryl Streep is my favorite actress.   *Example*

The baby slept peacefully <u>although</u> the party next door was a noisy one.   *Example*

<u>Although</u> Chicago is an interesting place, I don't want to live there.

<u>Because</u> I want to buy a new wardrobe, I decided to get a part-time job.   *Example*

Exercise 2

INSTRUCTIONS: In each space, write either *although* or *because*. Read each sentence carefully so that you can decide which word is appropriate. When you are finished, be prepared to explain your choices to another student.

1. _____tropical fish fascinate me, I enjoyed visiting the Shedd Aquarium in Chicago.

2. I never had a salt-water aquarium _____salt-water fish are difficult to keep alive.

3. _____ angelfish look delicate, they have done well in my fish tank.

4. I change some of the water every week _____chemicals accumulate in the aquarium.

5. I have only one fish tank _____I'd like to have several more.

Exercise 3

INSTRUCTIONS: The following sentences are incomplete. Add any appropriate words to finish the sentences. Remember that *because* indicates a logical result, and *although* indicates a result you don't expect.

Sentences with *If, When, Because,* and *Although*

1. We postponed our trip to Europe because_____.

2. We postponed our trip to Europe although_____.

3. Dennis is a terrific basketball player although_____.

4. Dennis is a terrific basketball player because_____.

5. I'm doing well in college math because_____.

6. I'm doing well in college math although_____.

7. Luisa enjoys her part-time job although_____.

8. Luisa enjoys her part-time job because_____.

9. I enjoy college because_____.

10. I enjoy college although_____.

Using Commas with *If, When, Because,* and *Although*

Before you learn a new comma rule, review what you learned about fragments in Unit 9. What is wrong with this sentence?

Because I spent my savings on a new surfboard. *Example*

This sentence is incomplete and should be labeled a fragment. It needs an additional subject and verb to make it complete. In the next example, this fragment has been expanded into a complete sentence. Can you find the new subject and verb?

> **Because I spent my savings on a new surfboard, my bank account is low.** *Complete sentence*

Here is the sentence again, with the main subject and verb underlined:

> **Because I spent my savings on a new surfboard, <u>my bank account is</u> low.** *Complete sentence*

Check sentences with *if, when, because,* and *although* to make sure that they are complete. The sentences should have two parts. One part is the word group immediately following *if, when, because,* or *although,* called a *subordinate clause*. In Unit 8 you learned to cross out this part of the sentence with a light pencil line. The other part of the sentence—what's left outside of your line—is the main subject and verb.

Now you are ready to start thinking about commas. All of the sentences shown next are punctuated correctly. Some have commas, while others do not. See if you can discover the difference between those sentences that have commas and those that do not. When you think you have figured out the difference, pair off with another student and compare your discoveries:

> **Because the art gallery was closed, I couldn't finish my humanities report.** *Correct*
>
> **Tom missed his plane because his car had a flat tire.** *Correct*
>
> **The audience applauded when Billy Joel stepped onto the stage.** *Correct*
>
> **When I was in high school, I played varsity football.** *Correct*
>
> **If you decide to sell your car, I'd like to buy it.** *Correct*
>
> **Those jeans will shrink if you wash them in hot water.** *Correct*
>
> **Although Carol Burnett is most famous for comedy, she has also done serious roles.** *Correct*
>
> **I didn't sleep well although I was tired.** *Correct*

Sentences with *If*, *When*, *Because*, and *Although*

Here's another opportunity to see if you've figured out these commas. Try to decide which of the following sentences need commas and which do not. The correct answers appear right after the practice version. After you've tried putting in the commas yourself, check to see if you were correct.

Although the pizza was overdone we enjoyed eating it.

Call me if you need a ride.

I studied French when I was in high school.

I went to the laundry because my washing machine is broken.

If I finish my report I'll be able to go to the movie.

I ran out of wallpaper although I measured the room carefully.

When I get your check I will mail your order.

Because I can do carpentry I save money on home repairs.

Answers:

Although the pizza was overdone, we enjoyed eating it.

Call me if you need a ride.

I studied French when I was in high school.

I went to the laundry because my washer is broken.

If I finish my report, I'll be able to go to the movie.

I ran out of wallpaper although I measured the room carefully.

When I get your check, I will mail your order.

Because I can do carpentry, I save money on home repairs.

Placing such commas is easy. Just find the position of the subordinate clause. (The cross-out technique is helpful here.) If the subordinate clause is located at the beginning of the sentence, place a comma after the last word in the clause, as shown here:

~~When my check arrives~~, I will pay these bills.   *Comma needed*

If the subordinate clause is located at the end of the sentence, don't use a comma at all, as shown in this sentence:

I will pay these bills ~~when my check arrives~~.   *No comma*

Exercise 4

INSTRUCTIONS: Place commas where they are needed in the following sentences. Remember that crossing out the subordinate clause can be helpful.

1. When I lived in San Francisco I often ate Chinese food.
2. The baseball manager lost his job although his team had been winning.
3. You will lose weight if you follow this program.
4. Because Miriam speaks Italian she is looking forward to visiting Rome.
5. I often watch soap operas although I hate to admit it.
6. We saw a beautiful sunrise when we got up this morning.
7. If we are out of milk I will pick some up tonight.
8. Although I usually enjoy concerts I didn't like that one.
9. Dad is watering the lawn because we haven't had rain lately.
10. I will call you when I'm ready to leave.

Exercise 5

INSTRUCTIONS: Read the following paragraph carefully, inserting commas where they are needed. Again, try the cross-out technique. Not every sentence contains a subordinate clause.

Toscanini

If you are interested in music you have heard of Arturo Toscanini. He was one of the most famous orchestra conductors who ever lived. Music lovers admired him because he interpreted music brilliantly. When he conducted a piece of music the audience usually cheered. Although the public loved Toscanini the performers soometimes didn't. Because Toscanini demanded perfection he was difficult to work with. Sometimes he ripped up musical scores and smashed batons to splinters. He even threw his pocket watch on the floor when he was angry. Once a friend gave him a box of cheap watches to smash when he was conducting. Nothing was more important to Toscanini than beautiful music.

Combining Sentences with *If, When, Because,* and *Although*

As you have seen, these words can be used to make short, choppy sentences sound longer and smoother. Even more important, they can forge meaningful connections between ideas.

Now you are ready to use these words to combine sentences. The steps are simple. First, decide which word (*if, when, because,* or *although*) would work best with the sentences you have been given. Which word would you choose to combine these sentences?

Our star player was out with an injury. We won the basketball tournament.   *Short, choppy sentences*

The best choice here is *although*. Now you can combine the sentences using the word you have chosen:

Although our star player was out with an injury, we won the basketball tournament.   *Two sentences combined into one*

Finally, use the cross-out technique to decide whether a comma is needed:

~~**Although our star player was out with an injury**~~**, we won the basketball tournament.**   *Correct sentence*

Exercise 6

INSTRUCTIONS: Use the words *if, when, because,* and *although* to combine the following short sentences. If the sentences need commas, insert them correctly. When you're finished, compare your work to another student's.

1. You have been to Puerto Rico. You have probably heard of José de Diego.
2. He was born there in 1866. Puerto Rico still belonged to Spain.
3. He was twelve. He wanted to be a heroic bullfighter.
4. He realized that politicians could be heroes too. He changed his mind about bullfighting.

5. Puerto Rico became part of the United States. Its citizens wanted to keep their Spanish culture alive.
6. José de Deigo was a lawyer and politician. He was also a scholar and poet.
7. Puerto Rico wanted to have a unique culture. It needed its own poets.
8. José de Diego was fluent in English, Latin, and French. He wrote poetry in Spanish.
9. You are interested in Spanish-American literature. You are familiar with his work.
10. José de Diego wanted to promote Spanish culture. He started a special language school called the Antillean Academy.

Exercise 7

INSTRUCTIONS: Use the words *if*, *when*, *because*, and *although* to combine the following short sentences. If the sentences need commas, insert them correctly. When you're finished, compare your work to another student's.

1. Arthur Conan Doyle studied ophthalmology. He was interested in the science of human vision.
2. He opened up a medical office in London. He did not practice medicine there.
3. No patients came to his office. He began writing detective stories to pass the time.
4. You enjoy reading mysteries. You have probably read Doyle's Sherlock Holmes stories.
5. Doyle revolutionized police science. He was a creative thinker.
6. The Sherlock Holmes stories became famous. They were used to train detectives.
7. Sherlock Holmes believed that stains and footprints could help solve crimes. Police departments began to study these clues.
8. Detectives today use scientific methods. Arthur Conan Doyle demonstrated how useful they can be.

Writing Sentences with If, When, Because, and Although

Now that you have had some experience with these four subordinate conjunctions, you are ready to write sentences of your own. Remember to check your sentences carefully to be sure that you have used these words correctly. Remember, too, that the cross-out technique can help you check your sentences for completeness and correct punctuation.

The next two exercises require you to write sentences using these four subordinate conjunctions. In Exercise 8, part of the sentence has already been written; your job is to complete it. In Exercise 9, you will create sentences that are entirely your own. Then you will be ready to include subordinate conjunctions in a paragraph you will write yourself.

Exercise 8

INSTRUCTIONS: Use the blank spaces to finish the incomplete sentences. Place commas where they are needed, and check your sentences carefully to make sure that you have used your subordinate conjunctions correctly.

1. If the store has a half-price sale next week_____
   _____.

2. _____because I spent hours watching them perform on television.

3. When the bank was giving away luggage to new customers
   _____.

4. _____although I'm really too old for teddy bears.

5. _____if I can find a part-time job.

6. Because I couldn't get a taxi_____
   _____.

7. Although I bought this shirt at a Salvation Army thrift store _____.

8. _____ when I was in elementary school.

9. _____ although she could afford a foreign sports car.

10. When I saw the smoke coming out of the oven _____.

Exercise 9

INSTRUCTIONS: Use each of these words in two sentences: *if, when, because,* and *although*. Use the cross-out technique to make sure your sentences are complete and to place your commas correctly.

Exercise 10

INSTRUCTIONS: Using the steps of the writing process, write a paragraph about a goal that is important to you. Here are some possible goals:

losing ten pounds
starting an exercise program
making the dean's list
saving seventy-five dollars
cutting back on TV
making two new friends
cleaning out a closet

Try to include a few subordinate clauses in your paragraph, such as the following:

because my goal is important to me
when I achieve my goal
although it won't be easy

During the revising step, use the cross-out technique to make sure your sentences are complete and your punctuation is correct.

Looking Ahead: Learning More Subordinate Conjunctions

Listed here are additional subordinate conjunctions that you can use in your sentences. Use the cross-out technique with these words to check your sentences for completeness and your commas for correct placement.

after	since	while
as	unless	whenever
before	until	wherever

Exercise 11

INSTRUCTIONS: Use each of the subordinate conjunctions listed above in a sentence. Make sure all your sentences are complete, and check your commas for correct placement.

Reviewing What You Have Learned

Exercise 12

INSTRUCTIONS: Answer each question.

1. What is a subordinate clause?
2. What are two ways in which subordinate conjunctions can improve your sentences?
3. Mark as *true* or *false*:

   _____ a. Always use a comma with a subordinate conjunction.

   _____ b. You may start a sentence with a subordinate conjunction.

   _____ c. The main subject and verb in a sentence never appear in a subordinate clause.

   _____ d. You should use subordinate conjunctions sparingly because they tend to confuse readers.

_____ e. The subordinate conjunction *although* indicates a cause-and-effect relationship between two ideas.

_____ f. Subordinate conjunctions are rarely heard in ordinary conversations.

4. Fill in the blanks:

   a. You should use a comma when a subordinate clause appears at the _____ of a sentence.

   b. The _____ technique can help you use commas correctly with subordinate clauses.

Exercise 13

INSTRUCTIONS: Use *if, when, because,* and *although* to combine the following sentence pairs. Use the cross-out technique to ensure that you have placed your commas correctly.

1. You are a football fan. You have heard of Johnny Unitas.
2. Johnny Unitas became Most Valuable Player. He was quarterback for the Baltimore Colts.
3. Unitas was one of the most famous players in the NFL. He started his career with a semipro team.
4. No professional team wanted him. He graduated from the University of Louisville.
5. Unitas was slender. The professionals overlooked his remarkable talent.
6. He got a job as a construction worker. He needed to support his wife and baby.
7. The Pittsburgh Steelers gave him a try in their preseason camp. They weren't impressed.
8. The Steelers didn't see his potential. The Colts did.
9. Unitas was sometimes discouraged in those early years. He didn't show it.
10. Unitas played brilliantly for the Baltimore Colts. Fans still talk about him.

Exercise 14

INSTRUCTIONS: This paragraph contains several short, choppy sentences. Use subordinate conjunctions to combine some of these sentences. Check each

Sentences with *If, When, Because,* and *Although*

sentence to make sure you have placed your commas correctly. When you are finished, read the paragraph aloud. Your ear will help you determine whether your punctuation is correct.

Many Sherlock Holmes fans confused fiction and reality. They thought Arthur Conan Doyle was really Sherlock Holmes. They asked Doyle to solve mysteries for them. Doyle was not trained as a detective. He solved many spectacular mysteries. Crown jewels were stolen from Ireland. Doyle found them. Scotland Yard asked Doyle to help solve a murder. Doyle's detective skills were extremely valuable. One case was particularly interesting. A young law student was jailed for cruelty to animals. Doyle proved his innocence. The young man had a severe vision problem. He couldn't see well enough to commit the crime.

Unit Eleven
Sentences with And, But, *and* Or *(Coordinate Conjunctions)*

SUMMARY

1. And, but, and *or* are called *coordinate conjunctions*, and they can add maturity to your writing.

2. When you join two sentences with one of these words, place a comma at the end of the first sentence.

3. *And* is a weak connector word. Develop the habit of using other words to join sentences.

4. Any of these words, including *but*, may be used at the beginning of a sentence.

Sentences with *And*, *But*, and *Or*

You use *and*, *but*, and *or* frequently in conversation and writing—so frequently that you probably haven't stopped to wonder what special purpose they have. These three words, which are often called *coordinate conjunctions*, are useful for combining sentences. The prefix *co* means "equal." Coordinate conjunctions join "equal" sentences: both sentences must have a subject and verb. The examples that follow show how these words can eliminate choppiness and add maturity to your writing. (Notice that the sentences are equal: each has a subject and verb.)

The tennis match was over. Mark was grinning   *Choppy*

The tennis match was over, and Mark was grinning.   *Better*

My new glasses are ready. I can't pick them up today.
Choppy

My new glasses are ready, but I can't pick them up today.
Better

The pitcher must improve his fast ball. He might get sent to the minors.   *Choppy*

The pitcher must improve his fast ball, or he might get sent to the minors.   *Better*

The combined sentences sound better than the short, choppy ones. In addition, the words *and*, *but*, and *or* add maturity to these sentences. For example, the word *but* tells readers to expect a shift in meaning in the next part of the sentence. The word *and* is quite different: it tells readers to expect more of the same.

To learn more about the meaning of these three words, examine the following sentence pairs:

Jack is studying karate, and he's learning quickly.   *Example*

Jack is studying karate, but he's not doing very well.
Example

I'll go to Kala's party, and I'll tell you about it on Monday.
Example

I'll go to Kala's party, but I'll probably have a miserable time.
Example

> **You can try to lose weight on your own, or you can ask your physician for help.** *Example*
>
> **I can help you with algebra right now, or I can work with you tomorrow afternoon.** *Example*

Read the example sentences again several times, both silently and aloud. Then spend a few minutes talking about the examples with another student. Try to explain why *and* was used to join the first and third sentences, *but* was used with the second, and *or* was chosen for the fourth and fifth. When you are finished, proceed with Exercise 1.

Exercise 1

INSTRUCTIONS: Insert a coordinate conjunction (*and*, *but*, or *or*) into each space in the sentences. When you are finished, be prepared to explain your choices to another student.

1. I bought a camera, _____ I don't know how to use it yet.
2. Tonight we can go to a restaurant, _____ we can eat at home.
3. A baseball scout watched us play, _____ I think he wants to talk to our star pitcher.
4. Anne has been looking for an apartment, _____ she hasn't found one she can afford.
5. The hotel rooms are reasonably priced, _____ the beach is right outside.
6. Jogging is great exercise, _____ it can be hard on your knees and feet.
7. We can drive to Savannah, _____ we can take the train.
8. Jack landscaped the new office building on Main Street, _____ he won a civic award.
9. Driving an ambulance looks easy, _____ it takes concentration and skill.
10. Wilma may work in a medical lab, _____ she may take a job in a doctor's office.

Sentences with *And, But,* and *Or* 147

Using Commas with And, But, Or

Commas are sometimes (but not always!) necessary with *and, but,* and *or*. To see why, try reading the following sentences aloud to another student:

> **Everyone made the swimming team but Ginger may not have time to compete this year.** *Example*
>
> **Yesterday I lost my temper and my nephew got mad at me.** *Example*

You may have stumbled over these sentences because the commas were left out. Now read the corrected sentences aloud, noticing how commas clarify their meaning:

> **Everyone made the swimming team, but Ginger may not have time to compete this year.** *Correct*
>
> **Yesterday I lost my temper, and my nephew got mad at me.** *Correct*

Commas are essential to good writing because they make sentences easier to read and understand. Now you are ready to discover when a comma is needed and learn to place it.

All of the example sentences given here are correct. Examine them carefully; notice that some contain commas but others do not. Can you determine why some sentences need commas but others do not?

> **Jane loves ice cream, but she rarely eats it.** *Correct*
>
> **Jane loves ice cream but rarely eats it.** *Correct*
>
> **You can ride with me or catch the bus later.** *Correct*
>
> **You can ride with me, or you can catch the bus later.** *Correct*
>
> **Greg bought a set of weights, and he works out regularly.** *Correct*
>
> **Greg bought a set of weights and works out regularly.** *Correct*

If you think you know the rule for using commas with *and, but,* and *or,* try inserting commas into the following sentences. The correct answers follow:

> The dog growled but nobody was there.   *Example*
>
> Lisa enjoys painting and has sold some of her work.   *Example*
>
> Anna quickly mastered racquetball and she loves it.   *Example*
>
> You can write an extra paper or you can take the final exam.   *Example*
>
> I wanted to major in hospital administration but changed my mind.   *Example*
>
> I will call you or visit you this weekend.   *Example*

Answers

> The dog growled, but nobody was there.   *Correct*
>
> Lisa enjoys painting and has sold some of her work.   *Correct*
>
> Anna quickly mastered racquetball, and she loves it.   *Correct*
>
> You can write an extra paper, or you can take the final exam.   *Correct*
>
> I wanted to major in hospital administration but changed my mind.   *Correct*
>
> I will call you or visit you this weekend.   *Correct*

Here is the rule for using commas with *and, but,* and *or*: *If you're combining two sentences with one of these words, use a comma. If you have only one sentence, omit the comma.*

You'll find it helpful to look for a subject and verb *before* the coordinate conjunction and another subject and verb after. Here are the sample sentences once again with subjects and verbs underlined.

> The dog growled, but nobody was there.   *Two complete sentences: The comma is correct*
>
> Lisa enjoys painting and has sold some of her work.   *One sentence: No comma*

Sentences with *And, But,* and *Or* 149

Anna quickly learned how to play racquetball, and she loves it.
Two complete sentences: The comma is correct

You can write an extra paper, or you can take the final exam.
Two complete sentences: The comma is correct

I wanted to major in hospital administration but changed my mind.   *One sentence: No comma*

I will call you or visit you this weekend.   *One sentence: No comma*

Here is another set of sentences for you to punctuate. Before you insert the commas, find the coordinate conjunction (*and, but,* or *or*) in each one. Then see if you have a complete sentence (subject and verb) both in front of the coordinate conjunction and in back. The punctuated sentences follow:

Lynn called you this morning but forgot to leave a message.   *Example*

Lynn called you this morning but she forgot to leave a message.   *Example*

Barry owns an ice cream shop and his wife helps him run it.   *Example*

Henry runs an office-cleaning service and has a long list of satisfied clients.   *Example*

Next year we will buy new carpeting or put no-wax flooring in the family room.   *Example*

Jack overcharged you or you wrote the wrong amount on the check.   *Example*

Answers

Lynn called you this morning but forgot to leave a message. Lynn called you this morning, but she forgot to leave a message.   *Correct*

Barry owns an ice-cream shop, and his wife helps him run it. Henry runs an office-cleaning service and has a long list of satisfied clients.   *Correct*

Next year we will buy new carpeting or put no-wax flooring in the family room.   *Correct*

Jack overcharged you, or you wrote the wrong amount on the check.   *Correct*

Exercise 2

INSTRUCTIONS: Underline the subjects and verbs in each sentence. Then place commas where they are needed, using the rule you have learned.

1. The primaries are coming up and I'm learning about the candidates.
2. The rain was refreshing but wasn't enough to end the drought.
3. You can hire someone to paint the house or I will do it next summer.
4. I baked the cake and Sandra decorated it.
5. Grace probably took your file home or left it in her office.
6. I don't like to admit this but I used to wish I could be a Mouseketeer.
7. Betty should accept Brian's proposal or break up with him.
8. The sofa needs vacuuming and the windows need washing.
9. The concert sounds great but the tickets are sold out.
10. Charlene went to Japan and found it fascinating.

Exercise 3

INSTRUCTIONS: Use your own ideas to fill in the blanks. Notice that some of the sentences have a comma before the coordinate conjunction. In these sentences, you will need a subject and verb both before and after *and, but, or*.

1. I love the beach, but _____
   _____.

2. I love the beach but _____
   _____.

3. Selden may open his own business or _____
   _____.

4. Selden may open his own business, or _____
   _____.

5. Leo does the lights for our theater productions and _____
   _____.

6. Leo does the lights for our theater productions, and _____
   _____.

Sentences with *And, But,* and *Or* 151

7. The manager should replace the pitcher now, or_____
   _____.

8. The manager should replace the pitcher now or_____
   _____.

9. I know I have musical talent, but_____
   _____.

10. I know I have musical talent but_____
    _____.

Exercise 4

INSTRUCTIONS: Use your own ideas to fill in the blanks. Notice that some of the sentences have a comma before the coordinate conjunction. In these sentences, you will need a subject and verb both before and after *and, but, or*.

1. I need to study but_____
   _____.

2. I need to study, but_____
   _____.

3. Warren helped me get ready for my physics exam, and_____
   _____.

4. Warren helped me get ready for my physics exam and_____
   _____.

5. Celia can answer your question, or_____
   _____.

6. Celia can answer your question or_____
   _____.

7. Frank's Restaurant has delicious food and_____
   _____.

8. Frank's Restaurant has delicious food, and _____.

9. The cruise sounds wonderful, but _____.

10. The cruise sounds wonderful but _____.

Starting Sentences with And, But, and Or

Many students remember hearing a teacher warn them against starting sentences with *and* or *but*. Those warnings probably were meant to help beginning writers avoid writing fragments with words. But are those warnings still valid?

The answer is *no*. (Did you notice that the last sentence in the previous paragraph began with *but?*) Professional writers often begin sentences with *and* or *but*—and you can, too. *And* and *but* are useful when you want to make a connection between one sentence and the next. Placed at the beginning of a sentence, they tell your readers what to expect. *And* tells your readers to expect a related idea. For example:

> **Taking a brisk walk each evening will benefit your heart and lungs. And walking is an excellent way to reduce the negative effects of stress on your body.** *Example*

But alerts your readers that a contrast is coming. For example:

> **I expected college to be much like high school. But I have more freedom in college than I ever did in high school.**
> *Example*

When you start sentences with *and* and *but*, follow a few simple rules. First, make sure you don't write fragments. Check each sentence for a subject and verb. Second, make sure you've chosen the right connector. Don't, for example, use *and* to join ideas that have nothing in common, like these:

Gillian has been saving money for a new car since January. <u>And</u> she plays tennis with my brother.   *Incorrect*

You can learn more about *and* and *but* by studying the work of professional writers. In the following excerpts, all the sentences beginning with *and* and *but* have been underlined:

From "The Artstruck Englishman"
by George Bernard Shaw

No doubt every man has a shy child in him, artist or no artist. <u>But every man whose business it is to work directly upon other men, whether as artist, politician, advocate, propagandist, organizer, teacher, or what not, must dramatize himself and play his part.</u>

From *The Old Man and the Sea*
by Ernest Hemingway

No flying fish broke the surface, and there was no scattering of bait fish. <u>But as the old man watched, a small tuna rose in the air, turned and dropped head first into the water.</u>

From *Leaving Home*
by Garrison Keillor

<u>And away he went.</u> It's a wonderful thing to push on alone toward the horizon and have it be your own horizon and not someone else's.

From "I Have a Dream"
by Dr. Martin Luther King

<u>But there is something I must say to my people who stand on the warm threshold which leads into the palace of justice.</u> In the process of gaining our rightful place, we must not be guilty of wrongful deeds.

From *The Eyes of the Dragon*
by Stephen King

No one, not Peyna, not Flatt, not Aron Beson, worried that the prisoner might somehow climb down. The Needle's curving stone wall was utterly smooth. A fly might have done it, but not a man. <u>And if he grew depressed enough to jump, would anyone care?</u> Not much.

From *I Know Why the Caged Bird Sings*
by Maya Angelou

But the crime that tipped the scale and made our hate <u>not only just but imperative was his actions at the dinner table.</u> He ate the biggest, brownest and best parts of the chicken at every Sunday meal.

Exercise 5

INSTRUCTIONS: Examine the first page of your local newspaper. Underline any sentence starting with *and*, *but*, or *or*. Follow the same procedure on the editorial page. What can you conclude about the acceptability of sentences that start with one of these words?

Reviewing What You Have Learned

Exercise 6

INSTRUCTIONS: Answer each question.

1. List two ways in which coordinate conjunctions can improve your sentences.
2. Fill in the blanks:

   Punctuation helps people _____ and _____ what you have written.
3. Fill in the blanks:

   Use a comma when you have a _____ and _____ both before and after a coordinate conjunction.
4. True or false:
   Always use a comma with a coordinate conjunction.
5. True or false:
   Never start a sentence with *but*.
6. Name the coordinate conjunction that should be used sparingly because it is a weak connector.

Unit Twelve
Sentences with Who *and* Which

SUMMARY

1. The words *who* and *which* are useful for combining sentences.

2. Sentences with *who* and *which* can add variety and interest to your writing.

3. A word group beginning with *who* or *which* is called a *clause*.

4. A *who* or *which* clause that can be "erased" from a sentence should be preceded and followed by a comma.

5. Who and *which* clauses used with proper nouns are *always* preceded and followed by commas.

The words *who* and *which* are useful for several reasons. First, they can combine short, choppy sentences. By now you have discovered how important it is to combine ideas in mature-sounding sentences. Second, *who* and *which* enable you to vary your sentence patterns. Most important, *who* and *which* are convenient tools for adding interesting information to your sentences.

Read the following sentence pairs aloud. Notice that the second sentence provides more information and sounds more sophisticated than the first. A word group beginning with *who* or *which* is called a *clause*.

Albert Schweitzer was a medical missionary.   *Example*

Albert Schweitzer, who had three doctorates, was a medical missionary.   *Sentence with a* **who** *clause*

Bill Cosby created one of the most popular television programs in history.   *Example*

Bill Cosby, who has a doctorate in education, created one of the most popular television programs in history.   *Sentence with a* **who** *clause*

Soldiers used "Mickey Mouse" as a password.   *Example*

Soldiers who invaded Normandy in World War II used "Mickey Mouse" as a password.   *Sentence with a* **who** *clause*

Ragtime music developed from African rhythms.   *Example*

Ragtime music, which sounds very American to us, developed from African rhythms.   *Sentence with a* **which** *clause*

Cats need to be treated by a veterinarian.   *Example*

Cats which shake their heads often need to be treated by a veterinarian.   *Sentence with a* **which** *clause*

You may have noticed that the commas in these sentences come in pairs. You may also have noticed that two of these sentences have no commas at all—the one about soldiers and the one about cats.

Using *Who* and *Which* with Proper Nouns

Who and *which* often appear in sentences that feature the name of a person or a place, known as a *proper noun*. Try reading these pairs of sentences aloud:

Michael Jackson has enjoyed a successful singing career. *Example*

Michael Jackson, who was a child star, has enjoyed a successful singing career. *Sentence with a* who *clause*

The Statue of Liberty stands in New York Harbor. *Example*

The Statue of Liberty, which was a gift from France, stands in New York Harbor. *Sentence with a* which *clause*

Cher is the mother of two children. *Example*

Cher, who won fame as an actress and singer, is the mother of two children. *Sentence with a* who *clause*

The Executive Mansion is the President's home. *Example*

The Executive Mansion, which most people call the White House, is the President's home. *Sentence with a* which *clause*

Spend a few minutes listening to another student read these sentences, and then read them aloud yourself so that your partner can listen to you. Notice that your partner pauses each time he or she comes to a comma. Even without seeing the sentence in front of you, you can probably hear the precise spot where each comma was placed.

Reading sentences aloud in this way is an excellent way to feel more comfortable with this type of sentence. Of course, you do not place commas just by the sound of the sentence. This unit gives rules that tell you exactly where each comma should go.

Writing Sentences with *Who* and *Which* and Proper Nouns

First, use the name of a person or a place as the subject of a sentence (the name should be one that begins with a capital letter):

Anne Frank was a Jewish girl.   *Example*

Next, on a separate line, write the word *who* (for a person) or *which* (for a place or thing) and a short description. Since Anne Frank was a person, use *who*. As you have already learned, the group of words you choose for the description is a clause:

who wrote a famous diary   *Clause*

Now rewrite your original sentence, putting your *who* clause after the name:

Anne Frank who wrote a famous diary was a Jewish girl.

(Note that this sentence has not been punctuated yet.) Finally, add two commas. One goes after the name (in front of the *who* clause); the other goes after the *who* clause:

Anne Frank, who wrote a famous diary, was a Jewish girl.
Completed sentence

Read the sentence aloud to make sure it sounds correct. Notice that commas surround the *who* clause. One goes in front of it, and one goes in back.

Here are three more examples to show you how to write these sentences:

Dr. James Naismith invented basketball.   *Example*

who was a teacher   *Clause*

Dr. James Naismith, who was a teacher, invented basketball.
Completed sentence

Sentences with *Who* and *Which*

> **Albert Einstein enjoyed playing the violin.**   *Example*
>
> **who was a great physicist**   *Clause*
>
> **Albert Einstein, who was a great physicist, enjoyed playing the violin.**   *Completed sentence*
>
> **John F. Kennedy was our thirty-fifth president.**   *Example*
>
> **who wrote** *Profiles in Courage*   *Clause*
>
> **John F. Kennedy, who wrote** *Profiles in Courage,* **was our thirty-fifth president.**   *Completed sentence*

Exercise 1

INSTRUCTIONS: Each of these sentences is followed by a *who* clause. Using the examples given before as a guide, combine the *who* clause and the sentence. Remember, each sentence needs a comma both before and after the *who* clause. When you are finished, read your sentences aloud (by yourself and to another student) so that you can *hear* the comma pauses.

1. Anne Murray sings country music.
   who is from Canada
2. Woody Allen has produced many successful movies.
   who used to be a stand-up comic
3. "Buffalo Bob" Smith hosted the *Howdy Doody Show.*
   who has many middle-aged fans
4. Sandy Duncan played Peter Pan on television.
   who is a talented actress
5. Tom Baker played Dr. Who on television
   who once lived in a monastery
6. Bob Newhart has starred in two television series.
   who was once an accountant
7. Alan Young did the voice of Uncle Scrooge for Walt Disney
   who starred in *Mr. Ed*
8. Bruce Springsteen is known as "the Boss."
   who has done several benefit concerts
9. Graceland is a popular museum in Memphis
   which was Elvis Presley's home
10. The Grand Canyon is located in Arizona.
    which was formed by the Colorado River

Combining Sentences with *Who* and *Which*

You have already learned that *who* and *which* are useful for combining short sentences. Now you are going to learn the steps for combining sentences with these words. Read the following examples, which show you step-by-step how to combine sentences with *who* and *which* clauses:

Dr. Jonas Salk is searching for an AIDS vaccine. He discovered the first polio vaccine.   *Two short sentences*

First, change the *He* at the beginning of the second sentence into *who*, and remove the period, like this:

who discovered the first polio vaccine   *Who clause*

Now add this *who* clause and two commas to the first sentence, just as you did in Exercise 1:

Dr. Jonas Salk, who discovered the first polio vaccine, is searching for an AIDS vaccine.   *Completed sentence*

Here is another step-by-step example.

Jane Fonda is a famous actress. She has stirred many political controversies.   *Two short sentences*

In the second sentence, change *She* to *who* and remove the period:

who has stirred many political controversies   *Who clause*

Now insert the *who* clause and two commas into the first sentence, as you did in Exercise 1:

Jane Fonda, who has stirred many political controversies, is a famous actress.   *Completed sentence*

Sentences with *Who* and *Which*

Follow the same steps in all of the sentences that appear here. Remember that these steps apply to a particular type of sentence—one in which a *who* or *which* clause follows the name of a person or a place.

Exercise 2

INSTRUCTIONS: Combine each sentence pair into a single sentence, using a *who* or *which* clause. Your new sentence should contain two commas. When you are finished, read your sentences aloud. You should be able to hear the comma pauses as you listen.

1. Louisa May Alcott wrote *Little Women*. She was a nurse during the Civil War.
2. Bronson Alcott did not believe in working for wages. He was Louisa's father.
3. Bronson briefly went to jail. He was against slavery.
4. Abba Alcott supported the family by working and begging for money. She was Bronson's wife.
5. Concord was the family's home. It is a town in Massachusetts.
6. Ralph Waldo Emerson was Louisa's hero. He was a famous New England writer.
7. Henry David Thoreau taught Louisa about nature. He was another important writer.
8. The Alcotts once lived in a commune. They were always interested in new ideas.
9. Orchard House was one of the Alcotts' homes. It is now a museum.
10. The Alcotts lived comfortably after *Little Women* was published. They had always been poor.

Exercise 3

INSTRUCTIONS: Combine each sentence pair into a single sentence, using a *who* or *which* clause. Your new sentence should contain two commas. When you are finished, read your sentences aloud. You should be able to hear the comma pauses as you listen.

1. Jimmy Brown was the fullback for the Cleveland Browns. He won the Rookie of the Year award in 1957.
2. Brown's fans admired his speed and strength. They loved to watch him break away from his tacklers.
3. Yelberton Abraham Tittle is better known as Y.A. Tittle. He often fooled the opposing football team with his screen passes.
4. Bronko Nagurski played for the Chicago Bears in the 1930s and 1940s. He had unusual talent.
5. Bronko could play both offense and defense. He was a tackle and a fullback.
6. Bronko's football career was outstanding. It did not challenge Nagurski enough.
7. Professional wrestling is very different from football. It became Nagurski's second career.
8. Terry Bradshaw played quarterback. He helped the Steelers win four Super Bowl games.
9. Dan Marino broke many records for the Miami Dolphins. He is famous for his quick release of the football.
10. Joe Montana came from a small town in Pennsylvania. He was a Super Bowl winner when he was only twenty-five.

Exercise 4

INSTRUCTIONS: Write ten sentences of your own containing *who* or *which* clauses after the name of a person or a thing. (Use names that are capitalized.) The sentences given previously can serve as models. Be sure to put commas before and after your clauses. When you are finished, read your sentences aloud. Your ear will help you determine whether you have punctuated them correctly. To understand why you must place a comma before and after *who* and *which* clauses, follow this simple principle: *Two commas mean erase.* You can "erase" the clause because the proper noun alone tells who or what the sentence is about. Even if you don't recognize the name, the capital letters tell you that the person, place, or thing has a unique identity. To help you understand this principle more clearly, the sentences you read earlier are printed again here. Use a pencil to cross out the *who* and *which* clauses with a light line. Then read the sentences again. You will see that the subject of the sentence is still clear because the name is enough identification.

Michael Jackson, ~~who was a child star~~, has enjoyed a successful singing career.

The Statue of Liberty, ~~which was a gift from France~~, stands in New York Harbor.

Cher, ~~who won fame as an actress and singer~~, is the mother of two children.

The Executive Mansion, ~~which most people call~~ the White House, is the President's home.

Using Who and *Which* in Other Sentences

You have learned an important principle about *who* and *which* clauses: *Two commas mean erase.* Even if you drop the clause, the subject is still intact.

Now you are ready to apply this principle to sentences whose subject is not a proper noun. As you read the following sentence aloud, notice that it contains a *which* clause surrounded by commas:

Swimming, which burns many calories, can help you lose weight. *Example*

Now read the sentence again, skipping over the words between the commas:

Swimming can help you lose weight. *Example*

Has the meaning of *swimming* changed? The answer is *no*. Whether or not you mention the calories burned, *swimming* still has the same meaning.

Here's another example to read aloud:

My wedding pictures, which seem old-fashioned now, fascinate my two children. *Example*

Remember that *two commas mean erase;* try reading the sentence without the clause:

My wedding pictures fascinate my two children. *Example*

The meaning of "wedding pictures" is still the same. The information in commas is not essential to the meaning of the sentence. The clause "which seem old-fashioned now" can be erased from the sentence. Therefore, the commas are correct.

Here's a sentence with a *who* clause that cannot be erased from the sentence. Notice that no commas surround the *who* clause:

Students who have completed their reports do not have to attend class tomorrow. *Example*

If you erase the *who* clause, the meaning changes:

Students do not have to attend class tomorrow. *Example*

But the sentence does *not* mean that all students can skip class; it means that a certain group of students—those who have completed their reports—are excused. The *who* clause can't be erased, so no commas are used.

In the following exercise, try punctuating similar sentences. Each time you see a *who* or *which* clause, try erasing it (a light pencil line can be helpful). Then ask if the meaning of the word or words in front has changed. If the clause can be erased, put commas around it.

Exercise 5

INSTRUCTIONS: Put a pair of commas around any *who* or *which* clauses below that can be erased from the sentence. When you have finished this exercise, read your sentence aloud.

1. Cars which are imported from Europe must be adapted to meet American environmental standards.
2. Recipes which require advanced skills can create embarrassment for beginning cooks and their guests.
3. Raccoons which are highly intelligent animals sometimes manage to live in large cities.
4. Orange juice which is a good source of vitamin C is a favorite breakfast drink.

Sentences with *Who* and *Which*

5. The ozone layer which protects us from the sun is being weakened by pollutants.
6. People who work in department stores receive a discount on the store's merchandise.
7. Hula hoops which used to be popular playthings are not bestsellers today.
8. Pediatricians who specialize in children's health must undergo special training.
9. Students who want personal attention should consider attending a community college.
10. Dental hygienists who help people care for their teeth must meet strict licensing requirements.

Exercise 6

INSTRUCTIONS: Put a pair of commas around any *who* or *which* clauses below that can be erased from the sentence. When you have finished, read your sentences aloud.

1. Self-winding watches which used to be popular have been replaced by battery-operated watches.
2. The man who runs the nursing lab cares a lot about his students.
3. My favorite doll which used to sit on my bed is now in a box in my closet.
4. Athletes who don't develop their academic skills may have disappointing careers later in life.
5. Microwave ovens which were high-priced at first cost less to buy now.
6. A dictionary which is more than ten years old should be replaced with a newer edition.
7. Foods which are high in fiber can help prevent cancer.
8. Football players who are near-sighted say that contact lenses help them play better.
9. Baseball players who use drugs may be suspended from the team.
10. Pizza dough which is hand-tossed tastes better than the frozen kind.

Reviewing What You Have Learned

Exercise 7

INSTRUCTIONS: Use *who* or *which* clauses to combine the sentence pairs. Be sure to place commas where they are needed. When you are finished, read your sentences aloud. Your ear will help you make sure you have punctuated them correctly.

1. Jogging is an aerobic exercise. It helps prevent heart disease.
2. President Howard Taft was a huge man. He had a custom-made bathtub.
3. Toothbrushes aren't designed properly. They don't clean teeth thoroughly.
4. Fireworks are traditional on the Fourth of July. They terrify many dogs every year.
5. Motorcycles backfire all night long. They keep people from getting sufficient sleep.
6. Palm oil is used in many foods and cleaning products. It comes from coconut palms.
7. Mickey Mouse is the most famous mouse in the world. He has passed his sixtieth birthday.
8. Calcium prevents osteoporosis. Calcium is found in milk and some cheeses.
9. Cars need tuneups. They get poor mileage.
10. Florence Nightingale became a heroine during the Crimean War. She reformed the British Army.

Exercise 8

INSTRUCTIONS: Rewrite the following paragraph, using *who* and *which* clauses to combine choppy and repetitious sentences. Include commas where they are needed. Be sure to read the paragraph aloud when you are finished:

> The college campus provides many opportunities for recreation. First, there are outdoor sports facilities. These facilities include tennis courts, a jogging track, and an archery range. Many students like to participate in sports with their friends. The campus also has a large Health Center. It is open from eight until five. Exercise equipment is available there. It helps students unwind and burn off their excess energy. Best of all, the campus has an excellent Student Center. It is open from seven in the morning until ten at night. The Student Center provides snacks and a comfortable place to talk. Many students like to visit with their friends there.

Exercise 9

INSTRUCTIONS: Following the steps of the writing process, write a paragraph about a person you admire. In the planning step, look for ways to emphasize the person's special qualities. If the person is someone you know, set up an interview, if possible. Family letters or photograph albums may also be helpful. If you haven't met the person, use the telephone or the library to gather information. In the revising step, include a few *who* or *which* sentences in your paragraph. If you need a refresher, look at the sentences you wrote for Exercise 4.

Exercise 10

INSTRUCTIONS: Insert commas where needed in the following sentences. The *two commas mean erase* principle will be helpful to you. When you are finished, read your sentences aloud to listen for the comma pauses.

1. Students who have earned A averages are eligible for membership in the honor society.
2. Tom Seaver who has had an outstanding pitching career occasionally serves as a baseball commentator.
3. Baking soda which makes cakes rise is also useful as a deodorizer.
4. MTV which televises rock videos is popular with young people.
5. Ron Howard who played Opie on *The Andy Griffith Show* is now a movie producer.
6. Poodle skirts which I wore in the fifties seem quaint now.

7. The book which we're reading in Spanish class describes life in fifteenth-century Mexico.
8. Dogs which most people think of as pets can be trained to assist both blind and deaf persons.
9. Ironing clothes which used to be a burdensome chore is not necessary with most modern fabrics.
10. Any salesperson who exceeds this year's quota will receive a new car.

Exercise 11

INSTRUCTIONS: Ten sentence pairs appear here. Insert the second sentence into the first, using a *who* or *which* clause. Insert commas where they are needed.

1. Toscanini was a famous musical conductor. He created a sensation when he was nineteen.
2. An Italian orchestra was ready to perform in a Brazilian theater. It didn't have a conductor.
3. The regular conductor resigned. He had been criticized in the newspapers.
4. The assistant conductor was booed by the audience. He tried to lead the orchestra.
5. Toscanini was an unknown cellist in the orchestra. He had never studied conducting.
6. The orchestra members convinced him to conduct that evening. They knew that Toscanini had talent.
7. Toscanini stepped up to the podium and dramatically closed the musical score. He knew he had to win the audience's approval.
8. The members of the audience were shocked. They realized that Toscanini was going to conduct from memory.
9. Toscanini won the crowd's approval. He conducted brilliantly.
10. The news of the triumph changed Toscanini's life. The news spread rapidly.

Unit Thirteen
Semicolons

SUMMARY

1. Semicolons are useful for combining two related sentences.

2. Semicolons can add sophistication to your writing.

3. A complete sentence must appear both before and after a semicolon.

4. The first word following a semicolon is not capitalized unless it is a proper noun.

Semicolons are useful punctuation marks; every student should know how to use them. (Did you spot the semicolon in the previous sentence?) Semicolons can add sophistication to your writing style by combining related ideas and varying the sentence patterns.

Using Semicolons

It's easy to insert semicolons into sentences. Simply rewrite two short sentences as a single long one. Replace the period with a semicolon, and change the capital letter to a small letter.

Do not try to combine fragments with a semicolon. You must have a complete sentence in front of the semicolon, and another complete sentence behind it. Study the following examples:

The semicolon is a useful punctuation mark. Every student should know how to use it. *Two short sentences*

The semicolon is a useful punctuation mark; every student should know how to use it. *One sentence with a semicolon*

Because the semicolon is a useful punctuation mark, every student should know how to use it. *No semicolon*

In the third example, the first idea is a fragment:

Because the semicolon is a useful punctuation mark *Fragment*

Once you understand that a semicolon combines two sentences, you'll find it easy to use capital letters correctly with semicolon sentences. Here's the principle to follow: *When you have two sentences, you have two capital letters.* (Each sentence begins with a capital letter.) *But when you have one sentence, you have one capital letter.* A group of words containing a semicolon is only one sentence, so it should have one capital letter. Study the following examples:

Carmen has a basketball scholarship. It's exciting to watch her play. *Two sentences—two capital letters*

Carmen has a basketball scholarship; it's exciting to watch her play. *One sentence—one capital letter*

Semicolons

  I play racquetball. My sister prefers tennis. *Two sentences—
   two capital letters*

  I play racquetball; my sister prefers tennis. *One sentence—
   one capital letter*

  The football game was exciting. We yelled until we were
   hoarse. *Two sentences—two capital letters*

  The football game was exciting; we yelled until we were
   hoarse. *One sentence—one capital letter*

Exercise 1

INSTRUCTIONS: Five sentence pairs appear here. Rewrite each pair as a semicolon sentence. Change capital letters to small letters when necessary.

1. My parents are taking dancing lessons. Every week they come home laughing.
2. Nicole needs to stop smoking. She has developed a chronic cough.
3. I finished reading the newspaper. It's on the kitchen table.
4. Cheryl is learning sign language. She plans to teach hearing-impaired children.
5. Simon registered to vote. He's very interested in the upcoming election.

 You can use semicolons confidently by remembering these two principles:

1. Make sure you have a complete sentence both in front of the semicolon and behind it. Try substituting a period for the semicolon. If the period works, a semicolon would be correct also.
2. Capitalize correctly. Remember that a semicolon is *one* sentence and should have *one* capital letter at the beginning (except for proper names).

 To see how these principles work, study these examples:

  Willis sprained his ankle; <u>H</u>e's using crutches today.
   Incorrect—He *should not be capitalized.*

  Willis sprained his ankle; <u>h</u>e's using crutches today. *Correct*

  Figure skating always thrills me; debi Thomas is my favorite
   skater. *Incorrect—a person's name* always *needs a
   capital letter.*

  Figure skating always thrills me; Debi Thomas is my favorite
   skater. *Correct*

You will need to replace your tires; when most of the tread is gone.   *Incorrect—the second part is not a complete sentence.*

You will need to replace your tires when most of the tread is gone.   *Correct—no semicolon*

Exercise 2

INSTRUCTIONS: Write five sentence pairs of your own. Then change each pair of sentences into a single sentence with a semicolon. (Use the sentences in Exercise 1 as models if you wish.) Make sure you have used capital letters correctly.

Exercise 3

INSTRUCTIONS: The following sentences contain semicolons. Mark **C** if the sentence is correct and **I** if the sentence is incorrect.

_____ 1. I know how to fix a burrito; so that the filling doesn't drip out.

_____ 2. Gena wants to be a news anchor; she has a job with a local television station.

_____ 3. Tonya missed class yesterday; because her baby was sick.

_____ 4. The hurricane caused extensive damage; which will cost millions to repair.

_____ 5. A traffic light was broken this morning; causing a traffic jam on Main Street.

_____ 6. A student in my aerobics class is blind; she and her guide dog go jogging together.

_____ 7. My children aren't allowed to watch horror films; which cause nightmares for weeks afterward.

_____ 8. Grandma bakes every weekend; and I love the way her house smells.

_____ 9. Our lawn mower needs to be serviced; the blade is dull and the oil is dirty.

_____ 10. A local newspaper did a fast-food survey; McDonald's has the best french fries.

Varying Your Sentence Patterns

You may wonder how often you should use a semicolon in a paragraph, a letter, or a school report. What guidelines should you follow? Here are some suggestions.

When you join sentences with a semicolon, make sure both ideas are related. The following sentences should *not* be joined with a semicolon because they contradict each other:

> **Theodore Roosevelt was an ardent conservationist; he hunted rare species of African animals.** *Incorrect*

Instead of joining the sentences with a semicolon, you could use *although* to show the contrast between the ideas:

> **Although Theodore Roosevelt was an ardent conservationist, he hunted rare species of African animals.** *Better*

Remember that the semicolon is a formal punctuation mark. It's appropriate for professional writing, business reports, and college assignments. But semicolons don't work well in most informal writing—friendly letters, for example. Notice the difference in tone in the following examples. In the first businesslike sentence, the semicolon is appropriate:

> **Our new product line is being tested; the results will be available next month.** *Example*

The next two sentences come from a family letter. Because of the friendly tone, they should not be joined with a semicolon:

> **We enjoyed looking at the pictures you'd sent. Jeff certainly is growing up quickly!** *Example*

Use semicolon sentences occasionally to vary your sentence patterns. As you've already learned, sentence variety makes your writing more interesting and more professional. A topnotch cook, for example, knows at least a dozen ways in which to prepare potatoes; you should be just as versatile when you write. During this course, you might try including one semicolon sentence in every paragraph.

Eventually, you'll likely write semicolon sentences (and other types of sentences) naturally and confidently.

As you read the following paragraph, notice that the sentences are short and choppy. It appears again, rewritten so that it has more sentence variety. Read both versions aloud. Can you hear the improvement in the second paragraph?

My Least Favorite Holiday

I'm embarrassed to admit it. Thanksgiving is the holiday I like the least. First, my mother is always grouchy beforehand. Company makes her tense. She is afraid they will criticize her cooking and housekeeping. Second, my sisters always complain about the menu. Barbara is against turkey. She's a vegetarian. Clare doesn't like sweets. She's always on a diet. Worst of all, our guests are always unpleasant. Uncle Robert drinks too much. He falls asleep before dinner. Aunt Grace bores me. She tells the same stories about her childhood every year. For these reasons, I dread Thanksgiving every November.

Here's the same paragraph again, with sentences combined to sound smoother and more mature.

My Least Favorite Holiday

Although I'm embarrassed to admit it, Thanksgiving is the holiday I like the least. First, my mother is always grouchy beforehand; company makes her tense. She is afraid they will criticize her cooking and housekeeping. Second, my sisters always complain about the menu. Barbara is against turkey because she's a vegetarian. Clare doesn't like sweets because she's always on a diet. Worst of all, our guests are always unpleasant. Uncle Robert, who drinks too much, always falls asleep before dinner. Aunt Grace bores me, for she tells the same stories about her childhood every year. For these reasons, I dread Thanksgiving every November.

Semicolons

Exercise 4

INSTRUCTIONS: Label these sentence types in the paragraph you just read:
a. Sentences with semicolons
b. Sentences with subordinate conjunctions
c. Sentences with coordinate conjunctions
d. Sentences with *who* or *which*

Exercise 5

INSTRUCTIONS: The following paragraph contains several short, choppy sentences. Improve the paragraph by combining some of the sentences to make longer ones. Try using a subordinate conjunction, a coordinate conjunction, *who* or *which*, and a semicolon:

Keeping a Journal

I was thirteen years old. My mother gave me my first diary. I've kept a diary or journal ever since. First, my journal stores many memories. Once in a while I browse through its pages. I'm reminded of many special moments in my life. For example, my senior class went to Disney World last spring. The whole story is told in my journal. Second, keeping a journal helps me solve problems. A few months ago Diane and I started fighting all the time. Every night I wrote about my feelings. I was able to see some patterns. She and I worked out our disagreements. Most of all, my journal seems like a friend. It never judges me. I can write anything. Sometimes I'm angry or depressed. Writing in my journal is a great comfort. I think I'll keep a journal as long as I live.

Semicolons can work well in paragraphs you write because many of your ideas are related to one another. As you read the following paragraph, underline any sentence pairs that you think might be combined with a semicolon:

My Former Roommate

I couldn't get along with my former roommate. He said our problems were my fault, but I'm convinced that no one could live with him. First, he was nosy. He constantly questioned me about my friends and activities. I never had any privacy. Second, he was sloppy. The apartment was always cluttered and dirty. It was embarrassing to have friends over. Worst of all, he was a plant nut. Every morning he got up at six to talk to his plants. I could never sleep late after a party or date. Last month I finally moved into another apartment. We don't miss each other at all.

If you decided to use a semicolon or two in this paragraph, you would have many sentence pairs to choose from. All of these pairs could be joined with semicolons:

He constantly questioned me about my friends and activities. I never had any privacy.   *Example*

He constantly questioned me about my friends and activities; I never had any privacy.   *Example*

The apartment was always cluttered and dirty. It was embarrassing to have friends over.   *Example*

The apartment was always cluttered and dirty; it was embarrassing to have friends over.   *Example*

Every morning he got up at six to talk to his plants. I could never sleep late after a party or date.   *Example*

Every morning he got up at six to talk to his plants; I could never sleep late after a party or date.   *Example*

Last month I finally moved into another apartment. We don't miss each other at all.   *Example*

Last month I finally moved into another apartment; we don't miss each other at all.   *Example*

Semicolons 177

Exercise 6

INSTRUCTIONS: This paragraph contains several choppy sentences. Choose two pairs of choppy sentences and rewrite them with semicolons. Be sure your capital letters are correct. (Note that you need not copy the whole paragraph.)

The Dentist

I don't dread going to the dentist as much as I used to. First, the pain is almost gone. Even the needle doesn't hurt anymore. Second, it's easier to relax. I wear a headset and listen to music while my dentist is drilling. One time I was enjoying Bon Jovi. I forgot I was at the dentist's office. Best of all, my teeth are healthier. My hygienist has taught me how to avoid cavities and gum disease.

Using "Intensifying" Words With Semicolons

The words *however, therefore,* and *consequently* (conjunctive adverbs) can be called "intensifying" words because they can add power to your sentences. Since these words often appear next to semicolons, students sometimes ask if they must be used with semicolons. The answer is *no*. You can easily insert these words into any sentence you choose, even if the sentence doesn't have a semicolon.

As you read the following sentences aloud, notice where you naturally pause:

Therefore we believe the law should be changed.   *Example*

Consequently the sales tax was raised.   *Example*

Place a comma after an intensifying word each time it appears in a sentence:

Therefore, we believe the law should be changed.   *Example*

Consequently, the sales tax was raised.   *Example*

Often, but not always, intensifying words appear next to semicolons, as in these examples:

> **Profits are up; therefore, we can expect a raise in January.** *Example*
>
> **Seat belts have been proven to save lives; however, many people still neglect to use them.** *Example*

You can add an intensifier to a sentence any time you think it will strengthen the meaning. Read the following sentence pairs aloud. Can you hear the improvement when the intensifying word is added?

> **The book was dull. I read all of it.** *Example*
>
> **The book was dull. However, I read all of it.** *Example*
>
> **Bart couldn't afford to live alone. He found a roommate.** *Example*
>
> **Bart couldn't afford to live alone. Therefore he found a roommate.** *Example*
>
> **Stacy had to finish a research paper. She stayed home to write it.** *Example*
>
> **Stacy had to finish a research paper. Consequently, she stayed home to write it.** *Example*

Intensifying words tell readers what to expect next. *Therefore* and *consequently* mean "as a result." *However* signals an unexpected outcome, just as *but* and *although* do. To understand how these words create expectations, try completing these sentences:

> **I expected to find a check inside the birthday card from my mother. However,_____.**
> *Example*
>
> **I expected to find a check inside the birthday card from my mother. Consequently,_____.**
> *Example*

Your first sentence should have described an unexpected result, such as this one:

Semicolons

> I expected to find a check inside the birthday card from my mother. However, she sent a note saying that she'd invested in a Treasury Bond for me.   *Example*

Your second sentence should have described a logical result, such as this one:

> I expected to find a check inside the birthday card from my mother. Consequently, I spent my whole food budget on some compact discs I wanted.   *Example*

Notice that the words *however, consequently,* and *therefore* do not join sentences by themselves. They merely strengthen the meaning of the sentence. To join sentences, you must substitute a semicolon for the period, as you did before. (Remember to change capital letters to small ones where needed.) Compare these two sentences, which are joined with a semicolon, with the version you just read:

> I expected to find a check inside the birthday card from my mother; consequently, I spent my whole food budget on some compact discs I wanted.   *Example*

Exercise 7

INSTRUCTIONS: Insert the words *therefore, consequently,* and *however* into these sentence pairs. When you are finished, read the sentences aloud.

1. The Meyerson account is important to our company. _____, we must handle it carefully.
2. Katherine isn't very good at learning foreign languages. _____, she's going to sign up for a French course.
3. I'm buying a new car next week. _____, I'll be making car payments for the next four years.
4. We've had very little rain this summer. _____, the mayor is declaring a water shortage.
5. Anthony is on academic probation. _____, he isn't doing much studying this semester.

6. Bethena sings beautiful musical solos in her church. _____, many people admire her talent.

7. The microwave oven I want to buy is on sale. _____, I can't afford it right now.

Exercise 8

INSTRUCTIONS: Choose *four* of the sentence pairs in Exercise 7, and join them with semicolons. Where necessary, change capital letters to small ones.

Exercise 9

INSTRUCTIONS: Write a persuasive paragraph proposing a change in college life. As you plan your paragraph, choose an audience for your ideas—classmates, professors, administrators, families, or readers of a newspaper or magazine. In th revising step, use one or two intensifying words and one or two semicolons. (Yo need not use them in the same sentence!) Make sure all of the capital letters are correct.

Reviewing What You Have Learned

Exercise 10

INSTRUCTIONS: Write *true* or *false* in front of each statement.

_____ 1. A semicolon can join a fragment and a sentence.

_____ 2. Never capitalize the word following a semicolon.

_____ 3. To check that you've used a semicolon correctly, see if it can be replaced by a comma.

_____ 4. Semicolons can add sophistication and variety to your sentences.

_____ 5. Semicolons work well in formal writing.

_____ 6. Semicolons should be used with subordinate conjunctions.

_____ 7. The words *however, therefore,* and *consequently* can be called "intensifying words."

Semicolons   181

_____ 8. The word *however* is always used with a semicolon.
_____ 9. You should use semicolons as often as possible in your paragraphs.
_____ 10. In most paragraphs, it's difficult to find two sentences that can be joined with a semicolon.

Exercise 11

INSTRUCTIONS: Label the correct sentences **C**, and make any needed corrections in the others.

_____ 1. I have more freedom now; than I did in high school.
_____ 2. Ted, who goes to school in Boston; cheers for the Red Sox every year.
_____ 3. I'm looking for a good babysitter; we're invited to a New Year's Eve party.
_____ 4. Jasper stopped drinking and driving; after he was stopped by the police.
_____ 5. Mrs. Santos was born in Mexico; She helps me with my Spanish.
_____ 6. This pumpkin pie is special; I started with a pumpkin from my own garden.
_____ 7. I enjoy reading UFO stories; I wonder if there's life on other planets.
_____ 8. Because Bruce Springsteen is concerned about human rights; he has done concerts for Amnesty International.
_____ 9. Leonard really enjoys his part-time job; delivering pizzas all over town.
_____ 10. Skateboards aren't a good idea on campus; Larry almost ran over his physics professor.

Unit Fourteen
Sentence Variety

> SUMMARY
>
> 1. Sentence variety adds sophistication and polish to written work.
>
> 2. Mastery of sentence variety enables writers to express themselves with precision.

Sentence Variety

The last four units have encouraged you to vary the sentence patterns you use in your writing. This unit provides an opportunity to practice the four patterns you have learned.

To appreciate the importance of sentence variety, read the following two paragraphs. The first has several short, choppy sentences. In the second paragraph, the sentences have been combined to make them sound more mature:

My Husband the Laundryman

My husband Hal is eager to help me at home. He has never learned how to do a load of wash. First, he usually forgets to sort the clothes. The colors run. Last week my favorite white blouse looked like strawberry-ripple ice cream. Second, he hurries too much. He often forgets to change the temperature setting. He washed his favorite T-shirts in hot water. They shrank two sizes. Worst of all, he sometimes forgets to put soap in the machine. I come home and unload the washer. I have to wash everything again. I love Hal very much. I wish he'd find other ways to help me.

My Husband the Laundryman

Although my husband Hal is eager to help me at home, he has never learned how to do a load of wash. First, he usually forgets to sort the clothes, and the colors run. Last week my favorite white blouse looked like strawberry-ripple ice cream. Second, he hurries too much; therefore, he often forgets to change the temperature setting. When he washed his favorite T-shirts in hot water, they shrank two sizes. Worst of all, he sometimes forgets to put soap in the machine. After I come home and unload the washer, I have to wash everything again. I love Hal very much, but I wish he'd find other ways to help me.

Varying Your Sentence Patterns

Think about sentence variety in the *editing step* of the writing process. As you edit a paragraph, look for choppy sentences that can be combined. Then use one of the sentence patterns you've learned to combine the sentences. In Unit 4, you were introduced to the varied sentence patterns that successful writers use. Here they are once again:

1. Sentences with *although, if, when, because* (subordinate conjunctions)

   Harriet wants to buy a new car although she can't afford the monthly payments. *Example*

   Although she can't afford the monthly payments, Harriet wants to buy a new car. *Variation*

2. Sentences with semicolons

   Harriet wants to buy a new car; she can't afford the monthly payments. *Example*

   Harriet wants to buy a new car; however, she can't afford the monthly payments. *Variation*

3. Sentences with *and, but, or* (coordinate conjunctions)

   Harriet wants to buy a new car, but she can't afford the monthly payments. *Example*

4. Sentences with *who* and *which*

   Harriet, who wants to buy a new car, can't afford the monthly payments.

Exercise 1

INSTRUCTIONS: Using the examples as a guide, combine the following sentence pairs in as many ways as you can.

1. Lewis is an avid football fan. Sometimes he watches two games at once.
2. Art proposed to Lynn. She turned him down.
3. Sugar is not a healthful food. Most Americans love desserts.
4. Earl is very successful. He restores and sells antique cars.
5. Labor Day is a time for picnics and barbecues. It is a popular holiday.

Sentence Variety 185

Exercise 2

INSTRUCTIONS: Combine the sentence pairs, using the word provided. The first pair of sentences has already been combined so that you can use it as an example.

1. I'm learning basketweaving. Handwoven baskets make beautiful gifts.

    Because I'm learning basketweaving because handwoven baskets make beautiful gifts.

2. Eileen first played volleyball at church camp. She is the star of the college team.

    WHO _____

3. I've seen all the *Star Trek* movies. I have videotapes of all the *Star Trek* shows.

    AND _____

4. Carl loves square dancing. He hasn't found the right partner yet.

    BUT _____

5. Later I may open my own law office. I may work for a law firm.

    OR _____

6. Beth's uncle is a cantor in a temple. He sings very movingly.

    WHO _____

7. Microwave ovens used to be expensive. They cost less now.

    WHICH _____

8. Liza and Ben bought a new house. They made a large down payment.

    WHEN _____

9. I have to write a book report. I haven't picked out a book.

   ALTHOUGH _____

10. Sarah is trying to get rid of her credit cards. They encourage her to charge things she doesn't really need.

    BECAUSE _____

Combining Sentences

You've already learned that semicolons are useful in combining short sentences, as shown here:

UFOs fascinate me. I wish I could see one.   *Choppy*

UFOs fascinate me; I wish I could see one.   *Better*

Words such as *however, therefore,* and *consequently* can add interest to your sentences, but they cannot be used to combine sentences. That job calls for a semicolon, as shown in these examples:

I can't afford to rent an apartment; consequently, I live with a roommate.   *Example*

Alan isn't perfect; we get along well, however.   *Example*

Exercise 3

INSTRUCTIONS: As you combine the following sentence pairs, use each of these words at least once: *although, because, but, who, which, therefore, consequently, however.* Make sure you punctuate each sentence correctly.

1. Bowling is my favorite pastime. It's a great way to make new friends.
2. Chuck helps me with algebra. He plans to teach math.
3. Paula has a fabulous wardrobe. She makes all her own clothes.
4. I planned to take horseback riding lessons. I found out I was afraid of horses.

5. A horse seems small when you look at him. He's very big when you sit on his back.
6. The basketball coach is interested in all his players. He has earned their respect and friendship.
7. I enjoy pumpkin pie all year. Restaurants serve it only in November.
8. My mother tried five liver recipes. We hated all of them.
9. My dad doesn't know much about cars. He always makes my mom talk to the auto mechanic.
10. Peanut butter and jelly sandwiches aren't very elegant. They always taste great to me.
11. My cat is eleven years old. She still plays just like a kitten.
12. I took piano lessons for five years. I can't play a single piece.
13. The doorbell rang. We didn't hear it.

Exercise 4

INSTRUCTIONS: Five topics appear here. Write three sentences about each topic. For each group, use each of these words at least once: *because, if, when, however, but, who, which.*

1. Getting up in the morning
2. Making new friends
3. Your favorite television show
4. Your future plans
5. Something that annoys you

Choosing Sentence Patterns

Since ideas can be expressed in so many ways, students sometimes wonder which pattern is best. The answer is that there are no "best" patterns. When you write a paragraph, feel free to choose the sentence patterns that work best for you.

Vary your sentence patterns. Don't put three *who/which* sentences into the same paragraph, for example. Also, choose the sentence pattern that suits your purpose. If you're writing a story, you'll find the word *when* very helpful, as in this example:

When Detective Starke heard the story, he knew a great mystery was waiting to be solved.   *Example*

In a letter to a newspaper about a political issue, the words *because, consequently,* and *but* might be useful, as in these examples:

Because our children are at risk, we must take action now.
Example

This is an urgent issue; consequently, we need your support.
Example

Our proposal sounds costly, but it will save millions over the years.   *Example*

Using Sentence Variety in Paragraphs

You've already learned that you should think about sentence variety in the editing step of the writing process. After you've planned your paragraph and made a rough draft, read it aloud. Listen carefully for choppiness, abrupt sentences, and repetitious sentence patterns. Proficient writers use several sentence patterns in most paragraphs: a *who/which* sentence, a semicolon sentence, and one with a subordinate conjunction, for example. As you revise your sentences, make sure you've punctuated them correctly. It's also a good idea to get feedback about your sentences from a friend or family member. Reading aloud is always helpful when you're revising.

Exercise 5

INSTRUCTIONS: The following paragraph contains several short, choppy sentences. Rewrite it, using a variety of sentence patterns.

Down with Technology!

New technology is changing our lives every day. I don't like these changes. First, I'm spending too much money on auto repairs. I bought a new car three years ago. The car has many electronic components. I can't service it myself. Second, the things I buy don't last very long. I had to replace our refrigerator door. It rusted after a year. My wife and I bought a kitchen table and chairs. The veneer is starting to come off. Worst of all, the environment is suffering. Our society uses vast amounts of gasoline. It uses vast amounts of electricity. Pollution is a serious problem. I think our advanced technology is a mixed blessing.

Exercise 6

INSTRUCTIONS: Following the three-step writing process, write a paragraph explaining how technology affects your life. During the editing step, try to include a variety of sentence patterns in your paragraph.

Reviewing What You Have Learned

Exercise 7

INSTRUCTIONS: Write two short sentences on a sheet of paper. Exchange papers with another student, and write as many variations of the sentences you are given as you can.

Exercise 8

INSTRUCTIONS: Write a short letter to a friend. When you are finished, rewrite the letter to make the sentences as varied as possible.

Exercise 9

INSTRUCTIONS: After watching a television program, write a brief description of what happened. Then rewrite your description, using a variety of sentence patterns.

Part Three
Avoiding Common Errors

Part 3 focuses on learning how to avoid common errors with verb endings, punctuation, sentence structure, and other matters of usage. Unit 15, "Correcting Run-on Sentences," includes a review of the sentence patterns you've already learned. The other units will help you master the usage rules most important to first-year college students.

Unit Fifteen
Run-on Sentences

SUMMARY

1. Every sentence must end with a period, a question mark, or an exclamation mark.

2. Run-ons happen when two sentences are written as one, without correct punctuation between them.

3. Skills in using punctuation correctly and knowledge of sentence patterns help in correcting run-on sentences.

4. Reading sentences aloud is helpful for detecting run-ons.

Avoiding Common Errors 193

A run-on sentence may be long or short: its length does not matter. It is incorrect because it continues to "run on" after it should have stopped, as shown here:

The toaster is broken I'll bake some biscuits.   *Run-on*

This sentence should have stopped after the word *broken*:

The toaster is broken. I'll bake some biscuits.   *Correct*

If you imagine the engine of a car "running on" after the ignition has been turned off, you'll find it easy to understand what a run-on is: a sentence that keeps going after it is supposed to stop. Run-on sentences are not acceptable in college writing; most instructors consider them serious sentence errors.

A car engine that "runs-on" can be fixed by changing the grade of gasoline or adjusting the engine so that it stops when it is supposed to. In the same way, a run-on sentence can be fixed by inserting a period and a capital letter so that the sentence stops in the right place, as shown in these examples:

The movie was excellent we'd like to see it again.   *Run-on*

The movie was excellent. We'd like to see it again.   *Correct*

If you wanted to, you could correct every run-on sentence in this way. Just put a period at the end (or a question mark or exclamation mark), and start the next sentence with a capital letter. Here are several more examples for you to read aloud:

Bill has a slow heartbeat he runs a mile every morning.
Run-on

Bill has a slow heartbeat. He runs a mile every morning.
Correct

Two teenagers created Superman in 1938 their creation still appears in comics today.   *Run-on*

Two teenagers created Superman in 1938. Their creation still appears in comics today.   *Correct*

Because you are trying to develop a mature and professional writing style, you will want to vary the ways in which you correct run-on sentences. This unit gives you several options to choose from. The good news is that you have learned these options; now you are simply reviewing them. The four sentence patterns you already know can be used to correct run-on sentences.

Spotting Run-on Sentences

The basic procedure for finding run-ons in your work is a simple one. Just make sure you have put a period or question mark at the end of every sentence you've written. If you suspect that you've written a run-on, try reading the sentence aloud. Often, your ear will tell you that you've come to the end of a sentence and need to insert a period. Another possibility is to underline all the subjects and verbs in your sentences. Your underlining will help you see where one sentence ends and another begins. (Remember that a sentence always has a subject and a verb, and that it always expresses a complete thought.)

Exercise 1

INSTRUCTIONS: Label each run-on **R**, and label each correct sentence **C**. (Reading these sentences aloud will help you spot the run-ons.)

_____ 1. In the future robots may handle several types of dangerous police work.

_____ 2. The robots will control riots police work will not be so dangerous.

_____ 3. Translations will be done by computers human translators will be needed too.

_____ 4. Computers will use business "games" to train managers and executives.

_____ 5. Factories will rely on computers they will also need skilled technicians.

_____ 6. First-year college students can expect to change jobs at least ten times during their lives.

_____ 7. Most colleges teach computer skills students are eager to learn them.

_____ 8. Computer technology is advancing rapidly in our society.

Avoiding Common Errors 195

_____ 9. Computers double in power every five years computer scientists need constant retraining.

_____ 10. The prices for many computers have dropped more people are buying them.

Correcting Run-on Sentences

You can correct run-on sentences just by making each sentence stop when it is supposed to. In most cases a period and capital letter will do very well. Of course, if you have written a question, you must use a question mark. An exclamation mark is another possibility, but exclamation marks are used sparingly in college and professional writing.

The following examples will give you some practice in identifying and correcting run-ons. The subject and verbs have been underlined for you. You will find it helpful both to study these examples and read them aloud.

<u>The computers are</u> down <u>we can't finish</u> our project now. *Run-on*

<u>The computers are</u> down. <u>We can't finish</u> our project now.
Correct

<u>Suzanne broke up</u> with Glenn <u>she gave</u> him back his ring.
Run-on

<u>Suzanne broke up</u> with Glenn. <u>She gave</u> him back his ring.
Correct

<u>I used</u> the last piece of bread <u>another loaf is</u> in the freezer.
Run-on

<u>I used</u> the last piece of bread. <u>Another loaf is</u> in the freezer.
Correct

Exercise 2

INSTRUCTIONS: Label each run-on **R** and each correct sentence **C**. Then correct the run-ons with periods and capital letters. You will find it helpful to underline all the subjects and verbs; you should also read the sentences aloud.

_____ 1. The Fourth of July is coming we should plan a cookout.
_____ 2. I never get an attractive suntan in the summer.
_____ 3. Amanda bought a new swimsuit and went on a diet.
_____ 4. Michael is a terrific swimmer he's won some medals.
_____ 5. We go to the beach every weekend it's fun there.
_____ 6. At the beach we played volleyball, swam, and built sand castles.
_____ 7. I'm afraid of jellyfish they sting badly.
_____ 8. Janice is a lifeguard she goes to the beach every day.
_____ 9. We've seen dolphins playing together in the coastal waters.
_____ 10. I like to jog on the wet sand in the morning.

Exercise 3

INSTRUCTIONS: Label each run-on **R** and each correct sentence **C**. Then correct the run-ons with periods and capital letters. You will find it helpful to underline all the subjects and verbs; you should also read the sentences aloud.

_____ 1. Last year my aunt who's fifty-three decided to learn how to drive.
_____ 2. She was nervous we all tried to reassure her.
_____ 3. Her driving instructor was nervous too we felt sorry for him.
_____ 4. He was a very young and extremely timid man.
_____ 5. My aunt yells when she's nervous she frightened her instructor.
_____ 6. Learning how to drive was hard for her she took lessons for months.
_____ 7. Her instructor worried because she failed her road test twice.
_____ 8. Finally she passed it we all celebrated.
_____ 9. She and her instructor have become good friends.
_____ 10. Now my aunt is a skillful driver who enjoys her new mobility.

Sometimes a run-on has a comma where the period should be. (Some instructors call this error a *comma splice*.) To correct this error, just replace the comma with a period and start the next word with a capital letter. Remember that you can't end a sentence with a comma—a period is necessary. Here are several run-ons that need a period rather than a comma:

Diane is moving, she found a better job.   *Run-on*

Diane is moving. She found a better job.   *Correct*

The baby is asleep, we mustn't make any noise.   *Run-on*

> The baby is asleep. We mustn't make any noise.   *Correct*
>
> Gary won the race, he's excited about his trophy.   *Run-on*
>
> Gary won the race. He's excited about his trophy.   *Correct*

Exercise 4

INSTRUCTIONS: Some of the sentences that appear below are run-ons. Label all run-ons **R** and all correct sentences **C**. Then use periods and capital letters to correct the run-on sentences.

_____ 1. Your mother called, she needs to talk to you.

_____ 2. The hiking trail is a marvelous place for birdwatching and nature photography.

_____ 3. Because my nursing instructor believes in the personal touch, she encourages us to get to know our patients.

_____ 4. My article for the campus newspaper will be printed next Wednesday.

_____ 5. We don't allow chewing gum in the building it can damage the floors and furniture.

_____ 6. I'll see you Tuesday afternoon when we meet to discuss your plans.

_____ 7. I had a shock this morning, there was no hot water in the locker room showers.

_____ 8. Lorraine can help you, she studied advanced calculus.

_____ 9. I worked in a library for two years, and I learned how to use many reference books.

_____ 10. All the basketball players who are going to the tournament should be here by two o'clock.

Exercise 5

INSTRUCTIONS: Some of the sentences that appear here are run-ons. Label all run-ons **R** and all correct sentences **C**. Then use periods and capital letters to correct the run-on sentences.

_____ 1. While the cake is cooling, I'll make the icing.

_____ 2. Stella just got a new job, she's very excited.

_____ 3. *Star Wars* is my favorite movie I've seen it six times.
_____ 4. Business managers who speak fluent Japanese are in great demand.
_____ 5. Betty has a teaching license, and she also has secretarial skills.
_____ 6. I love homemade bread, but I don't have time to bake it.
_____ 7. Although Sandy has been to Europe twice, she hasn't seen much of the United States.
_____ 8. Rain suddenly poured down we ran for the car.
_____ 9. I love Manhattan, the people there are fascinating.
_____ 10. Josephine is looking for a new job but hasn't found one yet.

Sometimes you may want to use words such as *because, but, who* and others to correct run-ons. The next examples will show you some of the options available to you.

First, here is a run-on sentence that needs to be corrected:

> **Tina Turner is in her fifties, she's still a popular rock singer.**
> *Run-on*

Here are seven possible corrections based on the sentence patterns you have been studying. Notice that two of the patterns (*although* and *who*) have variations:

> **Tina Turner is in her fifties. She's still a popular rock singer.**
> *Period and capital letter*

> **Tina Turner is in her fifties, but she's still a popular rock singer.** *Comma + but*

> **Although Tina Turner is in her fifties, she's still a popular rock singer.** *Although*

> **Tina Turner is still a popular rock singer although she's in her fifties.** *Although (variation)*

> **Tina Turner, who is in her fifties, is still a popular rock singer.** *Who clause*

> **Tina Turner, who is still a popular rock singer, is in her fifties.** *Who clause (variation)*

> **Tina Turner is in her fifties; she's still a popular rock singer.** *Semicolon*

How do you decide which type of sentence to choose? Remember, no one choice is best. All of the sentence patterns are correct. You will probably find it helpful to think about sentence variety as you decide. If you already have written two semicolon sentences in your paragraph, it may be time to use another sentence pattern.

Exercise 6

INSTRUCTIONS: Correct each run-on, using the suggestions you are given. An example is provided.

The weather gets hot, my family goes to the mountains.
WHEN When the weather gets hot, my family goes to the mountains.
AND The weather gets hot, and my family goes to the mountains.
SEMICOLON The weather gets hot; my family goes to the mountains.

1. The telephone was always busy I gave up.

    BECAUSE _____

    AND _____

2. Cat Stevens converted to Islam, he left the music business.

    WHEN _____

    WHO _____

3. Jessica speaks perfect French she lived in Paris for five years.

    WHO _____

    SEMICOLON _____

4. Yogurt is a nutritious food it is high in calcium and B vitamins.

    WHICH _____

    BECAUSE _____

5. Jack handed in a perfect lab report, his notes were messy.

    ALTHOUGH _____

    BUT _____

6. You may want to go to a university you may prefer a small college.

    OR _____

    SEMICOLON _____

7. I cooked an anniversary dinner for my parents, my sister helped me.

   AND _____

   WHEN _____

8. My uncle used to box professionally, now he's retired.

   BUT _____

   SEMICOLON _____

9. The dog barked loudly, no one was there.

   ALTHOUGH _____

   AND _____

10. Queen Elizabeth II was once a military officer, she repaired army vehicles during the war.

    WHEN _____

    WHO _____

Reviewing What You Have Learned

Exercise 7

INSTRUCTIONS: Here are the sentences from the first run-on exercise you did in this unit. Earlier, you labeled the sentences either *run-on* or *correct*. Now you can apply your knowledge of sentence patterns to correct the run-on sentences. Use the following words at least once: *because*, *although*, and *but*. In addition, correct at least one run-on with a semicolon.

_____ 1. In the future robots may handle several types of dangerous police work.

_____ 2. The robots will control riots police work will not be so dangerous.

_____ 3. Translations will be done by computers human translators will be needed too.

_____ 4. Computers will use business "games" to train managers and executives.

_____ 5. Factories will rely on computers they will also need skilled technicians.

Avoiding Common Errors

_____ 6. First-year college students can expect to change jobs at least ten times during their lives.
_____ 7. Most colleges teach computer skills students are eager to learn them.
_____ 8. Computer technology is advancing rapidly in our society.
_____ 9. Computers double in power every five years computer scientists need constant retraining.
_____ 10. The prices for many computers have dropped more people are buying them.

Exercise 8

INSTRUCTIONS: Label the statements *true* or *false*.
_____ 1. You can use a comma to join two sentences.
_____ 2. A very long sentence is called a run-on.
_____ 3. It is always possible to correct a run-on with a period and a capital letter.
_____ 4. Reading sentences aloud can help you spot run-ons.
_____ 5. If you correct a run-on with a subordinate conjunction, be sure to use a comma.
_____ 6. A semicolon should always be followed by a capital letter.
_____ 7. Sentences with the words *who* and *which* sometimes require commas.
_____ 8. Sometimes run-ons are acceptable in college writing.
_____ 9. *And, but, or,* can be used to correct run-ons.
_____ 10. Several sentence patterns can be used to correct run-ons.

Exercise 9

INSTRUCTIONS: This paragraph contains several run-ons, along with some short, choppy sentences. Using a variety of sentence patterns, rewrite the paragraph to sound smoother and more professional. Punctuate each sentence carefully. Finally, read your version aloud, making any other corrections that are needed.

Why I Need New Furniture

I'm having a hard time furnishing my new apartment. I've never had my own place before. I don't have any attractive furniture. First, the pieces my parents gave me are ugly. They gave me a sofa, bed, and table. All three are old-fashioned. The table is scratched the sofa is faded. Second, I don't have enough other pieces to fill up my apartment. The living room and bedroom have empty corners, I don't like that. Worst of all, my best friend has a lovely apartment I'm ashamed to have my friends see mine. I know my parents are helping me as much as they can. I still wish I had a beautiful condominium.

Exercise 9

INSTRUCTIONS: Write a paragraph describing a habit you would like to change. As you plan your paragraph, think of three reasons why you'd like to change that particular habit. Then, as you organize your paragraph, label the reasons *first, second,* and *most of all*. In the revising step, draw one line under each subject and two under each verb. Correct any fragments and run-ons you may have written.

Unit Sixteen
Present-Tense Verbs

> SUMMARY
>
> 1. Present-tense verbs describe actions that are happening now or that happen regularly.
>
> 2. Present-tense verbs end in *s* or *es*.
>
> 3. The irregular verbs *be, go, have,* and *do* follow different forms.
>
> 4. Verb endings must correspond with the subject.

Read the following sentences carefully, noting the *time* in which each takes place:

I walk to school every day. *Example*

I am a first-year student in college. *Example*

I walked to school every day last year. *Example*

You should have noticed that the first sentence describes something that happens regularly and is still going on. The verb *walk* is a present-tense verb. The second sentence also uses a present-tense verb, *am*. This sentence describes a situation going on now. The third sentence describes something that happened last year. Its verb, *walked*, is a past-tense verb (which you will study in Unit 17).

Choosing the Correct Ending

Present-tense verbs sometimes add an *s* ending. Study the following short sentences, and notice the *s* ending on *works*:

The girl works. *Example*

The girls work. *Example*

I work. *Example*

You work. *Example*

The phrase *1, 2, I, you* will help you decide when to add the *s* ending onto a present-tense verb. As you read these examples, notice that the *s* ending is added to *work* in the sentence about *one girl*:

The girl works. One (The subject is **one** girl)

The girls work. Two (The subject is **two** girls)

I work. I (The subject is **I**)

You work. You (The subject is **you**)

Here is a chart showing you how to use the phrase *1, 2, I, you*:

1	(s or es)	(a single subject such as *he, she, it, Jack, the teacher, the dog, the pencil*)
2	(no ending)	(the subject is two or more: *they, we, Jack and Sue, the teachers, the dogs, the pencils*)
I	(no ending)	
you	(no ending)	

Any subject can be labeled with one of these words: *one, two, I,* or *you*. When you write a sentence about an event happening now or an event that happens regularly, the phrase *one, two, I, you* will help you choose the correct verb ending. Add *s* or *es* only when your subject is one person or one thing.

The *1, 2, I, you* rule assumes the use of *standard English*—the type of English usually spoken on television and written in books, magazines, and newspapers. Not everyone speaks and writes standard English all the time. In everyday speech, some people use a variation of standard English that can be called *community dialect*. For example, some people say "He go" instead of "He goes."

Community dialect often uses the word *be* as a verb. For example, a person speaking community dialect might say, "She be working." In standard English, however, the word *be* is used as a verb only in commands, as shown here:

Be quiet. *Correct*

Be here in an hour. *Correct*

In other sentences, *be* must be paired with another verb, such as *will*:

She will be here in an hour. *Correct*

College professors generally expect you to use standard English rather than community dialect. As you pursue your career, you will probably continue to use standard English. By learning the rules in this unit and practicing them in your speech and writing, you can build confidence in your knowledge of present-tense verbs.

Exercise 1

INSTRUCTIONS: Underline the verb twice in each sentence. Then label the subject of each sentence **1, 2, I,** or **you**.

_____ 1. You help.
_____ 2. Sam helps.
_____ 3. I help.
_____ 4. The teachers help.
_____ 5. I swim at the Health Center twice a week.
_____ 6. John and Bill lift weights regularly.
_____ 7. Marianne walks two miles before breakfast every morning.
_____ 8. You need another math course next semester.
_____ 9. The computer lab stays open late on Thursday evenings.
_____ 10. Both nurses prefer the day shift.

Exercise 2

INSTRUCTIONS: Listed here are ten subjects. Label each one either **1, 2, I,** or **you**.

_____ 1. John
_____ 2. I
_____ 3. The baseball players
_____ 4. A spare tire
_____ 5. Mr. and Mrs. Clayton
_____ 6. The women
_____ 7. You
_____ 8. A rock star
_____ 9. The textbook
_____ 10. My parents

Exercise 3

INSTRUCTIONS: Write a short sentence about each of the subjects in Exercise 2, making sure your sentences are in the present tense. (Check to see that they describe something that happens regularly or is happening now.) Use *1, 2, I, you* to add *s* to the end of the verb when necessary.

Present-Tense Verbs

Choosing the S or ES Ending

Present-tense verbs sometimes have *s* or *es* endings:

Jane walks to school every day.   *Example*

Mrs. Brown teaches English.   *Example*

As you read the following sentences aloud, listen to your pronunciation of the verbs. Your ear can help you learn when to use an *es* ending at the end of a verb:

Susan reads her textbooks for help with her assignments.
   Example

Susan searches her textbooks for help with her assignments.
   Example

Joe cleans his car when he's expecting a visit from his parents.
   Example

Joe waxes his car when he's expecting a visit from his parents.
   Example

All four verbs—*read, search, clean, wax*—contain one syllable. Try adding *s* to all four while saying them aloud. You will find that you can pronounce *reads* and *cleans* as one-syllable words. But *search* and *wax* cannot be pronounced as one-syllable words with an *s* ending. You must add another syllable by adding *es*: *searches, waxes*. As you say these two words aloud, you'll be able to hear the *es* ending. (Remember to use the *1, 2, I, you* phrase to decide whether the ending is needed at all.)

You may also find it helpful to learn this rule: If a verb ends in *s, ss, x, sh, ch,* or *zz,* it needs an *es* ending. Otherwise, use the *s* ending. (Again, use the *1, 2, I, you* phrase to make sure the ending is needed.)

Exercise 4

INSTRUCTIONS: In each sentence, add either *s* or *es* to the verb in parentheses. Make sure each sentence is in the present tense.

1. John (wish) _____ that his roommate would change his study habits.

2. His roommate (like) _____ to study in the wee hours of the morning.

3. He also (insist) _____ on playing his radio then.

4. Worst of all, he (fix) _____ snacks in the student kitchen and wants John to eat with him.

5. Every evening John (preach) _____ about the virtues of a good night's sleep.

6. But his roommate (cherish) _____ his habit of studying after midnight.

7. He (say) _____ that he memorizes material better that way.

8. Since he (pass) _____ every test, he is apparently right.

9. John (think) _____ that lack of sleep will eventually cause him to change.

10. Meanwhile John (catch) _____ a few hours of sleep whenever he can.

Exercise 5

INSTRUCTIONS: In each sentence, add the proper ending (where needed) to the verb in parentheses. Make sure that each sentence is in the present tense when you are finished.

1. Every afternoon Charlene (rush) _____ to the library.

2. She (finish) _____ her assignments before I even start mine.

3. Charlene (plan) _____ to be an orchestra conductor.

4. In the evenings she (dash) _____ to various rehearsals on campus.

5. After she (toss) _____ a few granola bars into her purse, she's ready for a long evening of music.

6. She (pay) _____ a stiff fee for private lessons in conducting.

7. Her determination (show) _____ when someone makes fun of her plans.

8. She (glare) _____ at her challengers but says nothing.

9. To earn extra money, she (teach) _____ what she knows to other music lovers.

10. Charlene (dream) _____ of conducting a major orchestra some day.

Present-Tense Verbs   209

Exercise 6

INSTRUCTIONS: Place a different subject before each verb. Use the phrase *1, 2, I, you* to help you make your choices.

1. _____ have different preferences about eating.
2. _____ cooks most meals at home to save money.
3. _____ likes dorm food and always eats in the cafeteria.
4. _____ eat fast food whenever possible.
5. _____ splurge and eat in a nice restaurant once a month.
6. _____ heats frozen meals in the dorm microwave.
7. _____ gets food packages from home.
8. _____ work in a cafe and eat most meals there.
9. _____ drops in on friends at mealtimes, hinting about food.
10. _____ cooks for a professor's family and eats with them free of charge.

Exercise 7

INSTRUCTIONS: Write five present-tense sentences about activities you do every day—for example, your driving route or the buildings you walk past on campus. Then rewrite the same five sentences (still in the present tense) with a friend's name as the subject. Be sure to use the correct verb endings.

Using Irregular Verbs

To speak and write effectively, you must master four irregular verbs: *be, go, have,* and *do*. These verbs are irregular because they do not follow the pattern of most verbs in the English language. Fortunately, these verbs probably are familiar to you already. You may need to check, however, to be sure that you use *is* and *are, do* and *does* (as well as the other irregular verb forms) according to the rules of standard English.

The Verb *Be*

The label *be* applies to three present-tense verb forms: *am, is,* and *are.* In standard English, the word *be* by itself does not act as the verb in a sentence. There is one exception, as noted before: commands, such as "Be quiet" and "Be here at ten." Otherwise, *be* must be combined with another word, such as *can, could, will, might, may* or *to.*

The *1, 2, I, you* pattern is slightly different for this verb. Here are the forms of *be*:

1   *is*

2   *are*

I   *am*

you   *are*

Study the following examples:

Jack is busy.   *One person: use* **is**

Jack and Mary are busy.   *Two persons: use* **are**

I am busy.

You are busy.

Exercise 8

INSTRUCTIONS: Put the correct form of *be* after each of the subjects. Use the chart given above as a guide.

1. John _____ .
2. I _____ .
3. The baseball players _____ .
4. A spare tire _____ .
5. Mr. and Mrs. Clayton _____ .
6. The women _____ .
7. You _____ .
8. A rock star _____ .
9. The textbook _____ .
10. My parents _____ .

Present-Tense Verbs 211

Exercise 9

INSTRUCTIONS: Do Exercise 8 again, expanding each short sentence by adding any words you choose.

Exercise 10

INSTRUCTIONS: Put the correct form of *be* into the space in each sentence.

1. My car _____ a useful storage place.
2. Six library books _____ stacked on the back seat.
3. My brand-new cassette tape _____ in the tape deck.
4. You _____ sure to see at least one pair of running shoes on the floor.
5. I _____ in the habit of throwing exercise clothes onto the back seat.
6. My laundry _____ in the trunk.
7. Several letters and bills _____ lying on the dashboard.
8. Various canned goods _____ stored under the front seat.
9. Many quarters, nickels and dimes _____ hidden under the floor mats.
10. A flashlight, can opener, address book, and spoon _____ kept in the glove compartment.

The Verbs *Go, Have,* and *Do*

The label *go* applies to two present-tense verbs, *go* and *goes*. The label *have* applies to two present-tense verbs, *has* and *have*. Finally, the label *do* applies to two present-tense verbs, *do* and *does*.

These verbs vary slightly from the *1, 2, I, you* pattern. Refresh your memory about the spelling and use of these forms:

	Go		Have		Do
1	goes	1	has	1	does
2	go	2	have	2	do
I	go	I	have	I	do
you	go	you	have	you	do

Study the following examples:

    Jack goes to work.   *One person: use* **goes**

    Jack has a new car.   *One person: use* **has**

    Jack does his homework.   *One person: use* **does**

    Jack and Mary go to work.   *Two persons: use* **go**

    Jack and Mary have a new car.   *Two persons: use* **have**

    I go to work.

    I have a new car.

    I do my homework.

    You go to work.

    You have a new car.

    You do your homework.

Exercise 11

INSTRUCTIONS: Choose the correct form of the verb in parentheses.
1. Most college students (have) part-time jobs.
2. I (go) shopping for homebound people to earn extra money.
3. Mary (do) light housework for single people and young mothers.
4. Karen (have) a plant-tending service called "Green Thumbs Unlimited."
5. Don and Emmanuel (go) from house to house looking for yard work.
6. Lili (go) to children's parties and performs magic tricks.
7. She also (do) adult parties.
8. In a college town, you (have) many jobs to choose from.
9. Several friends (do) translations from a number of languages into English.
10. One even (do) computer programs for clients who speak Spanish.

Exercise 12

INSTRUCTIONS: Write ten sentences containing forms of the verbs *be*, *do*, *have*, and *go*, using the following subjects: I, you, we, they, the women, Gail, the students, a car, the beach.

Exercise 13

INSTRUCTIONS: Choose the correct form of the words in parentheses.
1. My mother (be) going to college full-time.
2. She and her best friend, Anne, (be) in the nursing program.
3. Anne and my mother (go) to all their classes together.
4. When Anne (go) to the nursing lab for extra practice, Mom (go) with her.
5. Anne and Mom even (do) their homework together.
6. Luckily my brother and I (have) interests of our own.
7. We (do) whatever we can to help Mom.
8. My brother and I (be) excited about Mom's plans.
9. We already (have) plans for celebrating her graduation.
10. I (have) a gift picked out for her.

Exercise 14

INSTRUCTIONS: Choose the correct forms of the words in parentheses.
1. I (have) no desire to go camping again.
2. My friends often (go) camping because they love the outdoors.
3. But the weather (have) to cooperate, or I won't go.
4. A sudden rainstorm (do) awful things to my parents' old tent.
5. Bugs (be) another problem.
6. Frank still (have) red bumps from our last encounter with mosquitoes.
7. We always (do) a lot of arguing about the food.
8. The menus (be) Don's responsibility, but he has no imagination.
9. He (have) a fondness for dull things like canned spaghetti.
10. A weekend (go) slowly when Don takes charge of the cooking.

Using Present-Tense Verbs with Prepositional Phrases

Earlier in this book, you were introduced to two important prepositions: *of* and *in*. You also learned three important facts about prepositions:

1. A preposition is a word (usually a short word) that may indicate direction or purpose. Examples include *by, with, for, to, of, in, into, along, toward,* and *near*.
2. The word group beginning with a preposition is called *a prepositional phrase*.
3. Prepositional phrases never contain the subject or verb of a sentence. When you are looking for the subject and verb, cross out any prepositional phrases first so that they will not distract you.

When you are choosing the correct verb for a sentence, your ability to identify prepositional phrases will be of tremendous help. Study this sentence:

Three apartments on the top floor are vacant. *Example*

On is a preposition, and *on the top floor* is a prepositional phrase that you should cross out before you find the subject and verb:

Three apartments ~~on the top floor~~ **are vacant.** *Example*

Now you can easily find the subject—*three apartments*—and the verb—*are*.

Try to find the subject and verb of this sentence:

One of the surprise guests is expected any minute. *Example*

You should have crossed out the prepositional phrase *of the surprise guests*:

One ~~of the surprise guests~~ **is expected any minute.** *Example*

One is the subject, and *is* is the verb.

Now you are ready to choose the correct verb form yourself. Read the following sentence, cross out the prepositional phrase, and decide whether *do* or *does* belongs in the blank space:

The watches on the bottom shelf _____ not have batteries. *Example*

You should have crossed out *on the bottom shelf*:

The watches ~~on the bottom shelf~~ **_____ not have batteries.** *Example*

Present-Tense Verbs

The *1, 2, I, you* phrase will remind you that watches (more than one) should have a verb without an *s* ending. The word *do*, therefore, belongs in the blank space:

The watches ~~on the bottom shelf~~ do not have batteries.
Example

Exercise 15

INSTRUCTIONS: Choose the correct form of the words in parentheses. Remember to cross out the prepositional phrases first, and use *1, 2, I, you* as a guide when you choose the verb.

1. One of my mother's hobbies (be) collecting antiques.
2. A glass case full of interesting antiques (stand) in our dining room.
3. Some valuable pieces from the eighteenth century always (attract) the attention of our visitors.
4. Her collection of antique vases (be) especially popular.
5. Every Christmas an old-fashioned tree with delicate glass ornaments (dominate) our living room.
6. The shelves in the den (display) antique toys.
7. My favorite pieces in her collection (be) the toy trains.
8. All of the neighborhood children (beg) to come and see them.
9. Collectors from many states (write) long letters to my mother.
10. Sometimes even visitors from Europe (ask) to view her antiques.

Exercise 16

INSTRUCTIONS: Choose the correct form of the words in parentheses. Remember to cross out the prepositional phrases first, and use *1, 2, I, you* as a guide when you choose the verb.

1. My favorite time of the year (be) autumn.
2. The hot months of summer (make) me yearn for cooler weather.
3. Autumn days with brisk mornings (refresh) me.
4. The vacant lots near my home (take) on a new beauty.
5. A spectacular array of wildflowers (bloom) throughout the fall.
6. The football field behind the school (become) noisy every afternoon as team members practice.

7. An occasional glimpse of migrating birds (cause) me to marvel at the wonders of nature.
8. Children with heavy schoolbags (stand) on corners, waiting for the school bus.
9. Piles of cold-weather clothing (come) down from my parents' attic.
10. The beauty of the changing autumn leaves (make) me happiest of all.

Sentences Beginning with There Or Here

As you learned in Unit 8, the words *there* and *here* never are the subjects of sentences. When a sentence begins with one of these words, you must look elsewhere in the sentence for the subject. After you have found the subject, you can choose the correct verb, using *1, 2, I, you* as a guide. Study the following example:

There (is, are) six patients waiting.   *Example*

The subject—*six patients*—is easy to find. Using the *1, 2, I, you* rule, you can see that the verb must be *are*:

There (is, <u>are</u>) six patients waiting.   *Example*

Here is another example:

Here (grows, grow) a fine maple tree.   *Example*

Your subject is *a fine maple tree*. Using the *1, 2, I, you* rule, you know that the verb must be *grows*.

Exercise 17

INSTRUCTIONS: Underline the verb in each sentence. Remember that *there* and *here* never are the subjects of sentences.
1. There (is, are) a big party at our house every New Year's Eve.
2. Here (is, are) the guest list for the party.

3. There (goes, go) my brother to hang the decorations.
4. Here (comes, come) the live band we hired.
5. There (seems, seem) to be some problems with the sound system.

Exercise 18

INSTRUCTIONS: Underline the correct verb in each sentence. Remember that *there* and *here* never are the subjects of sentences.

1. There (hangs, hang) the paintings my father has done.
2. Here (is, are) some awards my sister won in college.
3. There (stands, stand) a sculpture done by my mother.
4. Here (lies, lie) two rugs woven by my brother.
5. Unfortunately there (is, are) no art works by me in our house.

Reviewing What You Have Learned

Exercise 19

INSTRUCTIONS: Use each of the following verbs in a sentence: *am, is, are, go, goes, do, does, has, have.*

Exercise 20

INSTRUCTIONS: Use each of the following verbs in a sentence: *consists, consist, lists, list, exists, exist, grasps, grasp, collects, collect.* Read the sentences aloud when you have finished, pronouncing the verbs with particular care.

Exercise 21

INSTRUCTIONS: Write five correct sentences beginning with *here* and five more beginning with *there.* Be sure to find the true subject before you select your verb.

Exercise 22

INSTRUCTIONS: Choose the correct form of the word in parentheses.

1. I (hate) going to the laundry room in my apartment building.
2. The machine (wash) only a small load.
3. My landlord (refuse) to buy a bigger machine.
4. Someone (be) always using the machine when I'm ready to do my laundry.
5. Time (go) slowly while I'm waiting.
6. My clothes always (have) mysterious stains that don't wash out.
7. Detergent and bleach (do) not work for me.
8. My neighbors (say) that our hard water causes the stains.
9. We (want) the landlord to do something about the problem.
10. He (insist) that the water is fine here.

Exercise 23

INSTRUCTIONS: Write a paragraph describing a way that you enjoy spending time with others, either friends or family. Use the present tense throughout your paragraph. You can do this easily by using an *every* phrase near the beginning of your paragraph, as shown here:

Every Saturday night my family watches an auto race.

My friends and I go skiing every February.

In the revising step, use the *1, 2, I, you* rule to check your verb endings.

Unit Seventeen
Past-Tense Verbs

> SUMMARY
>
> *1.* Past-tense verbs are used for events that happened in the past.
>
> *2. Regular* verbs add *-ed* endings in the past tense—for example, *walked, looked, logged, danced.*
>
> *3. Irregular* verbs change in a variety of ways in the past tense—for example, *run* becomes *ran, sleep* becomes *slept, teach* becomes *taught.*
>
> *4.* Past participles are verb forms used with a helping verb.

When you talk or write about something that happened in the past, you almost always use a form of the verb that differs from its present-tense form. The following sentence pairs illustrate such verb changes. The first sentence in each pair uses a present-tense verb, while the second sentence describes something that already happened—the past tense. Read the sentences aloud, paying particular attention to the verbs:

I <u>drive</u> three friends to class every morning.   *Present tense*

Yesterday I <u>drove</u> Becky home.   *Past tense*

My wife and I always <u>watch</u> the evening news after dinner.
   Present tense

Last night my wife and I <u>watched</u> a football game.   *Past tense*

We usually <u>board</u> our dog at a kennel when we take a trip.
   Present tense

Last summer we <u>boarded</u> Skipper at our vet's office.   *Past tense*

Two of the verbs you just read, *watched* and *boarded*, are called *regular* verbs: They just add *-ed* to form the past tense. But the verb *drive* is different: The past tense is spelled *drove*, and there's no *-ed* ending. Verbs that don't add *-ed* in the past are called *irregular* verbs.

A few verbs don't change at all in the past tense. *Cut, cost, hurt, let,* and *put* are included in this group:

Today, my purchases <u>cost</u> thirty-two dollars.   *Present tense*

Last year, the same items <u>cost</u> only twenty-five dollars.   *Past tense*

Some students <u>cut</u> classes because they don't take college seriously.   *Present*

When I <u>cut</u> classes in high school, I ended up in trouble.   *Past*

People often <u>hurt</u> others without meaning to.   *Present tense*

Alton <u>hurt</u> my feelings with that remark.   *Past tense*

I <u>let</u> my children have sweets only on weekends.   *Present tense.*

Last night I <u>let</u> them stay up late to watch a movie.   *Past tense*

I <u>put</u> some money into my Christmas Club every month.   *Present tense*

Sherry <u>put</u> a thousand dollars into a savings certificate last year.   *Past tense*

Using Past-Tense Verbs Correctly

Chances are that you frequently hear verb errors such as these:

The final date for my book report almost <u>snuck</u> past me.   *Incorrect*

My cousins nearly <u>drownded</u> last summer.   *Incorrect*

Here are the correct versions of these sentences:

The final date for my book report almost <u>sneaked</u> past me.

My cousins nearly <u>drowned</u> last summer.   *Correct*

Check the dictionary when you have doubts about a verb you're using. The words *snuck, brung,* and *drownded* are always incorrect. Dictionaries describe them as *substandard* or *nonstandard*. Both terms signify that these verb forms are unacceptable for college and professional writing.

Study Tip: If any of these verbs create problems for you, copy the correct sentences onto an index card and tape it where you'll see it often. Also, start a verb notebook. Write down correct sentences with verbs you need to learn, and review the sentences daily.

Using Irregular Verbs in the Past Tense

The verbs listed below are irregular—they don't end in *-ed* in the past tense. As you complete the exercises in this unit, make a list of the irregular verbs you need to learn:

PRESENT	PAST
arise	arose
become	became
begin	began
bend	bent
bite	bit
blow	blew
break	broke
bring	brought
build	built
buy	bought
catch	caught
choose	chose
come	came
cut	cut
do	did
draw	drew
drink	drank
drive	drove
eat	ate
fall	fell
feed	fed
feel	felt
fight	fought
find	found
fly	flew
get	got
give	gave
go	went
have	had
hear	heard
hide	hid
hold	held
hurt	hurt
keep	kept
know	knew
lay	laid
lead	led
leave	left
lend	lent
let	let
lie	lay

PRESENT	PAST
light	lit
lose	lost
make	made
meet	met
pay	paid
put	put
ride	rode
ring	rang
rise	rose
run	ran
say	said
see	saw
sell	sold
send	sent
shake	shook
shrink	shrank
shut	shut
sing	sang
sit	sat
sleep	slept
speak	spoke
spend	spent
stand	stood
steal	stole
stick	stuck
swear	swore
swim	swam
take	took
teach	taught
tear	tore
tell	told
think	thought
wear	wore
weep	wept
win	won
wind	wound
write	wrote

Exercise 1

INSTRUCTIONS: Choose the correct past-tense verb for these sentences. (The present-tense form is supplied for you.)

1. The whole team (go) to Disneyland to celebrate.
2. Molly (grow) up in Brooklyn.
3. I (know) the answer to every question on the science test.
4. What happened to the book I (lay) on the table?
5. We (drink) an entire pitcher of iced tea with our pizza.
6. The birds (eat) all the seed in the feeder.
7. As the wind increased, the temperature (fall).
8. Ms. Daniels (give) everyone on her list a cannister of cookies.
9. My brother (cut) his foot on a seashell.
10. Everyone in the class (draw) a bowl of fruit.

Using *Be* in the Past Tense

You've already learned the present-tense forms of *be: am, is,* and *are.* (You also know that you can use *be* as a verb only in commands, such as "Be seated!" and "Be patient.") Now you are ready to learn the past-tense forms—*was* and *were:*

SINGULAR	PLURAL
I was	we were
you were	you were
he, she, it was	they were

Study tip: Copy these forms onto an index card, and tape it to a place where you'll see it often.

Exercise 2

INSTRUCTIONS: Insert the correct past-tense form of *be.*

1. That physics test _____ difficult for me.
2. Warren and I _____ on the fencing team in high school.

3. Francine _____ disappointed with her grades.
4. Kerry and Sheila _____ selected to be cheerleaders.
5. I _____ stunned by the bill from the garage.
6. They _____ busy all morning getting ready for the reception.
7. Calculus and trigonometry _____ offered last semester.
8. We _____ wise to take a study-skills course.
9. You _____ nominated to be vice-president of the class.
10. Both of you _____ in Professor Kelly's English class.

Exercise 3

INSTRUCTIONS: Choose the correct past-tense verbs. (The present-tense form is provided for you.)

1. I (arise) at six this morning.
2. I (blow) my nose so often that my face (Become) red.
3. I (buy) another houseplant at the flea market.
4. His father (choose) not to accept the offer.
5. Mr. O'Brien (come) to this country from Ireland.
6. My family (send) over a hundred Christmas cards last year.
7. Professor Ryan (let) us look at our notes during the test.
8. The pirate (hide) the treasure chest in a cave.
9. Same (have) the best painting in the art show.
10. Geraldine (weep) for joy at the news.

Using Past Participles

Words such as *given, seen, gone,* and *done* are *past participles.* They can be used only with forms of the helping verbs *have* or *be:*

has   am
have   is
had   are
              was
              were

As you read the following examples, notice that the verb forms have something in common: they refer to something that happens regularly or has happened recently. Such sentences are written in the *present perfect tense*. To *hear* the correct use of these forms, read these examples aloud:

I have *given* him all the help I can.   *Correct*

We have *seen* two dance performances this winter.   *Correct*

The sale items are always *gone* before we do our shopping.   *Correct*

Everything on Kelly's list is *done*.   *Correct*

All regular verbs have past participles to use with helping verbs. Just add *-d* or *-ed* to form the past participle:

Shorthand tests are <u>timed</u> after the second week.   *Correct*

Many people are <u>fascinated</u> by hypnosis.   *Correct*

Ginny's romance with Sherman is <u>finished</u>.   *Correct*

Libby's comments about our math class should not be <u>repeated</u>.   *Correct*

Regular verbs sometimes add a double letter in both the past tense and the past participle—for example, *grabbed, hugged,* and *rebelled*. When you're doubtful about how to form a participle, check the dictionary. Each verb is given in three forms: present tense, past tense, and past participle. If you look up *go*, for example, you'll find *go, went, gone*. The past participle is the third form, *gone*.

Study Tip: The past participles that cause the most confusion are *seen, given, gone,* and *done*. Copy correct examples onto index cards, and carry them with you to study.

VERB FORMS

PRESENT	PAST	PAST PARTICIPLE
arise	arose	arisen
become	became	become
begin	began	begun
bend	bent	bent
bite	bit	bit
blow	blew	blown
break	broke	broken
bring	brought	brought
build	built	built
buy	bought	bought
catch	caught	caught
choose	chose	chosen
come	came	come
cut	cut	cut
do	did	done
draw	drew	drawn
drink	drank	drunk
drive	drove	driven
eat	ate	eaten
fall	fell	fallen
feed	fed	fed
feel	felt	felt
fight	fought	fought
find	found	found
fly	flew	flown
get	got	got
give	gave	given
go	went	gone
have	had	had
hear	heard	heard
hide	hid	hidden
hold	held	held
hurt	hurt	hurt
keep	kept	kept
know	knew	known
lay	laid	laid
lead	led	led
leave	left	left

PRESENT	PAST	PAST PARTICIPLE
lend	lent	lent
let	let	let
lie	lay	lain
light	lit	lit
lose	lost	lost
make	made	made
meet	met	met
pay	paid	paid
put	put	put
ride	rode	ridden
ring	rang	rung
rise	rose	risen
run	ran	run
say	said	said
see	saw	seen
sell	sold	sold
send	sent	sent
shake	shook	shaken
shrink	shrank	shrunk
show	showed	shown
shut	shut	shut
sing	sang	sung
sit	sat	sat
sleep	slept	slept
speak	spoke	spoken
spend	spent	spent
stand	stood	stood
steal	stole	stolen
stick	stuck	stuck
swear	swore	sworn
swim	swam	swum
take	took	taken
teach	taught	taught
tear	tore	torn
tell	told	told
think	thought	thought
wear	wore	worn
weep	wept	wept
win	won	won
wind	wound	wound
write	wrote	written

Past-Tense Verbs

Exercise 4

INSTRUCTIONS: Correct any verb errors. If a sentence is correct, mark it **C**.

_____ 1. Kristin done went to the library to work on a report.
_____ 2. Cliff has seen all of Elvis Presley's movies.
_____ 3. Jake has gave diving demonstrations all over the state.
_____ 4. I done did all the algebra problems.
_____ 5. Patricia and Courtney have gone to a dude ranch for the weekend.
_____ 6. The sorority has gave a party for the senior citizens every December.
_____ 7. I seen him in his office before class.
_____ 8. They have went to Colorado to ski.
_____ 9. Melissa and Daryl have given me the directions.
_____ 10. Floyd has did everything I asked him to.
_____ 11. Gigi has shown the director all her best tap routines.
_____ 12. I have slept late every Monday this semester.
_____ 13. Buster has shaked his birthday present all morning.
_____ 14. If Professor Cally had wrote the words on the board, I would have understand them.
_____ 15. The coach has spoken to the dean twice about our playing schedule.

Exercise 5

INSTRUCTIONS: Write a sentence for fifteen of the past participles listed in the chart of verb forms.

Exercise 6

INSTRUCTIONS: Fill in the correct form of the verb printed in capital letters.
1. What (begin) as a joke ended as a tragedy.
2. Josie (catch) an awful cold while on vacation.
3. One thing (lead) to another, and I decided to volunteer.
4. Cory (lend) us a van so we could attend the play.

5. Beverly (hear) the test results yesterday).
6. My grandmother always (let) her cat sleep on the bed.
7. Hannah (spend) too much on my birthday gift.
8. I (teach) my dog how to fetch.
9. The hotel clerk (wake) us up right on time.
10. The elbows on my jacket (worn) out before the collar did.

Exercise 7

INSTRUCTIONS: Fill in the correct form of the verb.
1. On the way home, I (sleep) in the back seat.
2. The coach (take) Grace aside and congratulated her.
3. It was the first time May ever (hold) a baby, and she was nervous.
4. Chad was rude to Vicky and (hurt) her feelings.
5. Because I (keep) at it, I finally learned how to skate.
6. A tree limb (bend) the antenna of my car.
7. Shawn chipped a tooth when he (bite) down on some candy.
8. Debby and Sam (build) the parade float themselves.
9. For three weeks I (feed) those kittens with a nursing bottle.
10. Dennis (find) a ten-dollar bill on the golf course.

Exercise 8

INSTRUCTIONS: Fill in the correct form of the verb.
1. My car (cost) a great deal, but it's always in the shop.
2. Curtis (drive) all night long.
3. My baby sister's face (light) up when she saw the present.
4. Mitchell (tear) the phone book in half at the party.
5. After I heard the news, I (feel) very fortunate.
6. We went skating as soon as the pond (freeze).

7. Because of the snowstorm, we (think) the campus would be closed today.

8. The old pine tree (stand) in the center of a clearing.

9. Bells (ring) constantly when we were in Rome last year.

10. Professor Murphy's father once (sing) on Broadway.

Reviewing What You Have Learned

Exercise 9

INSTRUCTIONS: Answer these questions.
1. Write **R** in front of the sentences with regular verbs; write **I** in front of the sentences with irregular verbs.
   _____ a. The Eagles <u>lost</u> the game in the last minute of play.
   _____ b. I <u>enjoyed</u> Mark's graduation party.
   _____ c. Mr. Holmes <u>spent</u> forty years in the real-estate business.
   _____ d. After his bath, Fido <u>shook</u> himself dry.
   _____ e. We <u>pretended</u> not to know about the math assignment.
2. Underline the verb forms that must be used with helping verbs: *gone, did, went, seen, given, ran.*
3. List four verbs that do not change in the past tense.

Exercise 10

INSTRUCTIONS: Plan and write a paragraph describing your best experience in high school. In the revising step, work with a partner to make sure all your past-tense verb forms are correct. If necessary, use the dictionary to check your verbs.

Unit Eighteen
Pronouns

SUMMARY

1. Pronouns are small words that take the place of nouns.

2. The "thumb" rule is a guide for choosing the correct pronoun in a sentence.

3. Possessive pronouns such as *its, his, hers, ours,* and *yours* never have apostrophes.

Pronouns are important words—usually small ones—that we use every day. Pronouns simplify sentences by taking the place of nouns. For example, instead of saying "Jerry said that Jerry would come to the game," you can use the pronoun *he*. Then your sentence sounds like this: "Jerry said that *he* would come to the game."

Here is a list of pronouns you should know:

SINGULAR
I, me
you
he, him, she, her, it

PLURAL
we, us
you
they, them

Introducing the "Thumb" Rule

Take a look at the following examples. How do you decide which pronoun is correct?

Yesterday Penny and (I, me) did the homework correctly. *Example*

Let Penny and (I, me) help you this afternoon. *Example*

The "thumb" rule is a quick method for choosing the correct pronoun in a sentence. Here's how it works: Use your thumb to cover up the *and* phrase in front of the pronoun in a sentence. Because the sentence is shorter, you'll find it easy to choose the correct pronoun.

To find the correct pronoun in these examples, cover up *Penny and* with your thumb. Now the sentences will look like these:

Yesterday ~~Penny and~~ (I, me) did the homework correctly.

Let ~~Penny and~~ (I, me) help you this afternoon.

If you read each shortened sentence aloud, you'll be able to *hear* the correct pronouns:

Yesterday Penny and I did the homework correctly. *Correct*

Let Penny and me help you this afternoon. *Correct*

Here are two more examples to try:

Send Doug and (I, me) your new address as soon as you can.
Example

Sometimes Doug and (I, me) spend hours talking about cars.
Example

Use your thumb to cover up the words "Doug and":

Send Doug and (I, me) your new address as soon as you can.

Sometimes Doug and (I, me) spend hours talking about cars.

The simplified sentences now read:

Send (I, me) your new address as soon as you can.

Sometimes (I, me) spend hours talking about cars.

Here are the correct answers:

Send Doug and me your new address as soon as you can.
Correct

Sometimes Doug and I spend hours talking about cars.
Correct

Exercise 1

INSTRUCTIONS: In the second sentence of each pair, the words directly in front of the pronoun have been covered up. Circle the correct pronoun in each sentence.

1. Two friends and (I, me) took a camping trip last weekend.
2. ~~Two friends and~~ (I, me) took a camping trip last weekend.
3. Help Dave and (I, me) pick up this box.
4. Help ~~Dave and~~ (I, me) pick up this box.
5. Next month my parents and (I, me) will move to a larger apartment.
6. Next month ~~my parents and~~ (I, me) will move to a larger apartment.
7. The committee chose Dana and (I, me) for the job.

Pronouns

8. The committee chose ~~Dana and~~ (I, me) for the job.
9. Randall and (I, me) forgot to sign the petition.
10. ~~Randall and~~ (I, me) forgot to sign the petition.

Exercise 2

INSTRUCTIONS: Using the "thumb" rule, circle the correct pronouns in the sentences.

1. My friends and (I, me) collect toys for needy children every December.
2. Last night the librarian and (I, me) spent an hour searching for information about the space program.
3. Give Henry and (I, me) your bicycle, and we'll fix it for you.
4. Dr. Petrie said that Ralph and (I, me) have artistic talent.
5. My veterinarian and (I, me) were impressed with this medicine.
6. My mother reminded Jim and (I, me) about our dentist appointments.
7. Andrea and (I, me) are trying out for the college orchestra.
8. The package with the blue ribbon is from Cathy and (I, me).
9. You can trust Darlene and (I, me) with your secret.
10. What would happen if my family and (I, me) moved away?

The "thumb" rule will help you choose between *he* and *him, she* and *her, we* and *us, they* and *them*. Read the following examples to see how the "thumb" rule works with some of these pronouns (the correct pronoun is underlined):

Tell the Johnsons and (we, us) what dates are available.

Tell ~~the Johnsons and~~ (we, <u>us</u>) what dates are available.

The doctors said that the nurses and (they, them) should work together.

The doctors said that ~~the nurses and~~ (<u>they</u>, them) should work together.

Exercise 3

INSTRUCTIONS: Using the "thumb" rule, circle the correct pronoun in the following sentences.

1. Jill and (I, me) are taking a vacation together.
2. My neighbor said that (he, him) and his wife are going to put in a swimming pool.
3. When Jackie travels, (she, her) and her travel agent do a great deal of research first.
4. Our financial planner helped Kurt and (I, me) with our investments.
5. I think that you and (he, him) should start a business together.
6. The real-estate agent showed Patrick and (she, her) a fabulous house.
7. (We, Us) along with the assistant manager planned the advertising campaign.
8. This package is for Dennis and (she, her).
9. Tony and (she, her) are going to enter a figure-skating competition.
10. The videotapes helped both the professor and (we, us).

Using Pronouns in Formal Writing

In conversation, you often hear sentences like these:

It was me who called you.   *Informal English*

That was her I saw at the dance.   *Informal English*

Was it them in the red convertible?   *Informal English*

When you use formal English, the pronouns in these sentences must be changed. Here are the same sentences in formal English:

It was I who called you.   *Formal English*

That was she I saw at the dance.   *Formal English*

Was it they in the red covertible?   *Formal English*

Formal English is used primarily in official or business settings. Examples include an important speech, a letter to the newspaper, a business report, or a job interview. You expect to leave your casual clothes home when you work in a business; similarly, you should change from informal, everyday English to a more formal style when the need arises. Of course, no one expects you to speak formal English all the time. On a camping trip with close friends, you don't have to worry about proper pronouns or verb errors. But you should take the time to learn formal English now so that your skills are sharp when a formal occasion arises.

With the verbs *is, are, was,* and *were,* you can sometimes turn a sentence around to find the correct pronoun. Read the following examples aloud:

> **The honorary chairman was he.** *(He was the honorary chairman.)*
>
> **The most skilled horse rider is she.** *(She is the most skilled horse rider.)*
>
> **Happy travelers are we.** *(We are happy travelers.)*
>
> **It was she.** *(She was it.)*

Exercise 4

INSTRUCTIONS: Circle the correct pronoun.
1. It was (she, her) who answered the phone.
2. Give the message to (she, her).
3. Maggie said it was (I, me) who should make the presentation.
4. If it is (they, them), tell them we're ready.
5. It is (we, us) who benefit from the proposal.
6. Send (we, us) the refund quickly.
7. I heard (they, them) knocking on the door.
8. If the winners were (they, them), we would have protested.
9. A charming hostess is (she, her).
10. Hardworking students are (we, us).

Using Possessive Pronouns

Possessive pronouns show ownership. They include the following words, which you probably use often: *his, hers, ours, yours, theirs, mine, its*. You can use possessive pronouns in sentences such as these:

This book is mine.   *Example*

Those shoes are hers.   *Example*

Those books are yours, not ours.   *Example*

These pronouns show ownership, but they *never* have apostrophes. If you find yourself adding an apostrophe to one of these pronouns, stop and think about the word *his*. Remember that *his* never has an apostrophe, and you will remember not to use apostrophes in the other pronouns.

What about *its*? Like *his*, the possessive pronoun *its* has no apostrophe. Study the following examples:

Our no-wax floor is losing *its* shine.   *Correct*

The jacket I bought at Goodwill has all of *its* buttons.
   Correct

That sycamore loses *its* leaves every autumn.   *Correct*

Use an apostrophe in *its* only when you mean *it is*. You may find it helpful to think of the apostrophe as an *i*:

it is = it's

Study the following examples:

It's cold today.   *Example*

(It is cold today)

When the dog starts barking, it's time to feed her.   *Example*

(It is time to feed her)

If it's six o'clock, I have to leave.   *Example*

(It is six o'clock)

Pronouns

Exercise 5

INSTRUCTIONS: Write **C** if the sentence is correct, and write **I** if the sentence contains a pronoun error. Then correct the pronoun errors.

_____ 1. It's obvious that the property is ours.

_____ 2. That car of yours' needs to be washed and waxed.

_____ 3. The opera company begins it's fall season next week.

_____ 4. The trophy in the corner is hers'.

_____ 5. Which bicycles are theirs?

_____ 6. Phil's department met its quota ahead of schedule.

_____ 7. Our drama club lost its' star performer when Jennie graduated.

_____ 8. These packages are mine, and those are yours.

_____ 9. When its batteries are fresh, the radio works beautifully.

_____ 10. It's a pleasure to find a travel agency that treats it's clients so well.

Using Pronouns in Comparisons

It's important to choose the correct pronoun in comparative sentences, such as the following:

Jack is taller than I.   *Example*

Betty earns more than he.   *Example*

The Clarksons paid more for their car than we.   *Example*

You can select the right pronoun every time by "finishing the sentence." When you read a comparative sentence, finish the sentence by adding a pronoun and verb. Your ear will tell you which pronoun and verb to use. To see how "finishing the sentence" works, read these examples aloud:

Jack is taller than I [am].   *Example*

Betty earns more than he [does].   *Example*

The Clarksons paid more for their car than we [did].
   Example

Read the following examples aloud, and "finish" them with a pronoun and verb. Then compare your sentences to the correct answers:

Ted gave us more help than (she, her). *Example*

Marilyn had more acting lessons than (I, me). *Example*

Stacy's family has lived here longer than (we, us). *Example*

Ted gave us more help than *she* [did]. *Correct*

Marilyn had more acting lessons than *I* [had]. *Correct*

Stacy's family has lived here longer than *we* [have]. *Correct*

Exercise 6

INSTRUCTIONS: Finish the sentence and underline the correct pronouns. The first example is done for you.

1. Billy works faster than (I, me).
   Billy works faster than (I, me) [do].
2. Their basketball team trains harder than (we, us).
3. Peggy sings better than (he, him).
4. Allison earns more than (he, him).
5. The American athletes broke more records than (they, them).
6. A more experienced person might be better for that job than (he, him).
7. Cella doesn't study as hard as (I, me).
8. I've completed more assignments than (he, him).
9. Perry had fewer ideas than (she, her).
10. The sophomores scored more points than (we, us).

Checking Pronoun Agreement

English instructors often say that the pronouns in a sentence must "agree." The words *everyone, somebody,* and *each* are singular. They must be used with singular words such as *he, she,* and *it.* By contrast, the words *both* and *all* are plural. They must be used with plural words such as *they* and *them*. Read the following sentences aloud so that you can hear the differences:

Everyone brought their favorite recipe to the bridal shower.
Incorrect

Everyone brought her favorite recipe to the bridal shower.
Correct

Each of the fathers applauded when their child took a bow on the stage. *Incorrect*

Each of the fathers applauded when his child took a bow on the stage. *Correct*

Pronouns must be consistent. Don't switch from *me* to *you* in a sentence. Notice the difference between these sentences:

Niagra Falls thrilled me: you could hear the water pounding as it crashed over the rocks. *Incorrect*

Niagra Falls thrilled me: I could hear the water pounding as it crashed over the rocks. *Correct*

Avoiding Sexism in Pronoun Usage

In the past, professional writers used the male gender with *everyone, nobody,* and similar pronouns. Readers were supposed to understand that sentences with these words included both genders, even though they referred only to males, as in this example:

Everyone completed his assignment on time. *Sexist*

Today, this practice is changing; most writers would reword the previous sentence this way:

All of the students completed their assignments on time.

Writers today are concerned about the overemphasis on males in our language. Masculine expressions such as *firemen* and *policemen* are being changed to neutral ones such as *firefighters* and *police officers*. The words *humanity* and *humankind* are replacing the sexist word *mankind*. You can probably think of similar examples.

How can we eliminate sexism with pronouns such as *nobody*, *somebody*, and *someone*? Several possibilities exist. First, you can use *his or her* or a similar phrase, as in these examples:

Nobody has his or her homework today.   *Example*

If somebody asks for me, tell him or her to come back at one.   *Example*

Second, you can sometimes use the construction *s/he*, meaning *he or she*, as in this example:

Anybody can join if s/he has a 3.5 average.   *Example*

Third, you can alternate genders in your sentences. Dr. Benjamin Spock used this technique in his famous book *Baby and Child Care*. When he tells stories about infants and small children, Dr. Spock uses *he* and *him* half the time, *she* and *her* the rest.

Fourth, you can make your sentences plural, since *they* and *them* have no gender, as in these examples:

Any students can join if they have 3.5 averages.   *Example*

None of the students had their homework.   *Example.*

If people ask for me, tell them I'll be back at one.   *Example*

Finally, you can deliberately choose to be "incorrect" by writing and speaking sentences like these:

Nobody has their homework today.   *Example*

Does everyone have their book?   *Example*

Obviously, your choice will vary with your personal taste and your situation. The *him or her* construction sounds clumsy to some writers, who refuse to use it. Some businesses do not permit *s/he* in an official letter or report. If you write a book or magazine article, your editor may not permit you to alternate genders, as Dr. Spock did. On a standardized English test, you might lose points with the sentence "Nobody has their homework today."

Pronouns 243

As you think about sexism in language, you'll probably find it most helpful to emphasize two points: First, be aware of sexism, and strive to avoid it in your writing and speech. Second, remember that plural pronouns are usually an easy way to avoid sexism in your sentences, as shown here:

No students have their homework today. *Example*

Do all of you have your books? *Example*

Using Singular Pronouns

All of these pronouns are singular:

anyone	anything
someone	something
everyone	everything
no one	nothing
anybody	either
somebody	neither
everybody	each
nobody	every

In the following example, you can't use *their*, because *everybody* means one person:

Everyone who shops at The Bridal Boutique wants <u>her</u> wedding to be special. *Correct*

If you examine this sentence carefully, you'll find two clues to remind you to use *her* rather than *their*. First, the word *one* in *everyone* is singular. Second, the verb *is* reminds you that *everyone* refers to one person. You certainly wouldn't say "Everyone are ready."

Notice that *someone* and *anyone* also contain the word *one*. They, too, are singular.

To build confidence with using these singular pronouns, read these examples aloud several times:

Each boy thought <u>his</u> kite was better than the rest. *Correct*

All of the speakers had <u>their</u> speeches ready on time.
Correct

One of my aunts gave me a vase from <u>her</u> antique collection.
Correct

Exercise 7

INSTRUCTIONS: Underline the correct pronouns in the sentences.

1. All of the students are inviting (his, their) families to the ceremony.
2. Both doctors gave (her, their) opinions about the procedure.
3. Three executives gave (his, their) reports this morning.
4. Every daughter had a carnation for (her, their) father to wear to the banquet.
5. Nobody at the Boy Scout Jamboree refused to do (his, their) part to help out.
6. One of the campers entertained (his, their) tentmates with ghost stories.
7. Somebody in locker room left (her, their) running shoes under the bench.
8. One of the boxers is unsure about (his, their) condition for tonight's bout.
9. Each of the finalists said that (she, they) enjoyed participating in the Miss America Pageant.

Using I and You

It's both natural and correct to use the pronouns *I* and *you* in conversation and writing. If you study business letters and reports, you'll see both these pronouns often. You'll hear them often, too, in sermons, presidential speeches, and television editorials.

These pronouns are appropriate in many kinds of writing, but you must use them consistently. If you write a set of instructions telling a consumer how to file a complaint, use *he* or *she* or *you* throughout your instructions. Don't write a sentence like this one:

If a consumer has a problem, you should follow this procedure.
Incorrect

This sentence is *inconsistent* because it jumps from *a consumer* to *you*. Here's a better version of this sentence:

If you have a problem, you should follow this procedure.
Correct

The sentence could also be correct this way:

If a consumer has a problem, she should follow this procedure.
Correct

Here is another inconsistent sentence, followed by its correction:

I enjoyed working in the newspaper office. You could quickly make new friends there.   *Incorrect*

I enjoyed working in the newspaper office. I could quickly make new friends there.   *Correct*

Exercise 9

INSTRUCTIONS: Correct the pronoun errors in the sentences.
1. Before someone goes cave-diving, you should take a safety course.
2. I like to exercise in a swimming pool because you don't get hot and sticky.
3. My mother insisted that I learn how to swim because it's a skill that can save your life.
4. If you're a good swimmer, you might be interested in lifeguard training.
5. Synchronized swimmers have fun because you're swimming to music.
6. Before you dive into a lake, you should make sure the water is deep enough.
7. I took springboard-diving lessons so I could impress my friends.
8. The Red Cross uses part of its budget to promote water safety.

Exercise 10

INSTRUCTIONS: Write a paragraph about the changing roles of men and women in our society. You may choose one of three approaches:
1. Describe a change in gender roles you have observed.
2. Write a narrative about a person who has broken away from traditional roles.
3. Write a persuasive paragraph. You may argue for retaining some of the traditional distinctions between roles, or you may advocate change.

Reviewing What You Have Learned

Exercise 11

INSTRUCTIONS: Answer each question.

1. List five pronouns.
2. If you were using the "thumb" rule, which words in the following sentence would you cover up?

    Give Donald and (I, me) your answer tomorrow.

3. List five possessive pronouns.
4. Under what circumstances would you place an apostrophe in a possessive pronoun?
5. The word *it's* is a contraction of two short words. What are they?
6. How would you "finish the sentence" in the following example?

    Art gave me better advice than (she, her).

7. Explain the term *sexism in language*.
8. Write a sentence that contains sexist language. Then rewrite the sentence so that it could represent both males and females.

Exercise 12

INSTRUCTIONS: Underline the correct pronouns.

1. Gert reserved theater tickets for Harry and (I, me).
2. Gert is more efficient than (I, me).
3. But my reading speed is faster than (hers, her's).
4. (It's, Its) fortunate that Gert and (I, me) work together.
5. Our boss relies heavily on his computer and (we, us).
6. He admits that the computer has (it's, its) limitations.
7. Some employees fear that the computer will replace their friends and (they, them).

8. Those worries do not trouble my boss and (we, us).
9. Business need employees with skills like (ours, our's).
10. (It's, Its) clear that we have a bright future ahead.
11. All the officers agreed to commit (his, their) time to the project.
12. Both physicians presented (her, their) discoveries to the association.
13. Neither mother wanted (her, their) child to miss the school trip.
14. I like the college theater because it's small and (I, you) can sit close to the stage.
15. Students who miss classes should ask (their, your) professors about make-up work.

Unit Nineteen
Adjectives and Adverbs

SUMMARY

1. Adjectives and adverbs are descriptive words.

2. Adjectives describe nouns (persons, places, and things). They answer the question "What kind?"

3. Verbs can be changed to adjectives by adding *-ing*.

4. Adverbs describe verbs, adjectives, and adverbs. They answer the question "How?"

5. Adjectives and adverbs can be used to make comparative statements.

Adjectives and Adverbs 249

Adjectives and adverbs are descriptive words that can add interest to your writing. Adjectives are used with nouns—persons, places, and things. They describe nouns by answering the question "What kind?" In the following sentences, the adjectives are underlined. Can you identify the noun that each adjective describes?

> With a <u>sudden</u> snap, Alan shot the ball to Len. *Example*
>
> The <u>sleepy</u> kitten curled up in Anna's arms and fell asleep. *Example*
>
> Only a <u>sober</u> driver should take the wheel of a car. *Example*

Sudden describes *snap;* *sleepy* describes *kitten;* *sober* describes *driver.*
Adverbs describe verbs, adjectives, and other adverbs. Often, adverbs answer the question "How?" Many adverbs end in *-ly.* In the following sentences, the adverbs are underlined. Can you identify the words that these adverbs describe?

> Ben <u>suddenly</u> remembered a math assignment. *Example*
>
> Lucy finished the book and <u>sleepily</u> put it away. *Example*
>
> The Larsons <u>soberly</u> listened to the lawyer's warnings. *Example*

In the first sentence, *suddenly* tells how Ben *remembered.* In the second sentence, *sleepily* describes *put.* In the third sentence, *soberly* describes how the Larsons *listened.*

Adding Interest With Adjectives And Adverbs

Adjectives and adverbs can make your sentences interesting and memorable. Snow seems more real when you add the word *crunchy; sticky* might describe the fingers of a small child at a birthday party; a puppy's tail wags *joyfully* when his master comes home. These descriptive words fall into two categories. *Crunchy* and *sticky* are adjectives—words that describe *things* and answer the question "What kind?" *Joyfully* is an adverb because it describes how the dog's tail wags.

Think about adjectives and adverbs in the planning step of the writing process, as you prepare to write a paper. Quiet concentration can help you get in touch with the details that will bring your writing to life. How would you describe the bell that ended each of your classes in high school for example? Words such as *harsh, shrill,* and *clanging* can help you recall its sound.

Learning More About Adjectives

Listed here are three nouns followed by adjectives that could be used to describe them. Can you add any more adjectives to each list?

A kiss: tender, passionate, sultry, unexpected, lingering

A puppy: frisky, shy, playful, plump, gentle

A sundae: gooey, sweet, rich, cold, creamy

Exercise 1

INSTRUCTIONS: Write four descriptive words for each of the phrases. When you are finished, compare your list to a classmate's.

1. the student lounge
2. your room at home
3. your favorite food
4. a building you remember from childhood
5. a place you visited with a friend
6. a person you feel close to
7. a favorite piece of clothing
8. a song you like
9. a favorite possession
10. a special sound you remember

Exercise 2

INSTRUCTIONS: Choose one of the phrases in Exercise 1, and write four sentences about it. Try to make your sentences as vivid as you can.

Introducing -ing Adjectives

You've already seen that adjectives can add interest to your writing. A *smile* is quite ordinary, but a *sinister smile* sounds strange and mysterious. Because *sinister* describes *smile*—a thing—it's called an adjective.

Now you're ready to learn about another type of adjective—one that ends in *-ing*. Notice the *-ing* adjectives in these examples:

> The <u>grinning</u> nurse handed the baby to his <u>beaming</u> mother.
> *Example*

> The <u>glowing</u> colors of the portrait caught the critic's eye.
> *Example*

> Jeff held up the <u>winning</u> ticket for all to see.   *Example*

> Clare spent an hour on two <u>frustrating</u> math problems.
> *Example*

These adjectives developed from the verbs *grin, beam, glow, win,* and *frustrate.* Such adjectives always are placed next to the noun they describe: *grinning nurse, beaming mother, glowing picture, winning ticket, frustrating problems.*

Sometimes you must double a letter (*grin<u>n</u>ing, win<u>n</u>ing*) or drop a letter (*frustrating*) when you add *-ing* to a verb. Check a dictionary for the correct spelling of *-ing* words. Look up the verb, and then keep reading the dictionary entry.

Exercise 3

INSTRUCTIONS: Using the verbs in capital letters, insert *-ing* adjectives into the sentences. Use a dictionary to check the correct spelling.

1. The (wilt) flowers created a (depress) mood as the family waited for the doctor's report.

2. To save gasoline, I want to eliminate many of my (shop) trips.
3. Six of us met for a (plan) session yesterday.
4. When his (frown) father questioned him, the (tremble) boy admitted his mistake.
5. I want to improve my (save) habits so that I can buy a (flatter) new wardrobe.
6. (sing) waiters entertained us at the Italian restaurant.
7. The (set) sun amazed us with its brilliant colors.
8. (cheer) crowds greeted the (blush) beauty queen when she stepped off the plane.
9. The (dip) stock prices alarmed the investors.
10. You'll need to hurry to catch your (connect) flight.

Often, you can build a group of words around an -*ing* adjective. Compare these three sentences:

The boy walked away.   *Example*

The <u>shrugging</u> boy walked away.   -*ing adjective*

<u>Shrugging his shoulders</u>, the boy walked away.   -*ing word group*

Word groups using -*ing* can improve your writing in two ways. First, they add interesting information to your sentences. Second, they vary your sentence patterns. You can use an -*ing* word group to combine short, choppy sentences. Read the following sentence pairs aloud. Can you hear the improvement in the second sentence in each pair?

Heather drove to work. She heard a strange sound under the hood.   *Choppy*

Driving to work, Heather heard a strange sound under the hood.   *Better*

Notice that the verb *drove* was changed to an -*ing* form, *driving*. This change makes it possible to combine both sentences, as in the following examples:

Brandie telephoned her aunt. She dialed a wrong number.   *Choppy*

Adjectives and Adverbs

Telephoning her aunt, Brandie dialed a wrong number.   *Better*

Mark felt threatened. He ran from the fierce dog.   *Choppy*

Feeling threatened, Mark ran from the fierce dog.   *Better*

Read the following paragraphs to see how *-ing* word groups work. In the first version, several choppy sentences appear; the second paragraph is correct. Read both versions aloud, listening for the improvements in the second version:

Making Weekend Plans

No matter how carefully I plan, I can never please everybody with my weekend plans. I study all week and work part-time. I want to enjoy my weekends. But my mother and friends interfere with what I want to do. My mother expects me to work for her every Saturday. She spends all week struggling with the housework. She makes a pleasant home for all of us. I understand her feelings, and I wish I could help. But my girlfriend makes demands, too. She misses me during the week. She wants us to spend Saturday and Sunday together. I feel guilty saying no to her. Worst of all, my old friends drop in without warning. I try to get some rest on weekends. I often stay in bed on Sunday mornings. But they come to my house and wake me up. Although I love my mother and my friends, I wish I had more freedom on weekends.

Making Weekend Plans

No matter how carefully I plan, I can never please everybody with my weekend plans. Studying all week and working part-time, I want to enjoy my weekends. But my mother and friends interfere with what I want to do. My mother expects me to work for her every Saturday. Spending all week struggling with the housework, she makes a pleasant home for all of us. I understand her feelings, and I wish I could help. But my girlfriend makes demands, too. Missing me during the week, she wants us to spend Saturday and Sunday together. I feel guilty saying no to her. Worst of all, my old friends drop in without warning. Trying to get some rest on weekends, I often stay in bed on Sunday mornings. But they come to my house and wake me up. Although I love my mother and my friends, I wish I had more freedom on weekends.

Exercise 4

INSTRUCTIONS: Write a paragraph describing a conflict you face in your everyday life. When you revise your paragraph, include at least one *-ing* sentence in what you've written.

Exercise 5

INSTRUCTIONS: Use an *-ing* adjective to combine the following sentence pairs. Check a dictionary to make sure you spell each *-ing* adjective correctly.

1. Jody hoped to win the contest. She called the radio station.
2. Bert leaned on his shovel. He wiped the sweat from his face.
3. I ran for the bus. I stumbled and fell.
4. The Browns questioned the lawyer. They learned about the violation.
5. Scott began to speak. He defended the committee's decision.
6. Kyle forgot the rules. He touched the soccer ball with his hand.
7. We joked about our mistakes. We stopped worrying about them.
8. The storm rumbled in the distance. It approached our neighborhood.
9. The politician kissed three babies. He sought votes at the day-care center.
10. The new senator left her office. She faced a crowd of reporters.

Read the following sentence aloud. What's wrong with it?

I saw two shoestores walking down the street.   *Incorrect*

You probably realized immediately that shoestores can't walk down the street. (The misplaced *-ing* phrase is called a *dangling modifier*.) The sentence should be rewritten like this:

Walking down the street, I saw two shoestores.   *Correct*

When you revise your paragraphs, always make sure that *-ing* word groups are positioned correctly. Remember, an adjective word group must always be placed near the word it describes.

Here's another incorrect sentence. Rewrite it so that the *-ing* word group is positioned correctly:

Purring at her feet, Carla stroked the coal-black kitten.
Incorrect

Your corrected sentence should look like this:

Carla stroked the coal-black kitten purring at her feet.
Correct

Exercise 5

INSTRUCTIONS: Write **C** in front of each correct sentence. Rewrite each incorrect sentence so that the *-ing* word group is placed correctly.

_____ 1. Ringing the doorbell, Toni tried to remember everything she knew about selling Girl Scout cookies.

_____ 2. Crying helplessly, the young father comforted his little boy.

_____ 3. Sparkling in the early-morning sun, Cathy photographed the dew-covered flowers.

_____ 4. Throwing a curve ball, the pitcher retired the side.

_____ 5. Scattered around the playroom, Mrs. Smith picked up dozens of Lego toys.

_____ 6. Shouting instructions at the boys, Ted and Chris listened to their coach.

_____ 7. Excited about the sale, Donna skipped her last class.

_____ 8. Pecking at insects, the birdwatchers spotted the robin.

_____ 9. Scoring a goal, the crowd cheered the young hockey player.

_____ 10. Shining brightly in the sky, the moon illuminated the lake.

Learning More About Adverbs

Since adverbs describe verbs, adjectives, and adverbs, they may seem complicated at first. But in practice, adverb problems arise in only a few areas. First, some students confuse *good* (an adjective) with *well* (an adverb). Second, students occasionally misuse *real* (an adjective) and *really* (an adverb). Finally, students sometimes forget to add *-ly* (the adverb ending) where it is needed. This unit provides information for using them all correctly.

Good and *Well*

Because it's an adjective, *good* is used with persons, places, and things. You might have a *good* time at a *good* resort with *good friends*. Most students find it easy to use *good* correctly this way. But some uses of *good* are not quite so obvious. Read the following examples aloud:

> **The referee's call sounds good to me.**   *Correct*
>
> **The garlic bread in the oven smells good.**   *Correct*
>
> **Turquoise always looks good on you.**   *Correct*
>
> **I feel good about this report.**   *Correct*

People occasionally make the mistake of using *well* rather than *good* in sentences such as these. Remember that *good* is the correct word with these verbs: *sound, smell, taste, look, feel*. You may want to copy the example sentences above onto an index card to carry with you and study. Other verbs that use *good* (not *well*) are *seem, become,* and all forms of *be*.

When do you use *well*? The answer is that *well* is used with action verbs. You can sing, dance, study, and sleep *well*. All of these are true actions. Compare these two examples:

> **That homemade soup smells good.**   *Correct*
>
> **Philip cooks well.**   *Correct*

In the second example, Philip is performing a true action when he cooks. But the homemade soup in the first example can't literally *smell*. The sentence actually means that the soup *is* good.

Here are two more examples:

> **That red velvet dress looks *good* on you.**   *Corrrect*
>
> **Justine chose her college wardrobe *well*.**   *Correct*

In the second example, Justine performed a true action when she chose her college wardrobe. But a red velvet dress can't really *look*. The sentence actually means that the red velvet dress *is* good.

When a verb is a true action, use *well*. But with the special verbs mentioned above—look, sound, feel, seem, become, and *be*—use *good*.

Adjectives and Adverbs

One final note: sometimes the word *well* is an adjective meaning "healthy":

Jane was ill for two weeks, but she's well now. *Example*

Exercise 6

INSTRUCTIONS: Underline the correct word in these sentences.
1. Rick is a (good, well) fielder.
2. Rick fields his positions (good, well).
3. My Aunt Rita learned to cook (good, well) in Paris.
4. Aunt Rita is a (good, wel) cook.
5. My boss is a (good, well) woman.
6. She treats her employees (good, well).
7. If you like (good, well) movies, go to the drive-in soon.
8. That director did his job (good, well).
9. That suit looks (good, well) on you.
10. It fits you (good, well).

Exercise 7

INSTRUCTIONS: Underline the correct word in these sentences.
1. Jason studied his notes (good, well) and got a (good, well) grade on the test.
2. My father has a (good, well) ear for music.
3. He plays several instruments (good, well).
4. I did (good, well) in the target-shooting event.
5. I am a (good, well) shot.
6. That coach's team always does (good, well) on road trips.
7. The baseball team had a (good, well) season.
8. Your career plan sounds (good, well) to me.
9. You planned our holiday program (good, well).
10. Arlene seems (good, well) for the starring role.

Real and *Really*

Real means true. It is an adjective, and it should be used only when you describe something genuine: a real diamond, or real maple syrup, for example. *Really* is an adverb with two meanings: *truly* and *very* (both are adverbs themselves). When you use *real* or *really* in a sentence, ask yourself whether you mean *genuine* (real), *truly* (really), or *very* (really). Read the following examples aloud:

Daisy's aunt is a *real* countess.	Correct
I was *really* tired after the party.	Correct
Rachel's silk dress is *really* made of polyester.	Correct
Eric gave his wife a string of *real* pearls.	Correct

It's also helpful to *hear* how sentences are affected when these words are used incorrectly. If you substitute *real* for *really*, your sentences sound colloquial, not professional, as these examples illustrate:

Mario had a real good time at the party.	Incorrect
Mario had a <u>really</u> good time at the party.	Correct
Barney was real excited about the escaped convict.	Incorrect
Barney was <u>really</u> excited about the escaped convict.	Correct

Exercise 8

INSTRUCTIONS: Underline the correct word in these sentences. Remember that *real* means *genuine* and *really* means *truly* or *very*.

1. We were (real, really) fascinated when a professional writer visited our writing class.
2. He had been (real, really) successful as a science-fiction writer.
3. We learned that it takes (real, really) effort to break into publishing.
4. The results, however, are (real, really) worthwhile.
5. Writers need (real, really) mastery of the elements of English.
6. Planning and preparation are (real, really) important, too.

Adjectives and Adverbs 259

7. Science-fiction writers need (real, really) familiarity with scientific principles.

8. All professional writing demands (real, really) competence and in-depth knowledge.

9. Several students in our class have a (real, really) desire to be successful writers.

10. All of us want to be (real, really) prepared for the kinds of writing we'll be doing in our careers.

Adverbs Ending in -*ly*

It's important to add an -*ly* ending when you explain *how* something happens, as shown in these examples:

Harvey speaks German *fluently*.   **Correct**

I *quickly* grabbed my jacket and ran out the door.   **Correct**

Matt *swiftly* wrote the story and gave it to his editor.
Correct

Notice that *speaks, grabbed,* and *wrote* are verbs. When you tell *how*, you're describing a verb. The following exercises will help you master -*ly* adverbs.

Exercise 9

INSTRUCTIONS: After each verb, write five adverbs describing how each action could be done. (An example is provided for you.) Remember that most adverbs end in -*ly*. If you're not sure whether a word is an adverb, check the dictionary.

sang: beautifully, sadly, movingly, touchingly, loudly
Example

1. argued:
2. whispered:
3. played:
4. worked:
5. studied:

Exercise 10

INSTRUCTIONS: Choose one of the verbs from Exercise 9, and write three or four sentences using the adverbs that you've listed.

Adverbs with *Do, Does,* and *Did*

Go, make, and *work* are action verbs that must be used with *well* rather than *good.* The verbs *do, does,* and *did* are action verbs, too; and they also must be used with *well* rather than *good.* Take some time to practice using *well* with these verbs. Refer to these examples:

    I did good on my algebra quiz.   *Incorrect*

    I did <u>well</u> on my algebra quiz.   *Correct*

    Theo always does bad on biology tests.   *Incorrect*

    Theo always does <u>badly</u> on biology tests.   *Correct*

Exercise 11

INSTRUCTIONS: Underline the correct words. Remember that adjectives answer the question "What kind?" Adverbs with *-ly* answer the question "How?"

1. The comedian Jackie Gleason was known as the (Great, Greatly) One.
2. Gleason was a (superb, superbly) actor.
3. Eager to show off his new car, Doug (rapid, rapidly) drove away from the car dealership.
4. We stood on the pier and saw a (beautiful, beautifully) sunset.
5. I will do (good, well) if I stick to my schedule.
6. We managed to avoid a (bad, badly) accident.
7. Georges Simenon was a (masterful, masterfully) writer.
8. He wrote (brilliant, brilliantly).
9. The midwife (tender, tenderly) cradled the newborn baby.
10. Nancy's boss says that she is an (efficient, efficiently) worker.

Better, Best, Worse, Worst

These four words are often called *comparatives* because they are used in comparisons. Use *better* or *worse* when you compare two things; Use *best* or *worst* when you compare three or more things. Study the following examples:

Bob's taste in clothing is *better* than mine.   *Correct*

My sister Laura is the *best* shopper in my family.   *Correctly*

I always do *worse* on tests than Ben does.   *Correct*

In high school, my *worst* grade was in chemistry.   *Correct*

Because *worse* and *worst* sound so similar, you should take special care not to confuse them in comparisons. (This is also a good opportunity to remind yourself that *than*, not *then*, is a comparison word.)

Exercise 12

INSTRUCTIONS: Underline the correct words.

1. Giles is the (better, best) student in my calculus class.
2. Every year the parking problem here gets (worse, worst).
3. Sid knows where I can get the (better, best) deal on a car.
4. Plan A is the (worse, worst) of the two insurance programs.
5. Of the two finalists in the photography contest, I think Shane is (better, best).
6. Although cigarettes and sweets are both bad for your health, I think cigarettes are (worse, worst).
7. This is the (worse, worst) breakfast cereal I've ever eaten.
8. Our fencing team is having its (better, best) season ever.
9. Although I followed the doctor's instructions yesterday, I feel (worse, worst) today.
10. I think sports coverage has become (better, best) than it was before.

More, Most, -er, -est

You've already seen that *better, best, worse,* and *worst* are comparison words. Now you are ready to learn how all adjectives and adverbs can be used in comparisons.

Short adjectives and adverbs add *-er* or *-est* to the end—for example, *cuter, happier, faster, harder.* (Check the dictionary to verify the correct spelling when you add such endings.) Longer adjectives and all *-ly* adverbs don't add an ending. Instead, the word *more* or *most* is added in front, as these examples show: *most beautiful, most carefully researched, most gracefully, most cruelly.*

Remember to use *-er* or *more* when you compare two things, and use *-est* and *most* when you compare three or more things. Study these examples:

Toby is *cuter* than Tuffy. *Example*

Toby is our *cutest* kitten. *Example*

Ragtime composer Scott Joplin is *more popular* now than when he was alive. *Example*

"White Christmas" was Bing Crosby's *most popular* record. *Example*

Val is the *bigger* of the twins. *Example*

Bridget has the *most beautiful* voice I've ever heard. *Example*

Josh's paintings are *more beautiful* than Glenn's. *Example*

Warning: Never use *most* and *-est* with the same word. Notice that this example is incorrect:

Faye has the most loveliest house in our neighborhood.
Incorrect

Faye has the loveliest house in our neighborhood. *Correct*

Exercise 13

INSTRUCTIONS: Each sentence shows a word in capital letters. Insert the correct forms into each sentence. Use the dictionary to make sure your spelling is correct.

Adjectives and Adverbs

1. Roger works (hard) at his part-time job than I do.
2. Of all the people on our team, Cliff works (hard).
3. The Empire State Building used to be the (tall) building in the world.
4. Sherry dances (gracefully) than Greg does.
5. Cassie is (skillful) at the computer than I am.
6. I think Garfield and Snoopy are the (appealing) animals in the comics.
7. Watching a movie at home is (convenient) than going to a movie theater.
8. Although Gina and Lib did well in yesterday's race, Daisy ran (fast).
9. Tony's Sicilian pizzas are the (tasty) I've ever eaten.
10. Lottie shoots baskets (powerfully) than Jon does.

Reviewing What You Have Learned

Exercise 14

INSTRUCTIONS: Fill in the blanks.

1. Adjectives describe _____; adverbs describe _____, _____, and _____.
2. _____ answer the question "What kind?"
3. _____ answer the question "How?"
4. Adverbs often end in _____.
5. The word *good* is an _____.
6. the word *well* is an _____.
7. When you compare two things, use the ending _____ or the word _____.
8. When you compare three or more things, use the ending _____ or the word _____.
9. You can add *-ing* to a particular type of word to make an adjective. Name the type of word.
10. When you use an *-ing* word group in a sentence, you must check for two things. What are they?

Exercise 15

INSTRUCTIONS: Underline the correct words in the sentences.
1. Everyone in the band did (good, well) at the state competition.
2. Roy is the (better, best) of the two trumpet players.
3. That style looks (good, well) on you.
4. This year's Super Bowl will be the (most exciting, excitingest) game of the year.
5. The lawyer's explanation sounded (right, rightly) to me.
6. I feel (bad, badly) that Gene had to work the day of our class picnic.
7. A major-league baseball scout is (real, really) interested in signing Hal.
8. This candy is made with (real, really) walnuts and pecans.
9. I did (worse, worst) this semester than I expected.
10. I hope to do (good, well) next semester.

Exercise 16

INSTRUCTIONS: Underline the correct word in the sentences.
1. The swimming coach feels (good, well) about our team's performance this season.
2. At the statewide conference, Alan spoke (passionate, passionately) about the need for clean air and water.
3. I slept (sound, soundly) after my long trip.
4. That homemade bread smells (good, well).
5. My husband is (real, really) delighted with my academic progress.
6. Five-year-old Bonnie (sleepy, sleepily) asked for a glass of water.
7. Because she's the (smarter, smartest) of the four candidates, we chose Alicia to be president.
8. Of the two restaurants, Thoni's food is (tastier, tastiest).
9. Speech 105 is the (most difficult, difficultest) courses I've taken so far.
10. Doreen has (real, really) acting talent.

Unit Twenty
Apostrophes

SUMMARY

1. Apostrophes show that letters have been omitted in contractions such as *it's, can't,* and *shouldn't.*

2. Apostrophes sometimes signal ownership.

3. Apostrophes are placed either before or after the *s* at the end of the word.

An apostrophe is a small punctuation mark with two important uses. First, it signals the omission of letters in contractions such as *it's*, *can't*, and *shouldn't*. Second, the apostrophe signals ownership, as this sentence illustrates: Wendy's bicycle needs a new tire. The apostrophe means that Wendy owns a bicycle.

Using Apostrophes in Contractions

You probably hear and use contractions frequently. If you read the following sentence aloud, you'll notice that it sounds stiff and unnatural because it doesn't have contractions:

> **I am sharing an apartment because I cannot afford to pay the rent myself.**   *No contractions*

With the contractions *I'm* and *can't*, the sentence sounds more natural:

> *I'm* **sharing an apartment because I** *can't* **afford to pay the rent myself.**   *Contractions*

Contractions appear often in everyday conversation and informal writing. They're appropriate any time you want your writing to sound natural and conversational. (Many contractions appear in this textbook.) Contractions are *not* appropriate in more impersonal and formal writing—for example, in a research paper, an important speech, a business report, or a newspaper editorial. When you read, listen to the radio, and watch television, pay attention to when writers and speakers use contractions and when they do not.

Be careful to use apostrophes correctly when you write contractions. Apostrophes replace the missing letters in words. Here are a few examples:

aren't = are n̲o̲t̲   **we're** = we a̲r̲e̲

haven't = have n̲o̲t̲   **didn't** = did n̲o̲t̲

Apostrophes

Exercise 1

INSTRUCTIONS: Write contractions for the following phrases. If you're unsure about the correct placement of an apostrophe, check the dictionary.

1. would not _____
2. must not _____
3. it has _____
4. we had _____
5. they are _____
6. she had _____
7. cannot _____
8. does not _____
9. I am _____
10. we have _____

Exercise 2

INSTRUCTIONS: Write a sentence for each contraction in Exercise 1.

Using Apostrophes to Show Ownership

An apostrophe and an *s* usually are used together to show ownership, as shown here:

Amy's ring is an heirloom.   *Example*

Of course, Amy spells her name without the final *s*. In this example, the apostrophe and *s* work together to show ownership. Take a few moments to study the following examples:

>Miki's dream is to skate in the Olympics.   *Apostrophe*
>
>The dream of Miki is to skate in the Olympics.   *No apostrophe*
>
>Our team's defensive plays are weak.   *Apostrophe*
>
>The defensive plays of our team are weak.   *No apostrophe*
>
>My car's battery needs to be replaced.   *Apostrophe*
>
>The battery of my car needs to be replaced.   *No apostrophe*
>
>Doris's plans for next year didn't work out.   *Apostrophe*
>
>The plans of Doris for next year didn't work out.   *No apostrophe*

Each sentence can be written two ways—with an apostrophe or with *of*. If you use *of*, don't use an apostrophe.

Ownership can have several meanings. Usually we think of a person who owns an object—Amy's ring, for example. But ownership can have other meanings, too: a car's battery, Miki's dream, the team's defensive plays. You can speak of "the student's desk" even though the student doesn't legally own the desk; it's the student's, in a grammatical sense, as long as he or she is the one using it.

The apostrophe appears directly after the owner's name: *Miki's dream, Amy's bicycle.* It doesn't matter how many dreams Miki has, or how many bicycles Amy owns. The apostrophe is the same: *Miki's dreams, Amy's bicycles.* When you use an apostrophe to show ownership, the owner's name must be followed by the thing that is owned: *Amy's bicycle.* (Of course, you can add a description first—*Amy's blue bicycle.*) Take another look at this example:

>**Our team's defensive plays are weak.**   *Example*

The team "owns" its defensive plays, so the apostrophe is correct. When a word or name ends in *s*, add an apostrophe after the *s*. Then add a final *s*: *Doris's plans.* Notice that you can *hear* the extra *s* when you say the word or name aloud.

Exercise 3

INSTRUCTIONS: Some of the sentences below need apostrophes; others do not. Write *yes* if the sentence needs an apostrophe and *no* if the sentence does not.

_____ 1. Our cheerleaders routines may win an award this year.
_____ 2. Rhodas engagement ring is dazzling.
_____ 3. I bowled three games last night.
_____ 4. I think we should invite the Suttons to dinner next Saturday.
_____ 5. Did you get Sylvias message?
_____ 6. All the supervisors are meeting at three this afternoon.
_____ 7. A girls best friend is her mother.
_____ 8. College classes should be scheduled at the convenience of the students.
_____ 9. The princess marital difficulties were front-page news.
_____ 10. Young people need heroes to inspire them.

Placing Apostrophes Correctly

To place apostrophes correctly, look for the *last letter* of the owner's name (or the ownership word). It's helpful to make an *of* phrase out of the sentence, as shown here:

Marys running shoes are Nikes.   *Example*
(The running shoes of Mary are Nikes.)

Put the apostrophe after the last letter of *Mary*, and add an *s*:

Mary's running shoes are Nikes.   *Correct*

Here's another example:

Mr. Lewis career has been exceptional.   *Example*
(The career of Mr. Lewis has been exceptional.)

Put the apostrophe after the last letter of *Lewis*, and add another *s*:

Mr. Lewis's career has been exceptional.   *Correct*

Remember, don't use an apostrophe with *of*. Making an *of* phrase is a good way to find the last letter of the owner's name.

Exercise 4

INSTRUCTIONS: Here are the sentences from Exercise 3. Place apostrophes where they are needed. *Of* phrases are provided to guide you.

1. Our cheerleaders routines may win an award this year. (routines of our cheerleaders)
2. Rhodas engagement ring is dazzling. (engagement ring of Rhoda)
3. I bowled three games last night. (no *of* phrase)
4. I think we should invite the Suttons to dinner next Saturday. (no *of* phrase)
5. Did you get Sylvia's message? (message of Sylvia)
6. All of the supervisors are meeting at three this afternoon. (no *of* phrase)
7. A girls best friend is her mother. (best friend of a girl)
8. College classes should be scheduled at the convenience of the students. (no *of* phrase)
9. The princess marital difficulties were front-page news. (marital difficulties of the princess)
10. Young people need heroes to inspire them. (no *of* phrase)

Exercise 5

INSTRUCTIONS: Place apostrophes where they are needed. *Of* phrases are provided to guide you.

1. I always enjoy Lees parties. (parties of Lee)
2. Our government should listen to the peoples wishes. (wishes of the people)
3. If Dellas plans work out, she'll be spending the summer in Paris. (plans of Della)
4. My boss wit makes my job bearable. (wit of my boss)
5. Doris thirst for learning amazes me. (thirst of Doris)
6. The librarys hours may be expanded next semester. (hours of the library)
7. Dennis pranks exasperated his neighbors, the Wilsons. (pranks of Dennis)
8. Randys report is almost finished. (report of Randy)
9. Kristys tennis game has improved remarkably. (tennis game of Kristy)
10. My mothers knack for silly puns amuses all of our friends. (knack of my mother)

Apostrophes

Now you've learned a two-step procedure for placing apostrophes correctly. First, use the owner's name (or ownership word) in an *of* phrase. Then use the *of* phrase to find the last letter of the name, and place the apostrophe after it.

You can always place apostrophes correctly if you know how to spell the ownership word correctly. Sometimes you'll need to check the dictionary, of course. Right now, spend a few moments examining these singular and plural nouns. What observations can you make about them?

one girl   one woman
several girls   two women
one boss   one puppy
many bosses   five puppies

Notice that the plurals of English words vary. When you talk about more than one girl, you just add an *s*. But puppy changes to *-ies* in the plural, and woman changes to *women*—there's no *s* at all.

Many plural forms are already familiar to you. You probably say *bosses* quite naturally, without even thinking about it. (The last letter, of course, is the final *s*.) Some plural forms cause difficulty, however. For example, some people incorrectly say *womens* instead of the correct form, *women*.

The procedure for using apostrophes with plural nouns is the same one you've already learned: Find the ownership word, make it an *of* phrase, and place the apostrophe after the last letter. Add an *s* only if it is needed, as in *women's*. Try the following examples yourself. Make an *of* phrase, place the apostrophe, and then look at the correct answers that follow:

The libraries budgets throughout the city may be cut.
Example

The puppies will need their first shots soon.   *Example*

When womens shoes go on sale, I always buy several pairs.
Example

My new boss background is extremely impressive.   *Example*

The puppys ball rolled under the picnic table.   *Example*

Both classes scores were unusually high.   *Example*

Answers

The libraries' budgets throughout the city may be cut.
(budgets of the libraries)

The puppies will need their first shots soon. *(no of phrase, and no apostrophe)*

When women's shoes go on sale, I always buy several pairs.
(shoes of women)

My new boss's background is extremely impressive.
(background of my new boss)

The puppy's ball rolled under the picnic table. *(ball of the puppy)*

Both classes' scores were unusually high. *(scores of both classes)*

Notice that *s* is used with *men, women,* and *children* only when these words indicate ownership: *men's shoes, women's sizes,* and *children's illnesses.*

Another plural noun to remember is *people*; its ownership form looks like this:

The *people's* arguments did not influence the governor.
Example

Study tip: Write these words on an index card and study it several times a day.

Exercise 6

INSTRUCTIONS: Write an *of* phrase for each sentence. Then place apostrophes where they are needed.

1. My superintendents moods make my life miserable.
2. The mens cars are parked illegally.
3. Both babies temperatures are normal.
4. When a new product fails to meet peoples expectations, the manufacturer can lose millions of dollars.

Apostrophes 273

5. The candidate did not dare to disagree with his partys philosophy.
6. Ralph always enjoys taking part in his stepchildrens games.
7. Contest entries will be disqualified if they are submitted after the deadline.
8. Many laws changed when Americans started becoming sensitive to womens issues.
9. The cities problems were studied by a special task force in the legislature.
10. The cities problems are caused by poor planning and inadequate financing.

Using Apostrophes in *Of* Expressions

Ownership includes any *of* relationship. Study the following examples:

a week's delay   (delay of a week)

two years' salary   (salary of two years)

Nassau County's leaders   (leaders of Nassau County)

the table's surface   (surface of the table)

The procedure for placing these apostrophes is the same as the one you've already learned. First, make an *of* phrase; second, look for the last letter, and place your apostrophe after it.

Exercise 7

INSTRUCTIONS: Place apostrophes where they are needed.

1. After a moments hesitation, I stammered out the answer. (hesitation of _____)
2. Two weeks vacation is never enough for me. (vacation of _____)
3. That medicines side effects can be serious. (side effects of _____)
4. An instants delay caused the whole squad to lose their lives. (delay of _____)
5. That trucks road taxes total over $5,000 annually. (road taxes of _____)

Exercise 8

INSTRUCTIONS: Place apostrophes where they are needed.

1. You have one days sick leave remaining.
2. Five years experience is required for this position.
3. My toddler never gives me a minutes peace.
4. The years close brought with it many tearful partings.
5. The policys errors caused endless confusion.

Using Apostrophes With Family Names

Apostrophes used with family names follow the same principles you've already learned. Study these examples:

The Wilsons sold their house and bought a condominium.
Correct (no *of* phrase—no apostrophe)

The Wilsons' house sold quickly because of its location.
Correct (house of the Wilsons)

Mr. Santos's contract expires in March. *Correct* (contract of Mr. Santos)

The Cohens sent us a postcard from Las Vegas. *Correct* (no *of* phrase—no apostrophe)

Use an apostrophe only when the name shows ownership, as in *Mr. Santos's contract*. Remember, too, that the thing owned must follow the name immediately. Can you see why there's no apostrophe in this example?

The Simpsons bought a restaurant downtown. *Correct*

The Simpsons is a plural form, not an expression of ownership. Don't use an apostrophe in such a sentence.

One common mistake is using an apostrophe to mean more than one family member. Can you find the error in this sentence?

The Reynolds' lent us their snowblower last Sunday morning.
Incorrect

Here's the correct version:

The Reynoldses lent us their snowblower Sunday morning.
Correct

Since the name Reynolds ends in *s*, add *es* to form the plural. Read the sentence aloud a few times so that you can hear the extra syllable. (Instead of adding *es*, you can just write "The Reynolds family" or "Mr. and Mrs. Reynolds.") No apostrophe is used because no *of* relationship is implied.

Add *es* in the same way to form the plural of names that end in *z*. The name Martinez, for example, becomes "The Martinezes."

Family names are important in our everyday lives, so you need to familiarize yourself with these forms. (Wouldn't it be embarrassing to discover that you've signed your holiday greetings cards incorrectly for the last five years?) The following exercise will help you sharpen your skills.

Exercise 9

INSTRUCTIONS: Place apostrophes where they are needed.

1. The Carters ice-cream store is a popular spot.
2. When the Tylers finished restoring the big house on the corner, the whole neighborhood celebrated.
3. Dr. Simpsons compassion is famous in our community.
4. I found a bouquet of roses on my porch at lunchtime; the card was signed simply "The Smiths."
5. Betty Levins French poodle is a playful little rascal.
6. Sometimes the Willises take me shopping with them.
7. When I had my broken leg, Gina Ellis did all my grocery shopping.
8. Dr. Nelsons enthusiasm for baseball was a big surprise to me.
9. The Blacks two children are both in the Air Force.
10. Should we have "The Johnsons" or "The Johnson Family" imprinted on our holiday greeting cards?

Exercise 10

INSTRUCTIONS: Place apostrophes where they are needed.
1. When the actress's scripts arrived, we rehearsed the play.
2. Professor Morris's classes always fill up quickly.
3. Did you hear that the bakery's employees are on strike?
4. Two days' work was lost when the computer malfunctioned.
5. The boss's complaints eventually led to far-reaching changes in our company.
6. A business's profits can take a sudden drop with no warning.
7. I've known the Thompsons since 1974.
8. Last month's bills weren't sent out until yesterday.
9. A special commission is examining the county's expenditures.
10. I stayed at the Fowlers' party until three in the morning.

Reviewing What You Have Learned

Exercise 11

INSTRUCTIONS: Answer the following questions:
1. Write an *of* phrase for each of the following sentences. Then place apostrophes where they are needed.
    a. Our softball team's record is the best in the league.
    b. Women's fashions are displayed upstairs.
2. Place an apostrophe into the following sentences:
    a. The men's group meets for breakfast every Tuesday.
    b. Women's sports are beginning to receive more funding from colleges.
    c. Children's quarrels can get out of hand very quickly.

Apostrophes

3. True or false:
   _____ a. Always use an apostrophe when you sign your family's name on a holiday greeting card.
   _____ b. When you're placing apostrophes, ownership can refer to any *of* relationship.
4. Fill in the blanks:
   a. In an *of* phrase, look for the _____ of the owner's name.
   b. Family names that end in *s*, like *Morris*, add _____ to form the plural.
5. Form contractions for these words and phrases: could not, cannot, I am, you are, does not.

Exercise 12

INSTRUCTIONS: Add apostrophes where they are needed.
1. She always holds her childrens birthday parties at a skating rink.
2. The womens superior attitude infuriated me.
3. Both patients questions were difficult to answer.
4. The dictionaries prices were too steep for my budget.
5. This buildings exits are clearly marked.
6. The employees lounge opens at 7:30 in the morning.
7. My neighbor couldn't wait until her grandchildrens visit ended.
8. The actresses told our drama club about the difficult times early in their careers.
9. Parents never forget the thrill of watching a babys first step.
10. The puppies yelping kept me up all night.

Exercise 13

INSTRUCTIONS: Plan and write a paragraph about an object you've always wanted to own. In the editing step, make sure all your apostrophes are placed correctly.

Unit Twenty-One
Words Often Confused

SUMMARY

1. Many English words and phrases sound alike but have different meanings. They are called *homonyms*.

2. The English language also includes words that are similar but are used differently. Examples include *among* and *between*, *less* and *fewer*, and several others.

3. The *a/an* pair requires special attention.

Words Often Confused

Many English words sound alike but have different meanings and spellings. For example, *there, their,* and *they're* sound alike; so do *too, two,* and *to.* These words are called *homonyms,* and you must use them carefully in writing.

To sharpen your skills, it's a good idea to keep a list of words that create special problems for you in your notebook for further study. You should also resolve to check this textbook or a dictionary any time you feel doubtful about one of these words.

Set 1

WORD	MEANING
accept	receive (a verb)
except	other than (a preposition)

I've never had the chance to accept an award. *Example*

The car was in good shape except for its seat covers. *Example*

all ready	prepared (an adjective phrase)
already	by this time (an adverb)

The tent was pitched, and they were all ready to hike. *Example*

Although it was only eight, I had already prepared for bed. *Example*

advice	recommendation (a noun)
advise	to give counsel (a verb)

Since advice is free, people are always willing to give it. *Example*

Ward Cleaver often had to advise Wally and the Beaver. *Example*

Note that these words are pronounced differently. Listen for the *ice* in *advice.*

WORD	MEANING
affect	influence (a verb)
effect	result (a noun)

    Damp weather can affect people with arthritis. *Example*

    Slow, dreary music creates a spooky effect. *Example*

Effect can be a verb, too, although students rarely use it this way. It's wise to double-check a dictionary when you use either of these words.

among	in or through the midst of (a preposition)
between	in the interval separating (a preposition)

    We had only five dollars among the three of us. *Example*

    The house sits between two enormous oak trees. *Example*

brake	stop (a verb)
break	shatter (a verb)

    Get ready to brake the car; there are many children on this block. *Example*

    Don't drop the vase because it could break. *Example*

does	form of *do* used with singular subject (a verb)
dose	a measured amount of medicine (a noun)

    My dad does not drink, smoke, or gamble. *Example*

    Be certain to take the prescribed dose tonight. *Example*

Exercise 1

INSTRUCTIONS: Underline the correct words in the sentences.

1. The mechanic checked my car and said it was (all ready, already) to go.
2. I told her not to bother because I had (all ready, already) cleaned that room.
3. We got up early, but it was (all ready, already) evening when we reached the farm.

Words Often Confused

4. During rainy weather you should (break, brake) motor vehicles gently.
5. It seems that every summer someone is going to (break, brake) my heart.
6. Tracy agreed to (accept, except) full responsibility for the program.
7. During spring (break, brake), everyone (accept, except) Shawn is going to the beach.
8. I tried to (advice, advise) her, but she ignored me completely.
9. I always feel lost (between, among) the baseball and hockey seasons.
10. Hormones have been discovered that (affect, effect) the growth of plants.
11. What (effect, affect) will the policy have on the stock market?
12. We divided the work (between, among) the four of us.
13. Who (does, dose) your hair?
14. A (does, dose) of this medicine should soothe your throat quickly.
15. Everything is ready for the picnic (accept, except) the potato salad.
16. Please (accept, except) my apology.

Exercise 2

INSTRUCTIONS: Write a sentence for each of the words in Set 1. When you're finished, compare your sentences with another student's, and make any corrections that are necessary.

Set 2

WORD	MEANING
clothes	garments (a noun)
cloths	pieces of fabric (a noun)

I have lots of nice clothes, but nothing fits me.   *Example*

I made several dusting cloths from an old beach towel.
    Example

WORD	MEANING
desert	bare, sandy land (a noun); to abandon (a verb)
dessert	sweet dish served after lunch or dinner (a noun)

Animals have evolved in amazing ways to survive in the desert. *Example*

The nervous recruit decided to desert his unit. *Example*

Strawberrry shortcake is my favorite dessert. *Example*

You may find it helpful to think of two lumps of sugar with your dessert and coffee—one *s* for each lump.

fewer	a smaller number (an adjective)
less	a smaller amount (an adjective)

They have fewer chairs than we do. *Example*

They have less furniture than we do. *Example*

hear	to listen (a verb)
here	at this place (an adverb)

Did you hear the news? *Example*

I left my books here. *Example*

it's	contraction of *it is* or *it has* (a verb)
its	belonging to it (a pronoun)

It's a shame there are so many unwanted dogs and cats. *Example*

Since the swim team lost its star, nobody has won a trophy. *Example*

loose	roomy (an adjective, rhymes with *moose*)
lose	to misplace (a verb, rhymes with *fuse*)

Because I dieted successfully, all my clothes are loose. *Example*

These are important papers that I don't want to lose. *Example*

WORD	MEANING
passed	went by (a verb)
past	the time before now (a noun)

We passed several enormous trucks on the highway.
Example

In the past, there were few famous women athletes.
Example

Exercise 3

INSTRUCTIONS: Underline the correct words in the sentences.

1. (Here, hear) are the (clothes, cloths) you ordered for our vacation.
2. During the winter, we see (less, fewer) birds around here.
3. My sister wants to (loose, lose) twenty pounds before summer begins.
4. We shouldn't expect our (passed, past) successes to be repeated in the future.
5. Greg (passed, past) the ball in a surprise play that stunned the other team.
6. The department hasn't met (its, it's) quota this month.
7. This (dessert, desert) has (less, fewer) sugar than most.
8. I made a resolution not to (loose, lose) my temper so easily.
9. Did you (hear, here) about the championship game?
10. The (desert, dessert) often gets surprisingly cold at night.
11. Sometimes (its, it's) difficult to make the right decision.
12. The (cloths, clothes) I sew with are in that cabinet.
13. (Here, Hear) are the catalogs you wanted.

Exercise 4

INSTRUCTIONS: Write a sentence for each of the words in Set 2. When you're finished, compare your sentences with another student's, and make any corrections that are necessary.

Set 3

WORD	MEANING
peace	harmony (a noun)
piece	fragment (a noun)

    I wonder if we will ever see the world at peace. *Example*

    The county bought a piece of property from us. *Example*

principal	person running a school (a noun); borrowed money (a noun); most important (an adjective)
principle	law or rule (a noun)

    We're paying both the principal and the interest on our loan.
       Example

    Ms. Fogarty is the principal of our high school. *Example*

    His principal problem is tardiness. *Example*

    My guiding principle is fairness. *Example*

quiet	silent (an adjective)
quite	very (an adverb)

    I was worried about babysitting, but they were quite charming children. *Example*

    You have to be quiet in the library. *Example*

than	in comparison with (a preposition)
then	at that time (an adverb); as a consequence (an adverb)

    This wallpaper is lighter than the kind we have now.
       Example

    If you enjoy classical music, then you'll like this concert.
       Example

Words Often Confused

WORD	MEANING
their	belonging to them (a pronoun)
there	in that place (an adverb)
they're	contraction of *they are* (a verb)

I don't think their motive is an honorable one.   *Example*

Right there is where the accident happened.   *Example*

Because they were late again, they're quarreling.   *Example*

though	(in spite of the fact that (a conjunction)
thought	an idea (a noun); past tense of *think* (a verb)

Though it was difficult, I went to school and worked part-time.   *Example*

I thought we would have snow today.   *Example*

Exercise 5

INSTRUCTIONS: Underline the correct words in the sentences.

1. (Their, There, They're) claiming that (their, there, they're) camera was stolen.
2. My high-school (principal, principle) was a person of (principal, principle).
3. (Their, there, they're) isn't much more that can go wrong with my old car.
4. I find it (quite, quiet) pleasant to spend a (quite, quiet) evening with friends.
5. The roads are still icy (though, thought) the temperature is starting to rise.
6. (Though, Thought) he has a newer car, his payments are lower (than, then) ours.
7. Have a (piece, peace) of this apple-raisin cake.
8. The pathway to (piece, peace) starts with each individual.
9. If (their, there, they're) are no questions, we can proceed to the next unit.
10. The (principal, principle) of unselfishness should be learned early in life.

Exercise 6

INSTRUCTIONS: Write a sentence for each of the words in Set 3. When you're finished, compare your sentences with another student's, and make any corrections that are necessary.

Set 4

WORD	MEANING
to	in a direction toward; for the purpose of (an adverb)
too	excessive; also (an adverb)
two	the number 2 (a noun, an adjective, a pronoun)

I want to see that movie again. *Example*

The prices are too high here. *Example*

Shirley will be joining us, too. *Example*

I paid only two dollars for this book. *Example*

your	belonging to you (a pronoun)
you're	contraction of *you are* (a verb)

Does your roof still leak? *Example*

If you're on time, they'll certainly take you along. *Example*

weather	atmospheric conditions (a noun)
whether	if (a conjunction)

The weather report is right only half the time. *Example*

I wonder whether Sumi will enjoy her visit here. *Example*

were	past tense of *are* (a verb)
we're	contraction of *we are* (a verb)

The Cartwrights were in London for the royal wedding.
Example

If we're late, everyone will stare at us. *Example*

Words Often Confused

WORD	MEANING
whose	belonging to whom (a pronoun)
who's	contraction of who is (a verb)

Whose jacket is that? *Example*

Who's going to volunteer? *Example*

Exercise 7

INSTRUCTIONS: Underline the correct word in the sentences.
1. (Weather, Whether) satellites are useful to forecasters.
2. A rooster (who's whose) flock is under attack may become aggressive.
3. Of course it matters (weather, whether) we get red or green.
4. When (we're, were) on vacation, time goes quickly.
5. Which appliances (we're, were) on sale last week?
6. When (your, you're) ready, let me know.
7. Is that (your, you're) Corvette in the driveway?
8. Lyle's book report is ready (too, too, two) be typed.
9. The reservations are finished, and I picked up the tickets, (to, too, two).
10. This carton is (to, too, two) big for the trunk of my car.

Exercise 8

INSTRUCTIONS: Write a sentence for each of the words in Set 4. When you're finished, compare your sentences with another student's, and make any corrections that are necessary.

Introducing a Special Pair: A and An

A and *an* often are used incorrectly in speech and writing. *A* is used with words that begin with consonant sounds, such as *a baby, a horse, a carton of milk*. *An* is used with words that begin with vowel sounds, such as *an apple, an elbow, an earring*.

When you write, remember that spelling and pronunciation don't always match. For example, *hour* sounds like *our*—it has no *h* sound. Therefore, you would write, "We went for *an* outing" and "We were gone for *an* hour." Reading your work aloud will help you use *a* and *an* correctly. Trust your ear, not your eye, to use *a* and *an* correctly with phrases such as the following: a European vacation, a one-sided argument, a unicorn, a united front, a ukulele, a useful tool, an hour, an herb.

Mastering Additional Words and Expressions

a lot	*Never* write *a lot* as one word.
all right	*Never* write *all right* as one word.
being that	Use *because* instead.
can't hardly	Use *can't* or *hardly* by themselves, never together.
hisself, theirself	Use *himself* and *themselves* instead.
I'm	Always omit the *a* in *am* in this contraction.
used to, supposed to	Always add the *d* at the end. Don't write *use to* or *suppose to*.

Exercise 9

INSTRUCTIONS: Underline the correct words in the sentences.

1. If they (accept, except) my offer, I may make (alot, a lot) of money.
2. I (past, passed) all my courses (accept, except) biology.
3. (It's, Its) best to get (advice, advise) from someone with experience.
4. Because (it's, its) peak is covered with snow, that mountain is hard (to, too, two) climb.
5. We (use, used) to live in New York when my sisters and I (we're, were) small.
6. (It's, Its) very (lose, loose); I haven't tied it down yet.
7. My dream is to take (a, an) European vacation after I graduate.

Words Often Confused

8. After (a, an) hour, I was ready for (a, an) break.

9. (Were, We're) always (quite, quiet) content to spend New Year's Eve at home with a few friends.

10. Someone (who's, whose) cruel to animals is often cruel (to, too) people

Reviewing What You Have Learned

Exercise 10

INSTRUCTIONS: Correct the mistakes in words and expressions.
1. When I'am concentrating hard, I can't hear a thing.
2. Lester couldn't hardly here a word I said.
3. Were suppose to meet Liz at three-thirty.
4. If you have alot of work left to do, call us.
5. So far, were doing alright in our Spanish course.
6. Being that Harry built up that business by hisself, I have to give him credit for his accomplishment.
7. Sailors have many sayings about the whether.
8. The cat was nervous because one of its' kittens was missing.
9. Last night I read my children a story about a princess and an unicorn.
10. My mother always makes a apple pie and a pumpkin pie for Thanksgiving.

Exercise 11

INSTRUCTIONS: Underline the correct words in the sentences.
1. My boss gives us (less, fewer) raises (than, then) yours does.
2. The love letters were hidden (between, among) piles of old-fashioned (clothes, cloths).
3. Stanley (who's, whose) a carpenter, built a beautiful home for his family.
4. Rosalie (does, dose) beautiful portraits in oils and watercolors.

5. Our committee has (a, an) idea for rescheduling popular classes.
6. I'd order (dessert, desert), but the prices (here, hear) are (to, too, two) high.
7. Charlene and Denise made those decorations all by (theirself, themselves).
8. This (past, passed) year, Archie (past, passed) all his courses.
9. I've paid off most of the (principal, principle) on my student loan.
10. (I'm, I'am) happier now (than, then) when I was in high school.

Exercise 12

INSTRUCTIONS: Write a story—funny, exciting, or serious—using as many of the words in this unit as you can. In the editing step, check each word carefully to make sure you used it correctly.

Unit 22
Capital Letters

SUMMARY

1. A capital letter marks the first word in a sentence and the words in a title.

2. Names of persons and the word *I* are always capitalized.

3. Capital letters are used for places on a map and places named in signs.

4. The days of the week, holidays, and months are capitalized; seasons are not.

5. Brand names are capitalized.

6. Capital letters are used for clubs, organizations, nationalities, countries, religions, and languages.

Most capitalization rules are straightforward and simple. Capitalize the names of people and the word *I*. Also capitalize the days of the week, months of the year, and holidays. (Don't capitalize seasons.) Names of countries, religions, and languages are always capitalized.

To evaluate your own understanding of these basic rules, try the following exercise.

Exercise 1

INSTRUCTIONS: Use capital letters where necessary in these sentences.

1. every tuesday, tarsha and I have lunch together.
2. tran nguyen began learning english in vietnam.
3. my friend holly was born the day after christmas.
4. for muslims, ramadan is a holy month.
5. my french professor spent july and august in belgium.
6. johnny carson started his career as a magician.
7. i worked all summer to save the money for tuition.

Capitalizing the Names of People

It's easy to capitalize most names: Dan Rather, Rosa Parks, Stevie Wonder, and so on. The same principle applies to names with titles—for example, Mother Teresa, Grandma Moses, and Dr. Spock. Capitalize any word that is used as a person's name, but don't capitalize a title preceded by a possessive pronoun (*my, our, your, his, her, their*). Study these examples:

My <u>grandpa</u> landed at Normandy on D-Day.   *(No capital letter)*

Last Sunday I went fishing with <u>Grandpa</u>.   *(Capitalized)*

Your <u>doctor</u> can help you quit smoking.   *(No capital letter)*

If <u>Dr.</u> Morris is here, I'd like to see her.   *(Capitalized name)*

Let's ask <u>Brother</u> Thomas to lead us in prayer.   *(No capital letter)*

My <u>brother</u> is a news anchor in Bridgeport.   *(Capitalized name)*

Capitalizing Place Names

You'll find it helpful to think of a map when you're capitalizing place names. Any location, region, site, or natural formation that appears on a map should be capitalized—for example, Texas, Sea World, London, Mt. McKinley, Route 66, Canada. But don't capitalize general locations, such as *uptown, nation, community, neighborhood*.

Thinking of signs can be useful when you're capitalizing. You've seen many signs that say, for example, *Springdale, Central High School, Holiday Inn, Carl's Market, Westview Church of God.* These all use capital letters. But don't use capital letters for general places—*town, high school, inn, market, church*, and the like—unless they're part of a specific place or building.

Watch out for these words: *north, south, east, west.* They are capitalized when they indicate specific locations: West Virginia, East Orange, South Dakota. The word *the* often indicates a specific geographic area that should be capitalized. If you travel to *the West*, for example, you might visit California, Colorado, or Oregon. A trip to *the South* might take you to Miami, Atlanta, or Baton Rouge. But don't use capital letters to indicate direction. If you're driving to a city forty miles west of your town, for example, use a lower-case letter for *west*.

Exercise 2

INSTRUCTIONS: Insert capital letters where they are needed.

1. last summer we had a family reunion out west, in the town where my mother grew up.
2. relatives came from every part of the united states, including the south and new england.
3. my favorite relative, uncle albert, even flew in from europe.

4. the reunion began on friday evening.
5. we gathered in the local high school cafeteria for a buffet and family talent show.
6. when aunt clare and uncle donald did a comedy duet, everyone roared with laughter.
7. most people spent the night at the sheraton hotel on the north side of town.
8. early saturday morning we gathered for a picnic at lions park.
9. we all had fun looking at the old photo albums that grandma had brought with her.
10. everyone was amused at the T-shirts that my cousin stan had designed for us.

Exercise 3

INSTRUCTIONS: Insert capital letters where they are needed.
1. my favorite teacher at cardinal hayes high school was sister mary paul.
2. our family doctor took her children to busch gardens.
3. this nation's leaders must consider the impact their decisions may have on tomorrow's world.
4. lester was captain of the baseball team last year.
5. for several years, captain fowler headed a research project.
6. was your grandfather born in scandinavia?
7. ask grandmother if she wants to celebrate her birthday on saturday.
8. did i tell you that uncle john had been a prisoner of war?
9. my sister is a speech therapist.
10. tracy elementary school has a national reputation for excellence.

Capitalizing the Names of Groups

Always capitalize the names of specific clubs, associations, and organizations. (A good rule is to ask yourself if the name could be printed on stationery.) Religious, national, and ethnic groups also should be capitalized. Study these examples:

Capital Letters

    Abe belongs to the Business Leaders of America.   *Example*

    Abe belongs to a club that meets on Tuesdays.   *Example*

    Delonda is interested in Chinese cooking.   *Example*

    Shawn likes to experiment with foreign foods.   *Example*

    My mother appreciates her senior citizen discounts. *Example*

    Next week the Senior Citizens Activities Board will hold their monthly meeting.   *Example*

    Anna is proud of her Hispanic heritage.   *Example*

Exercise 4

INSTRUCTIONS: Insert capital letters where they are needed.

1. my father has made many lasting friendships thorugh the rotary club in town.
2. our veterinarian, dr. hightower, once served as a capitain in the air force.
3. captain trask of the salvation army is concerned about homelessness in this area.
4. i was a campfire girl for five years; both my brothers were scouts.
5. that italian restaurant serves the best pizza.
6. queen makeda of sheba was a famous african ruler more than two thousand years ago.
7. students of african-american literature should be familiar with ralph ellison's writings.
8. my english professor spent a summer studying the folklore of the seminole indians.
9. after lenore's trip to the east, she began to read books about buddhism and hinduism.
10. the mexican foods served at taco bell are very different from the dishes i ate in mexico last year.

Capitalizing Titles and Brand Names

Do you know the difference between *facial tissue* and *Kleenex*, *cola* and *Coke*? Manufacturers usually capitalize their brand names to distinguish them from similar products.

In titles, capitalize the first and last word and every important word in between. Don't capitalize prepositions or the words *a*, *and*, or *the*, except if they fall at the beginning of a title. Course titles in a school catalog should be capitalized. Otherwise, don't capitalize school subjects and majors, except for languages. Remember that English is always capitalized. Study these examples:

> **We had Rice Krispies for breakfast.** *Example*
>
> **My mother sometimes cooks with crisped rice cereal.** *Example*
>
> **Clara is taking Home Economics 101.** *Example*
>
> **Next semester I may take a home economics course.** *Example*
>
> **Do you plan to take technical writing or English literature?** *Example*
>
> **Only a gifted clarinetist can play** *Rhapsody in Blue.* *Example*
>
> **Grieg's** *In the Hall of the Mountain King* **is one of my favorite musical pieces.** *Example*

Exercise 5

INSTRUCTIONS: Insert capital letters where they are needed.

1. my baby brother stops crying as soon as we put a band-aid on his bruises.
2. you'll find that tide, bleach and spot remover can solve most laundry problems.
3. did you read *at the back of the north wind* when you were a child?
4. fatima wants to be a nurse, but she's having trouble passing human anatomy 101.
5. is microbiology required in the nursing program?

Capital Letters

6. i read *of human bondage* last summer.
7. when i was little, my grandfather taught me all the verses of "the marines hymn."
8. does your mother still play her *sergeant pepper's lonely hearts club band* album?

Reviewing What You Have Learned

Exercise 6

INSTRUCTIONS: Insert capital letters where they are needed.

1. before the beatles became famous, they called themselves the quarrymen.
2. *as tears go by* is a surprisingly tender song by the rolling stones.
3. the baptist church in town sponsors a big homecoming picnic every july.
4. if you drive two miles west of town on highway 544, you'll come to an enormous shopping mall.
5. it's hard for me to believe that british children used to study greek and latin; english is hard enough for me.
6. archie bunker's favorite lunchtime treat is a hostess twinkie.
7. women are becoming involved in such community organizations as kiwanis and sertoma.
8. this nation celebrates thanksgiving as an official holiday.
9. the mormon church, whose members are known as the latter day saints, has headquarters in utah.
10. can you identify aunt bea, opie, ernest t. bass, and deputy fife?

Index

"A" and "an," 287–88
Adjectives, 90, 249, 250, 251–55, 262
   contrasted with adverbs, 255–58
Adverbs, 249, 250, 259–62
   contrasted with adjectives, 255–58
Agreement of pronouns, 240–41
Angelou, Maya, 154
Apostrophes, 238, 265–77. *See also* Contractions
Audience, 60

Background information, 54
Backwards reading, 33, 82, 112
"Better" and "best," 261

Capitalization rules, 291–97
Carter, Jimmy, 11–14
Cassette recorder: as study aid, 10
Clauses, 113–26, 156; subordinate, 133–36. *See also* Prepositional phrases
Coherence, 23–25, 26, 27, 32
Colloquial, 5, 6
Commas, 8, 133–36, 147–52, 157, 162–68, 177, 196. *See also* Semicolons
Comma splice, 196
Commands as sentences, 108
Community dialect, 205
Concluding sentence, 29
Conjunctions
   coordinate, 67, 144–54, 175, 184
   subordinate, 67, 118–22, 127–43, 175, 184
Content, 32
Contractions, 75–76. *See also* Apostrophes
Control, 6
Coordinate conjunctions, 67, 144–54, 175, 184
Course guidelines, 9–11
Creativity, 19
Cross-out technique, 105

Details, 21, 54, 56
Dialect, community, 205
"Do," "does," and "did" with adverbs, 260

"-er" and "-est" endings, 262
Endings
   "-er" and "-est," 262
   "-ing" for adjectives, 251–53
   "-ly" for adverbs, 259
   for verbs, 204–08
Examples, 38, 39, 40, 43–46, 48, 49, 54
Exercises, 4, 5, 6, 8, 11, 14, 15, 19, 20, 24–25, 26, 27, 28, 29, 31, 33, 34, 35–36, 40, 42, 43, 44–50, 53–54, 55, 58, 61, 68–70, 73, 74–79, 81, 83, 85–86, 87, 88–99, 102, 103, 105–10, 113–18, 120–26, 136–43, 146, 150–52, 154, 159, 161–63, 164–68, 171–72, 175–77, 179–81, 184–90, 194–202, 206–13, 215–18, 224–25, 229–31, 234–37, 240, 244, 245–47, 250–52, 254–55, 257–64, 267–70, 272–77, 280–81, 283, 285–90, 292–97, 130, 132–33
Experience: used in writing, 18, 19, 25

Flexibility, 17
Formal English, 236–37
Fragments. *See* Sentences, fragments
Freewriting, 20

Gender and pronouns, 241–43
Gerunds, 90
"Good" and "well," 256–57

Hemingway, Ernest, 153
Homonyms, 279–87

"I" and "you," 244–45

Ideas
    creation of, 25, 29
    organization of, 27
    supporting, 26–28, 38, 39, 41, 42, 43–46, 48, 49, 60
Indentation, 38. See also Paragraphs
Infinitives, 89, 115
Information, background, 54
"-ing" endings for adjectives, 251–53
Intensifying words, 177–80
Interest, 21, 66, 249–50
Interpreting, 56
"Invisible" subjects, 108

Keillor, Garrison, 153
King, Dr. Martin Luther, 153
King, Stephen, 153

Lists: creation of, 21
"-ly" endings for adverbs, 259

Monotony, 66, 188–89. See also Sentences, varying pattern
"More" and "most," 262

Neatness, 33

"Of" expressions, 273–74
"One, two, I, you" rule, 204–07, 210–11, 215
Organization, 7, 24, 32
Organizing words, 27, 41, 49, 54, 88
Outline, 27, 28, 29

Paragraphs, 17
    coherence of, 23–25, 26, 27, 32
    definition of, 6, 38
    descriptive, 52, 52–55
    editing of, 82
    narrative, 52, 55–58
    parts of, 38, 39–50
    persuasive, 52, 59–61
    types of, 52
    unity of, 22–23, 24, 26, 32
    variety of sentences in, 188–89

Participles
    present, 90
    past, 225, 226–28
Personality, 18
Planning, 5–6, 17, 18–19, 20–28, 250
Planning sheet, 21
Possessive pronoun, 238–39, 292
Preparation, 19. See also Planning
Prepositional phrases, 104–05, 213–15
Prepositions, 104, 213–14
Pronouns, 232–47
    agreement of, 240–41
    in comparisons, 239–40
    and Formal English, 236–37
    and gender, 241–43
    possessive, 238–39, 292
    singular-plural, 233–34, 243–44
    using "I" and "you," 244–45
    using "who" and "which," 122–23, 157–68
Proper nouns, 157, 158–63. See also Capitalization rules
Punctuation. See Apostrophes; Commas; Semicolons

Questions: in the planning stage, 21

"Real' and "really," 258–59
Research, 18. See also Experience
Revising step, 17, 18, 31–33, 80, 91, 183, 188
    reading backwards, 33, 82, 112
    help from others, 32, 82
Rough draft, 28–31
Rules of capitalization, 291–97

Sarnoff, Dorothy, 11–14
Semicolons, 169–81, 184, 186. See also Commas
Sentences
    beginning with "and," "but," and "or," 152–54
    beginning with "there" and "here," 107–08, 216–17
    combining, 186–87

commands as, 108
comparisons in, 239–40, 261–62
complete, 8, 80
concluding, 29
correctness of, 68
editing of, 79–82
effective, 63–70
fragments, 72–73, 92–93, 112–26, 152, 170
improving with verbs, 97
inconsistent, 244–45
miniature, 76, 79, 102
patterns, 65–66
present perfect tense, 226
run-on, 192–202
topic, 26, 38, 39, 40, 46–49
varying patterns of, 65, 66, 129, 156, 170, 173–77, 182–90, 198–99, 200–02, 252–53
with multiple subjects, 103
with multiple verbs, 96
Sexism, avoidance of, 241–43
Shaping, 56
Shaw, George Bernard, 153
Slang words, 5–6
Speaking: compared with writing, 5–6
Spelling, 8, 10, 32, 82
Spock, Dr. Benjamin, 242
Standard English, 205
Subjects, 76–77, 83
 choice of, 18
 definition of, 73
 finding in a sentence, 102, 105, 108–10, 214
 importance of, 72
 invisible (understood), 108
 missing in fragments, 113–15
 multiple in a sentence, 103
Subordinate clauses, 133–36
Subordinate conjunctions, 127–33

Talent: writing as a, 4
"Thumb" rule, 233–35

Time words, 57, 88
Topic sentences, 26, 38, 39, 40, 46–49

Understood subjects, 108
Unity, 22–23, 24, 26, 32
Usage rules, 5, 8, 68. *See also* Punctuation; Spelling

Verbs, 83, 98–99
 action, 74–75, 85
 actions of the mind, 85
 definition of, 73–74
 endings of, 204–08
 existence, 74, 75, 85
 finding in a sentence, 87–88, 105, 214
 helping, 85, 86, 88, 95
 importance of, 72, 85
 look-alikes, 89–92, 95
 missing in fragments, 115–18
 multiple-word, 95
 nonstandard, 221
 past tense, 219–31; irregular, 220, 221–23; regular, 220; past perfect tense, 226
 present tense, 203–218, 222–23; irregular, 209–13
 substandard, 221
 to improve sentences, 97
 types of, 85

"Well" and "good," 256–57
"Who" and "which," 155–68
"Worse" and "worst," 261
Writing, 17
 as a learned skill, 4
 compared with speaking, 5–6
 descriptive, 53
 importance of, 1–15
 steps in, 8, 16–36, 79–82, 82, 183, 188

"You" and "I," 244–45